CONTENTS

EDITOR'S INTRODUCTION ... 5

FOREWORD: ROGUE TROOPER FROM THE SONIC FRONTIER, WE SALUTE YOU ... 10

PROLOGUE ...16

1. FROM RUSSIA, WITH LOVE... 19
2. MY FIRST EVENT... 33
3. THE HOUSE AND GARAGE CLUB... 42
4. UP SHIT CREEK WITHOUT A PADDLE... 49
5. THE BEACH AND TRUE LOVE... 57
6. ULTRAVIOLENCE AND A WEDDING... 82
7. SADDAM'S BUNKER... 105
8. THE GRAHAMS... 116
9. THE WHIRLPOOL OF DARKNESS ... 142
10. THE UNIT AND THE MACHETE WARRIOR... 155
11. ELAINE... 165
12. MOUNTAINS OF THE WHITE STUFF... 180
13. WHAT IS A RAVE?... 187
14. JUSTICE FOR CRIMINALS? PROTEST TO SURVIVE!... 191
15. BOSNIA OR BUST... 230

16. SPIRALLED ON A DMT TRIP. . . 253

17. NAPLES, ROBBERY, MAFIA AND DRUGS EVERY DAY. . . 261

18. A TOUCH TOO MUCH. . . 282

19. MADNESS IN DELHI. . . 300

EPILOGUE ... 307

AFTERWORD 1 ... 331

AFTERWORD 2 ... 341

ACKNOWLEDGEMENTS . . . 366

'Keith was one of the most remarkable and inspiring characters in UK rave culture history – an intrepid motivator who led a thrilling life to a heartbreaking conclusion.'

Matthew Collin (author of Dream Machines, Rave On and Altered State)

'Keith fearlessly brought the healing energy of music to where it was most needed. Whether that was across borders into war-torn Bosnia, or through police roadblocks to fill the empty spaces in Britain's soul.'

Mark Angelo Harrison (author of A Darker Electricity: The Origins of the Spiral Tribe Sound System)

'I think in any life, and especially the party scene, just occasionally we come across someone whose charisma, energy and sheer lust for life takes your breath away. They say that those stars which burn the brightest burn the fastest and that was Keith. A rare soul, a legend, a tragic loss...'

Harry Harrison (author of Dreaming in Yellow: The Story of the DiY Sound System)

'Keith was that rare character: a person you'd meet once and remember for the rest of your life. A lot of people will rightly admire him for being a lifelong raver, and the most interesting person at any party. But his appetite for life was only matched by a real, no-BS compassion for other people. We could all be more like Keith.'

Ray Philp (RBMA/Microplastics)

First published by Velocity Press 2025

velocitypress.uk

Printed and bound in Great Britain by Clays Ltd, Elcograf S.p.A.

Cover design: Hayden Russell
Cover photo: Matt Smith
Editor: Ian Donnelly
Proofreader: Paris Ferguson
Typesetting: Paul Palmer-Edwards

PRINT ISBN: 9781913231910
EBOOK ISBN: 9781913231927

GPSR
Publisher: Velocity Press, London, United Kingdom
EU Authorised Representative: Easy Access System Europe - Mustamäe tee 50, 10621 Tallinn, Estonia, gpsr.requests@easproject.com

Editor's Introduction

BY IAIN DONNELLY

I first met Keith at a Desert Storm party in August, 1991. I was living in Paisley at the time and we'd heard a rumour of a party being held at the 'Monkey House' (Formakin Estate) in nearby Bishopton. We'd already heard of Desert Storm holding Glasgow's – and possibly Scotland's – first illegal rave earlier that summer. We had our own – rather disorganised – sound system called Kaya Tribe, and though we hadn't met any of the DS crew yet, they were already heroes and what we aspired to.

Once we got some confirmation that it was more than a rumour, we made arrangements to head down that night. I was particularly excited as it was my birthday the next day, so the prospect of partying all night at an illegal event was a huge bonus. When we got to the venue, there was already a crowd of around 500 with more arriving all the time. We found out later that Keith had used the old 'We want to make a music video' story with a promise of no more than one hundred people in attendance. I think the final tally was just over 1,000 and so I would have loved to hear Keith explain that one away.

Andrew Weatherall supposedly played, but I was so far gone on a combination of vodka, Buckfast and E that the Queen herself could have been on the decks and I wouldn't have noticed. I do remember dancing non-stop for most of the night though, and I also remember meeting Keith for the first time.

When I told him I was a DJ and that we had our own small sound system, his friendliness and interest seemed genuine. And that is a word I always will associate with Keith; genuine. He gave me his number and arranged to meet up for a drink the following week. That meeting for a drink set the foundations for a friendship that lasted for the rest of his life.

Keith never had an agenda. He never had any real self-interest at the heart of his actions or plans. You could say he was a form of freedom fighter, and if he had been born in another time or place, he would have been at the forefront of some cause there and then too. Keith just wanted people to party, to have fun, to be free.

I was never part of Desert Storm as I was involved with other systems, first Kaya Tribe in Paisley and then later Glasgow's infamous Breach of the Peace, who to a great extent took up the DS mantle when Keith relocated to Nottingham. But we linked up regularly for gigs and/or sets. Kaya did a joint party with DS in Glasgow's Mugdock Park, an event which though it didn't have the largest turnout, is one of my favourite gigs of that era. By this time, Desert Storm had graduated from their famous transit van which frequently appeared outside The Arches in Glasgow to tempt clubbers to afterparty adventures like some sort of techno Pied Piper. Their new transport was a 7.5-tonne truck with plenty of room inside for a full sound system, decks and obligatory generator. It soon gained the name 'RDV', or rapid deployment vehicle.

My favourite memories of that truck include the magical moment at Letham Free Festival when Keith came hurdling over the nearest wall screaming at us to shut up the truck as the police had just invaded the site at the top of the hill, some 500 metres from our location. The beauty of that truck is that within five minutes of Keith arriving with his warning, the whole system was shut down and the truck locked up tight with all of us scattered to various locations nearby. Another was the famed Beltane celebration in Edinburgh, where we drove round the streets with techno blaring, Keith at the wheel and me on the decks, first ending up outside the wonderful Sativa club night, then heading up to Calton Hill to continue the fun there. Sadly, the organisers of Beltane didn't think we fitted in with the woad-painted warriors juggling fire and we were asked to leave after an hour or two.

Keith eventually decided it was time to leave Glasgow, mainly due to the increasing encroachment by organised crime who wanted a slice of the action at every level from door money, to selling drugs. That encroachment went against everything Keith believed in, and he saw the perpetrators as no better than the authorities and police who just wanted to shut us down.

Once he left Glasgow in the mid-90s, our meetings were less frequent but were still endowed with that same genuine friendship he exhibited from day one. As Desert Storm spread their wings across Europe and the teknival circuit, his visits home were usually confined to coming to see his mum, though he always found time to meet up with various friends and former DS crew members. The gradual spread of internet access made things easier, both for Keith to keep in touch and for us to follow his exploits. It also made organising parties a lot simpler and also easier for partygoers to find out what was happening that particular weekend. Before the internet was widespread, the main point of info was the United Systems phone line, which would list what events were happening in various regions of the UK. The downside of that was any copper could also call it up and find out what us naughty boys were up to.

With the coming of the Criminal Justice and Public Order Act 1994, the rave scene suddenly became politicised as a whole. While parts of the act were progressive and much needed, most of the spotlight remained on the draconian parts of the bill. These included changes to an accused person's right to silence, greater stop and search powers for the police, greater rights for the police to take intimate body samples and a crackdown on the travelling community as a whole. But the parts of the bill which got the most attention were those that focused on the 'rave community'. Much of that came as a result of the legendary Castlemorton rave of May, 1992. But even after the crackdown on that, no one expected what they would include in the bill to come. The police could stop any vehicle within five miles of a rave and turn it around. They could stop any gathering of people listening to music at night (out with legal events). But perhaps most bizarrely, they sought to criminalise music by genre with their definition of music which is 'wholly or predominantly characterised by the emission of a succession of repetitive beats'.

Keith revelled in the widening politicisation of a movement he had always seen as political. Desert Storm from that point were at the forefront of almost every campaign, from the demos against the bill in July and October of 1994, to being an integral part of the burgeoning Reclaim the Streets movement that followed. The former of these movements was the catalyst for Keith's – and Desert Storm's – almost unimaginable trip to Bosnia, a trip that will go down in the annals of free party history.

Over the next fifteen years or so, our contact was intermittent and more digital than real life. We'd have the odd chat via messenger, or later on as Keith became a little more paranoid, via a secure messaging service such as hushmail. In 2012, I left the UK to live in Southeast Asia and contact became purely digital. Then, in early 2015, a mutual friend messaged me to say that Keith needed a ghost writer/editor to sort out his life story. By that point, I had released two novels so that, combined with our long friendship, made me an ideal candidate.

I sent Keith a message asking why he had forgotten (or not realised) that I was a writer. Then on 10 May, 2015, I received a Facebook message saying simply:

hi to my new ghost writer... open hushmail account and email kevinroberston23@hushmail.com ASAP. kds23

Over the months that followed, we exchanged multiple emails discussing how to convert Keith's often disjointed writing into something that would read easily. The bones of a good book were there, but Keith tended to throw down words onto paper like a dysfunctional Beat Poet. It was my job to find order in the chaos.

Keith being Keith, it was never going to be a smooth journey. Throughout 2015 and most of 2016 there were various hurdles in the way, from dealing with evictions, to being jailed, to festival appearances. I'd always known the journey would take us a couple of years, but I never expected it to end so abruptly.

On 19 September, 2016, I awoke and did the routine checking of emails and Facebook. As I scanned through the usual inane nonsense, one post suddenly jumped out at me. Someone had posted that Keith had taken his life – though this was later changed at the inquest to 'death by misadventure' – the previous day, 18 September, 2016.

I was left sitting with a folder full of Keith's life story and with no idea what to do with it. It was only later, when Andrew from DS got in touch, that the project gained new life and, more importantly, permission from Keith's family to proceed.

What you are about to read is that story. I have tidied the chapters up and added to it here and there, and Andrew and the DS family have helped fix some continuity errors where needed as well as also adding to the story as a whole. But it is Keith's story, told mostly in his own words...

Keith Robinson – DJ, producer, freedom fighter, activist, but most of all... friend. I miss you, buddy.

Iain Donnelly, Siem Reap, Cambodia, February 2023

Foreword: Rogue Trooper From The Sonic Frontier, We Salute You

BY MATTHEW COLLIN

Meeting Keith Robinson represented the beginning of a new journey; a trip that carried me off in directions previously unimagined. Maybe it was the same for other people who called him a friend – he was the kind of man you instinctively trusted to take you up and away into the bewitchment and intrigue of the unknown. Others knew him much better than I did, of course, but I'd like to tell you some of what I remember.

We met for the first time one Saturday afternoon in May 1996, in the unlikely surroundings of the Trent Bridge Inn near the Nottingham Forest football ground. It was a match day, and the boozer was packed out with sturdy lads in replica shirts downing as many pints as they could before kick-off. We ordered some lager, and then we ordered some more.

Many years later, I went back through my notes from that time, and this is how I remembered my impressions of him from that first meeting:

> *'Keith at twenty-seven years old, lean and hard-bodied from his self-imposed itinerant existence, honed to peak physical condition like a fighter ready to enter the ring; the optimum weight for his chosen profession. He had a collected, authoritative manner and the force of personality to inspire people to follow him. A man who thrived on perpetual motion and someone, it seemed to me at the time, who could make things happen.'*

People sometimes say that pop stars and political leaders have charisma. Well, in the three decades that I've been working as a journalist, I've interviewed a fair number of prime ministers, presidents and rock 'n' roll heroes, and Keith Robinson had more charisma than almost all of them. Seriously, he *glowed* with it – it was like some irrepressible force, a vital energy that you could almost feel pulsing out of him. He made you believe that joining him on whatever journey he was talking about at that moment was exactly the right thing to do, however sketchy the plan and whatever risks might have been involved.

So inevitably I suppose, that meeting in a pub in Nottingham led to me joining the Desert Storm crew in their truck heading down to France for a Teknival somewhere south of Reims, and then going north to Glasgow for a free party in a concrete underpass below the M8 motorway – and all the while, his relentless energy driving us all onwards.

'*The more I got to know about Keith, the more fascinating he became*,' I wrote later. '*Raised in flux, he was a restless soul, always plotting the next coup. He was also utterly fearless. Policemen and customs officers were simply stuffed dummies around which he would dance, weaving his anarchic patterns while they blundered in his wake, unable to comprehend the maverick logic that drove him forwards.*'

For me at least, our first meeting in the mid-'90s came at exactly the right time, when I was looking for new inspiration. I had revelled in the collective euphoria of the early days of acid house and the rave scene, but by this point, the loved-up visions of those hazy times seemed to be fading as the culture became increasingly commodified.

Keith had a very different view of how things should be. He was an idealist. He *believed*. And he had the willpower and the daring to act on his beliefs. He also drew people of like minds towards him so that together they could make things happen that he could not achieve alone. I sometimes think that even if he had never been interested in electronic music at all, he would have had the same impact on people around him in any sphere of cultural life that he chose to be his own.

Most people who know anything about Desert Storm sound system are aware that they made several arduous and risky trips down to Bosnia and Herzegovina during the horrific war there in the 1990s to put on parties and bring what they saw as 'cultural aid' to the conflict-traumatised Balkan country – forging a direct connection between young people of different nations on the level of the basic human desire to celebrate and dance.

'People in Bosnia have been cut off from enjoyment and fun through being involved in this nightmare of war for so long,' he explained to me afterwards. 'Going there for a few weeks is not that risky, but the cumulative risk of being there all the time gets to you psychologically. Day in, day out, with this constant threat of death, nothing to do, a nightmare just trying to survive – it's going to get to your head, isn't it? So, someone comes in with a bit of music and enthusiasm, it gets you going, gives you something different to do for a while...'

Desert Storm's missions to Bosnia and their involvement with the demonstrations against the oppressive Criminal Justice Bill and the Reclaim the Streets environmental protest movement in the mid-'90s showed how, with enough dedication, commitment and sheer good fortune, his idea of a kind of idealist hedonism could actually *work*... for a while, at least. The fact that people are still talking and writing about all this stuff – about the times when sound system crews put their liberty on the line for their beliefs – shows what a remarkable episode it was in the history of popular culture.

The ideas that were set in motion back then still resonate even now, and not just in the free parties and Teknivals and cultural protest movements of Western Europe. What some people don't know about Desert Storm's sorties to Bosnia is how they had a lasting impact in the capital, Sarajevo, where their daredevil exploits helped to inspire the emergence of a local techno culture in the city. There's some visual evidence of this in a documentary film called 'Rave Against the Machine', about young people struggling to survive psychologically during the three-and-a-half-year siege of Sarajevo, and about how music worked as a kind of lifeline, helping them to 'keep a sense of sanity and to do something creative, not to become crazy', as the Bosnian techno DJ Jasmina Mameledzija once told me.

In the film, Bosnian punks, rockers and ravers talk about how music, gigs and parties helped them to hang on to some idea of a better reality amid the deranged brutality of the war. Some of them also talk about the people who managed to bring something special to Sarajevo from outside the besieged enclave, driving in through the mountains in an old white truck with a lightning-flash logo on its side, packed with humanitarian aid supplies – and a sound system.

'Desert Storm!'

'They came here from nowhere...'

'They were the first, the very first ones who brought electronic music to Sarajevo. It was the first time that we were faced with something new – some new sound...'

Some of the footage in the film, shot from the Desert Storm truck, shows the crew rolling through downtown Sarajevo one afternoon, rig blasting music fierce and proud, cheeky Bosnian kids jumping aboard, men in camouflage uniforms waving, pensioners peering up in bemusement – and then Keith Robinson dancing through the raddled streets as the truck cruises onwards, pumping his arms and raising his fist to the sky in sheer glee at the absurd glory of the moment.

It's all there in those images from Sarajevo – all those good feelings, all those moments of righteous euphoria. It snaps them all back into focus, with Keith right there in the centre of the frame, this blazing meteor of pure creative energy – irresistible, unstoppable.

Like all of us I suppose, he was shaped by the times in which he lived and the environment in which he grew up. But unlike many, he realised that he had the power to somehow reshape that environment himself, to bend some of that reality to his will and to turn his own life into a narrative full of wonder.

From the couple of decades I was lucky enough to know him, what I remember most vividly isn't so much the parties, but the conversations. Those long, free-ranging talks about music and social justice, families and relationships, chance and magic, destiny and duty... it got deep at times; in fact, it almost always did. As he once put it himself: 'These questions are a minefield... When you start asking them, you bring everything into question – what is it all about?'

More than anything, what I regret is that I'll never have one of those conversations again, and never hear that mischievous voice answering the phone then launching straight into a riotous recollection of his latest improbable escapade, a tale inevitably beginning with those familiar words: '*You'll never believe what happened...*'

Yes, I miss the man. And I know I'm not the only one.

Mattew Collin

PUBLISHER'S NOTE

Due to certain chapters being incomplete upon delivery of the manuscript following Keith Robinson's passing, the Publisher has summarised, where necessary, any unwritten events or information to improve clarity for the reader. All words in this book are Keith's own unless stated otherwise.

Prologue

Clutching my machine gun, I crept along the line of trees, keeping as close to the irrigation ditch as I could, ready to dive in at the first sign of trouble. And trouble was coming, that was for sure. Myself and the rest of the lads from Waterloo Company had been patrolling the deadly fields of Helmand's Green Zone in Afghanistan for only half an hour and already it wasn't looking good. A few minutes ago, a plume of white smoke had billowed from a compound, a sure sign that we were being marked (the Taliban put up smoke to mark our forward line). We turned east and again another plume of smoke. Taliban ICOM chatter came over the net... 'We have eyes on the ISAF patrol'. Now the civilian population was bugging out in every direction except the one we were headed. My mouth went dry and my heart rate quickened. The silence around us was deafening as the world around us seemed to hold its breath. We approached a small compound with three males sitting behind it. I looked at them and noticed they were laughing grimly and nudging each other while staring at us. These fuckers knew what was about to happen as well as I did.

As we passed the compound, I thought to myself... any minute now. Our officer obviously felt it too and ordered us to cross the road into cover to the north. As the first two troops in the patrol stepped into the road... *ratatatatatat...* the evening quiet was ripped asunder as the opening volley fell among us. Chaos ensued, rounds were zipping past my head and splashing into the dirt around me as we scrambled for cover. I got my foot caught up with another soldier as we threw ourselves into the ditch. The ditch was nice and deep and I got right down in the dirt. The volume of fire was immense and was numbing my brain. Then I heard the dreaded words, 'MAN DOWN...

MAN DOWN'. Oh shit, someone's been hit; I could hear screaming over the incoming fire.

Just as I was starting to wonder who it was, I heard a dull thump in the distance. Oh no, incoming RPG... *crump, bang*... I was showered in earth and the shock wave took the air from my lungs and my ears started ringing. As the dust settled, I looked to my right and saw the wall of the compound smashed to fuck. More firing points erupted to the southeast and northeast. Now we were surrounded on three sides. It occurred to me that maybe we were going to die here. But I didn't want to die, I had too much to live for; my new album must come out, I've got raves to do, I haven't even written the book I've been supposed to be writing for a long time and not to mention I've got to father a kid. FUCK THIS! I felt my anger rise and a red mist descended. FUCK THESE PEOPLE, TRY TO FUCKING KILL ME, WOULD YOU. YOU BASTARDS! I clutched my weapon and scrambled up the side of the ditch.

Hours later, exhausted and covered in mud, we staggered back into the base. I needed to tell my story. After the kit check and debrief, I went straight to my bed space, turned on my laptop, opened up Microsoft Word and typed up these words...

1

FROM RUSSIA, WITH LOVE

For me, it all started in a dingy hotel room in Moscow in 1968. A hotel room where two people did the wild thing. One of them, my mother, was a slightly out-there hippy chick, researching her chosen specialist subject, communist political systems, a subject which was, as you can imagine, not the easiest at the height of the Cold War! The other, my father, was a dodgy Marxist political activist from Sudan who had escaped from jail with the help of the Soviets and been spirited away to Russia in the dead of night, so to speak.

So it was wham, bam, thank you, ma'am, and my mother split on the next flight to America. Probably left him sitting in bed smoking a cigarette, wondering what had just happened as off she went to the good old US-of-A, to go to festivals, smoke pot, find out she was pregnant, then head back to the UK to have the kid.

Flash forward to a hospital room on 6 August, 1968. My birth, by all accounts, wasn't easy; feet first, umbilical cord wrapped round the neck, two weeks early. But I made it, son of a Scottish mother with Viking roots and a Sudanese insurgent father. Would you predict that this child would become a bank clerk or a civil servant? No, neither would I.

The early years were not that remarkable; We lived in a quaint little town called Drymen which was near Glasgow and on the edge of Loch Lomond. Mother went to work teaching at the university, while I did, well, baby things, I guess, but which of course I can't remember. Though from what I've been told, I was a quiet, well-behaved infant, all sweetness and light. I'm not so sure about this, because one of my earliest memories is of riding the stairs in my baby bath, and crashing through the window on the landing and falling some distance into the garden, badly hurting myself.

But all this tranquil living was too much for my mother, so she hatched a plan to buy a ruined farmhouse and outbuildings on the slopes of the Campsie Hills, again near Glasgow, that looked down the valley onto a small Loch. You reached it via an old byway called the Tak-Me-Doon Road, aptly named as it was the only route down from the high plateau of the hills above. Turning off the main road, the tree-lined Tak-Me-Doon road wound steeply up past quaint old millhouses, a bluebell wood and finally a right turn onto a bumpy track which led out of the trees and down to the farm. It was peaceful, idyllic and basically in the middle of nowhere. The idea was to do up the farmhouse, stables and kennels, and to supplement her teaching income by stabling horses and having boarding kennels for dogs. Seems like a nice plan, no? The place was even called Riskend Farm, what could possibly go wrong? But as they say, or as Burns said, 'The best laid schemes o' mice an' men gang aft a-gley' (editor's note: this means 'No matter how carefully a project is planned, something may still go wrong with it'). And this one started out badly and got worse. The house in Drymen was duly sold and the farm was bought with some form of bridging finance, and all that remained was for the new owner of the old house to pay up and move in. He moved in all right, but managed to get the keys off the lawyer without handing over the cash and then proceeded to squat the place! Work had already started on the farmhouse. We had intended to live in a few rooms while the rest were done up double time by a team of highly skilled and highly paid builders. The work, of course, ground to a halt like a train wreck, and with no cash coming in, the builders promptly downed tools and left the job, leaving us living on a building site and in a world of shit.

I might have only been three and a half at the time but it didn't take a genius to work out that mummy was far from being a happy bunny.

So that winter was spent living in the yard of the farm in a tiny caravan with no power, freezing cold and bathing in the kennel sink, with the wolves almost literally at the door. The other slight hitch with the plan was the quarry behind the farm; Riskend Quarry it was called, and although out of sight above and behind the house, it was far from out of hearing or mind and, on a daily basis, huge explosions would echo around the hills like thunder as they dynamited the granite, shaking the caravan, then raining small pebbles half a mile onto the roof. Endless Risk Quarry would have been a better name. I, of course, thought the detonations were great fun and would laugh and jump around with joy, unable to understand why my mother would begin weeping uncontrollably after each blast.

Then there was the nearest town, Kilsyth. This was a rough old mining town, now mineless and well past its prime. It was a town that time forgot. Although the date was the early 1970s and the rest of the country had been experimenting with cannabis, miniskirts, cocktails and disco music for some time, they forgot to tell Kilsyth. It was a dry town. That meant it had no bars, discos or even an off-licence! Now, as anyone who has been to the western central belt of Scotland will testify, they like a wee drink at the weekends. But not in Kilsyth. Drink does the devil's work apparently, and so it was banned in 1913 with the passing of the Temperance Act. Weird place, but strangely the weirdest person in the whole town was not the local vicar, religious fanatic or even a dour Presbyterian spinster, it was me. In a town of 10,000 souls, I was the only black one, and so it began.

But after that initial winter of discontent, things began to gradually improve. The weasel that squatted in our old house finally paid up and, after a while, we even got used to the daily explosions. This may have been partly due to Mum submitting a complaint to the quarry which led to them blasting a vein of rock a little further from the property. Work progressed on the farm house too and soon we were properly moved in; at first living in just one room, and then, as each room was finished, we had more and more of the house to use. You have to give my mother her due, she likes to follow a plan through, and the house was more than comfortable. Being an old place, built in 1806, it had many *olde worlde* features like six-feet-thick stone walls and the beautiful old wood-burning range in the living room. Once the wooden floors had been sanded, walls painted and the multitude of barns cleared out, the place became quite a posh country pile. Throw in a horse and some dogs and you had the good life.

Time went by, and for a young kid the place was paradise. An entire complex of old barns to play in, woods, fields, rivers, the loch and, once I'd made some friends in the local area, it was game on. We started a gang, the Alpha Betas. There were two sections of three. I, of course, commanded Alpha, and we took over the old grain loft in one of the barns and fortified it against attack. We were pretty well tooled-up for little kids. Fibreglass bow and a quiver of proper arrows, metal bars, catapults and, in pride of place above the dart board, an old rusty sword. The staircase up to the loft was protected by barbed wire and the door securely bolted from the inside. You could even drop rocks on intruders from a slit above the door, and as a last resort, the grain hatch could be opened in the floor and a rope lowered for escape. It may have been those early childhood adventures which prepared me well for brushes with the law in later years.

The area for about five miles was our territory. Back then, there wasn't a paedo behind every bush as they would have us believe today. So we were free to roam at will so long as we were back in time for dinner. And roam we did. There wasn't a fallen tree, path, stream, hay barn, rubbish tip or abandoned building that we had not explored. I could still find my way round that area perfectly today, even on a dark night.

Construction seemed to be the order of the day; the local dump was scoured for pram wheels, and wilder and wilder go karts were built, all tested on the super steep, death defying, now tarmacked track leading down to the farm. We were also addicted to building rope swings, and not your pitiful little back garden ones either. The one in the largest of the barns was truly scary, and others spanned ravines such as in the local nature reserve, Colzium Park. I even designed and built a boat, which I and one of my friends sailed out to the island in the local loch in and camped for the night. On the smaller side, I was right into Lego, and once I got my hands on technical Lego, I was off. Building guns that fired Lego blocks at a robot target that trundled towards you till you shot it in the right place, then it would retreat away, and many other weird and wonderful contraptions.

Musically, I had access to my mother's collection of vinyl, mostly 7" singles; The Beatles, Rolling Stones and such like, which I played to death on one of those old Dansette record players that stored the records in a stack and released them one at a time to be played. But the first record I actually bought – I'm ashamed to admit – was the Smurfs single, a mindless dog of a tune, but what the fuck; I was only a nipper.

For almost as far back as I can remember, I was into comics.

I had a copy of Spiderman, UK issue 3, before I could even read! I used to get the American Marvel and DC A5 comic books mail order, not to mention piles of Commando monthly. But it was in 1978 that I came across the first issue of 2000 AD and that changed things. Looking back now, the content was ultra-violent to say the least, and I remember having nightmares about the issue where the Angel Gang torture Judge Dredd's poor horse, but there was something new in 2000 AD; the artwork and the Mad Max apocalyptic-style look at the future really affected me, and I later used the emblem for one of Rogue Trooper's enemies, the Norts (short for northerners), as the emblem for my sound system, Desert Storm. It's a powerful image of a mushroom cloud with a lightning strike coming out of it. An image that I and others in Desert Storm have tattooed on our arms. How powerful it was I didn't quite realise at the time, and it was only when someone wrote into an events mag in Glasgow years later, claiming, 'Don't be fooled by Desert Storm's fluffy free party image, they are really Nazis who are into the occult and their emblem [the mushroom cloud with the lightning strike], was first used by a battalion of the Waffen SS'. This sparked my interest, and with a little digging I found out that although it was true that it had been used by the Nazis, Hitler had stolen it from a much older source, as he had with the Swastika, and in this case it was a Nordic power symbol for Thor, god of thunder, lightning and, appropriately, storms.

Comics, bizarrely, also got me interested in electronics, particularly an advert in the back of one for a product called Denshi Block, which was a blank circuit board into which you plugged electronic components according to a set plan given in the instructions, forming different devices, such as radios, mini amplifiers, even a device to sound a warning when your bath was full up! All good stuff.

My mother put the barns to use as well, organising a series of barn dances. Crazy knees-up affairs, often lasting the entire weekend, with bands and rivers of drink.

Holidays were spent in Cornwall, same caravan each year, and lazy days at Bedruthan Steps Beach, a place of extreme natural beauty, accessed via a winding stair cut into the living rock which took you hundreds of feet down to the bay where huge pillars of stone jutted out of the sea. I'm sure the British weather was better then, because there was hardly a day of those holidays when it wasn't blazing sunshine, or at least that's how I remember it.

Yup, all sounds idyllic, doesn't it? The perfect childhood and it was, until my mother decided to marry one of her students, an American called Howard. He was a blond-haired, blue-eyed, apple pie-eating, red, white and blue all-American asshole, and to say the least, we didn't see eye to eye. I really didn't see it coming; he used to visit from time to time, and that was almost cool, but when my mother told me he was moving in permanently, that was another matter. It was hate at first sight, or first sight after he moved in, and the feeling was mutual. He had been brought up in some huge strict New England family nightmare, and he obviously thought I was a feral kid who had more freedom than was good for him and needed to be reined in. The battle went on for many years, often violently, but he had underestimated his adversary, and in the end I drove him to insanity, and he had to check into the nuthouse. Oops.

Anyway, the best thing that came out of my mother and this relationship was my little sister Sarah, born in 1979, again blonde with blue eyes. When our family walked down the street, you would see people look over approvingly. Mother: white with dark hair – check; father: white, tall, blond and blue eyes – check; daughter: white, blonde and blue eyes – check; then the son: dark curly hair like a microphone, brown eyes and black skin – eh? You could see them do a double take. 'Where does he fit in then?' which was a shit attitude because I was there first.

Then came trouble on the ranch. The quarry had run out of useable granite on the far away slope from the house and started blasting closer to the farm again, much closer, and one day they must have miscalculated the quantity of explosives and, I kid you not, a rock bigger than a basketball landed in the yard and bounced twenty feet, crashing into the house wall and leaving a huge crater in the yard. Luckily, the walls were six-feet-thick (your average new build semi would have been flattened), but even still there was quite considerable damage to the place. The police were duly called and the image of six cops struggling and sweating as they heaved and dragged the massive boulder, suspended in a net, across the yard and into the back of their van is burned into my mind. Obviously, my mother and stepfather feared for our lives, and with good reason, if a boulder like that fell on your melon from a mile and half away, they'd be scraping you up with a spoon, so they decided to take it further and called in the quarry inspectors. Bad idea.

The quarry was one of the biggest employers in the town, and the money from it filled a lot of bellies. The problem was, as I said earlier, that the rock in the far hill had run out and the only way to continue in business was to blast closer and closer to the house. The quarry owner wasn't about to pick up sticks and close it down, so the first move he made was to pull some strings with the local police and the boulder disappeared and with it our evidence, I mean how can you lose a one-hundred-kilo rock? But undeterred, we moved forwards with our quarry inspector complaint – we always were a stubborn lot – and they had to start sending a worker down to the farm with an air horn to warn us of impending blasts. When the horn sounded we all had to run inside, like in an air raid, but the rocks kept coming.

It was looking bad for the quarry, and as the hearing approached, they decided to change tack and vandalised our water supply, then they sent a group of large men in the night to smash our windows, and in the ensuing confrontation with my stepfather, shotguns were mentioned if we didn't clear out of dodge. This gave me time to get my bow and as they fled across the fields, they did so with my arrows flying past their heads. But with the quarry, the townsfolk and the cops all rallied against us, we were fighting a losing battle, and it wasn't long before we had sold up and moved on.

The new place was a little further north, in a small town called Callander, a very picturesque tourist town situated on a popular route into the highlands. Sunset over Callander as it sinks behind the heather-coloured slopes of Ben Ledi is a sight worth seeing, but the novelty wears off quite quickly, I can tell you. Nice place for a visit, but fuck living there. I did a lot of outdoor things, like camping at Loch Lubnaig where the swimming is top notch. And there was a place hidden in the hills above the town, called the Scout Pool (at the northernmost point of the Bracklinn Falls Circuit), where for maybe millions of years a waterfall has carved out a huge bowl in the rock. It's here I learned to high dive, achieving forty-feet plunges into the dark water. Speaking of scouts, I had a good time with them as well, going on skiing trips and a three-week camp in the then West Germany where I got pissed for the first time and snogged some gorgeous blonde whose name I forgot.

But by now I was thirteen, and I soon got bored, which allowed my dark side to surface. I did things like construct a shotgun out of stolen twelve-gauge shells and metal piping, which is insane, I know. I got myself a black widow catapult, a vicious piece of kit, and turned to vandalism, and it wasn't long before I came to the attention of the cops for smashing windows. The whole moving idea had been a bad plan, it was just too far for my mother to commute to work in Glasgow, so we were off again. This time a move to the big city itself, sunny Glas Vegas, into a nice semi-detached house made of huge sandstone blocks in the sleepy west-end suburb of Jordanhill. It had a good school and it was supposed to be a fresh start for us all.

The first day there, I got my pocket money and jumped on a bus to head to the city centre where I got a powerful baptism into Glasgow life. There I was walking down one of the main shopping streets minding my own business when I found myself being jostled by a large group of youths much bigger than myself. Unfortunately for me, they were the infamous football casuals of Glasgow Rangers Football Club. Now this was not good. There are only really two teams in Glasgow; Rangers and Celtic. It is run on sectarian lines like a mini Northern Ireland. Protestants on the Rangers side and Catholics (and everybody else) on the other, and between the two there is proper hatred. Unfortunately, the Rangers' casuals tended to be a little racist, and proceeded to kick my head in, spit in my face and shout racist shit. This, as you can imagine, was a bit of a shock for the country boy, but as I crawled out of the crowd on my hands and knees, blood streaming from my nose, I could think of only one thing: Glasgow Celtic, a team I support to this day. Welcome to the big city.

School was hard at first – not the work, I'm no idiot – but fitting into a group of people who had been together for years wasn't easy, and it didn't help matters that there were only a couple of other black kids. I quickly realised you couldn't fight them all, so I got in with a crowd a year above me, especially with a kid called Bruce Tonner who was the second-hardest guy in the school. He was small, built like an athlete and looked a bit like a monkey, but by fuck could he fight and he became my best mate. This evened the odds and meant that I could take them one at a time, while my new mates would watch over to make sure no one else jumped in. It didn't make me Mr Popular with my year, but after I cracked a few heads, I got left alone.

Those were great times, my group of friends were tight and we spent all our spare time together. Many of us had hijacked our parents' garages and turned them into our own spaces; mine had seats, a stereo, dart board, fridge, punching bag, etc., and we would spend our time roaming the area moving from garage to garage. This was when my interest in mechanics started, and before long I had bought an old motorbike and done it up, and we would ride it on any available bit of waste ground we could find. Also around this time, my interest in chemistry came to the fore. I had always been a straight-A student in the subject and it seemed only natural to decide to do some experiments at home. At first it was just bringing home some magnesium wire and lighting it in the back garden, but then I progressed to gunpowder.

I'd obtained the recipe from the school library and the ingredients – potassium nitrate and sulphur – were stolen from the lab. I made the charcoal myself. The mixture was duly made and I decided to do a small test in my bedroom before I constructed what you could only have called a bomb. Pushing aside a small quantity from the main pile, I lit a match. Unfortunately, the match head snapped and fell into the mixture and the result was mind blowing. A metre-high green-and-orange flame flashed into being in my bedroom, nearly taking my head off as the place filled with smoke. I shat myself, sure the house was going to burn down, but luckily all that happened was a massive hole burned on my thick wooden table. That was the end of my mixture, and it was too sketchy to nick any more ingredients. Undeterred, I moved on to a new plan with new ingredients

Sodium chlorate (weed killer) and sugar. Now, if you know anything about explosives, you will know this is serious shit. The mixture, when lit, expands to 40,000 times its size in a fraction of a second. If you contain that within something such as an empty fire extinguisher, you have a bomb.

My mates were all keen, and soon we had the empty fire extinguisher primed with the mixture (a quarter full to allow the reaction to start), and a fuse constructed by a line of the powder running down a length of masking tape, and off we went to the nearest waste ground. Light the fuse and run like fuck, and luckily we did. The resulting explosion was huge, bringing people running out of their houses into the streets thinking there had been a gas explosion, and leaving a large crater in the ground. We had to leg it quickly too, as the sirens of cop cars and ambulances were converging on us from all angles. Now people usually get caught for shit like this because they blab to other people and large it up, then it gets out and you're nicked, but we knew this was serious shit and none of us said a word to anyone.

Now it should have stopped there, but it didn't, and an even larger device which we nicknamed the H-bomb was constructed, and with the aid of an older friend's car it was transported to an old quarry outside town and placed in a burned-out car to see what would happen. This bomb was a little more temperamental and refused to go off; four times we had to make a new fuse, four times we had to go back to the bomb, which was madness, but on the fourth go, we had a feeling this was it and ran well back and threw ourselves to the ground. It detonated with a bang so loud I can't describe it, and when the dust cleared the old car was gone! A full five seconds later, shrapnel started falling around us and into the water in the quarry. How none of us were killed I will never know, but finally we had scared ourselves, and that was the end of bomb making.

But back in the neighbourhood more trouble was brewing. A friend of ours, Mad Dog, had been expelled from school, and had been sent to the neighbouring school, Hyndland Academy, our sworn enemies. Now as he was a black kid like me and a couple of years younger, I felt quite protective of him, and since he was receiving daily beatings at his new school, I decided to organise some payback. The word was passed around and one evening fifty or so of us formed a posse and headed along the railway track to kick some heads in. The Hyndland lads always hung out in the bike sheds behind their school, so we split into two groups and came at them from both sides. We took them totally by surprise and gave them a proper bloody nose. Feeling pleased with ourselves, we headed back home thinking that was the end of it. Yeah, right.

The next day, I was lucky to make it to school alive. I was halfway there, just passing the local petrol station, when I heard a shout of 'there's the fucker, do him'. Looking across the street, I saw a group of guys running across the road armed with baseball bats, bricks and bottles, and these weren't the school kids we'd battered the night before, this was their big brothers and then some. I mean, one of them had a beard for fuck's sake! You could tell these boys meant business. My only chance was to make it into the garage. It was a close thing, but I just squeezed in through the door, slammed it in their faces and locked it from the inside, leaving them helplessly trying to smash through the shotgun-proof glass as I gave them the finger. That night there was a gang going round houses in Jordanhill with a table football cloth, trying to find out where I lived so they could use my head as the ball. Oops. They didn't get me though, and although the feud simmered for many years, for the moment it faded into the background and life went on.

Well, you may think all this 'when I was a lad' stuff is just a necessary but pointless intro before we get into the juicy drugs, sex and rave bits, but think again. Because I firmly believe, for reasons that will become clear later on, that without this basic grounding in construction, woodwork, electronics, sailing (well, maybe not sailing), etc., not to mention the exposure to the barn dances (a kind of rave, at least from the organisational point of view; flyers, site, bar sound system, punters, etc.) then what came after might never have happened for me, and my part in the wave of subculture that swept the UK and Europe like an unstoppable tsunami of energy, changing the attitudes and lifestyles of hundreds of thousands of people, would have been nil, and in my arrogance I believe the wave would have been a few metres smaller, and the power a little less. Now, this is where I get a little cosmic; I also believe that this was not an accident, and fate had set out this path for me, even before I was born.

But then, as people that know me could tell you, I'm a little crazy...

2

MY FIRST EVENT

I was fifteen when I organised my first party. My parents had gone away for the weekend leaving me all alone with the house. The flyers simply read: 'Garage Party, this Saturday at 6 Manor road, Jordanhill. All welcome, bring your own booze, starts 7.30 p.m.'. I made fifty flyers and gave them out at school. I naively thought fifty flyers meant fifty people, yeah, right. More like 250 plus. Bring your own booze, they sure did. The pitiful crate of beers and two bottles of wine I had acquired was gone by 7.45 p.m., the garage was overflowing onto the street and the music was pumping. Older lads arrived on motorbikes and were smoking dope while downing bottles of vodka on the lawn. I had promised myself that I wouldn't let anyone into the house, but after a few vodka and oranges, I didn't give a shit anymore.

It was your typical house party gone wrong: people shagging on your mother's bed, puking up in the hall (although he got a slap for that one), house bursting at the seams. You could tell kids had raided their parents' drinks cabinets – taking a bit from each bottle and mixing it – by the vile-looking brown concoctions they were drinking. Being the organiser was great kudos, and before long I was snogging the face off the neighbour's daughter. It was a top night. Now the date for this event was early September and we were having an Indian summer. In Scotland, this is perfect weather for magic mushrooms (usually Psilocybe semilanceata, also known as liberty caps). Bruce Tonner – it would be him – had been out picking the shrooms and proceeded to make a tea by boiling them up in the kitchen. The stuff tasted disgusting, like drinking liquid soil, and it was honestly really hard to keep it down, but I managed, continued partying and thought no more of it. Well, for about forty-five minutes anyway. At first there was just a rainbow-like sheen around objects in the house, then things like the walls started to move backwards and forwards as if they were breathing. This was alarming to say the least. I went to find Bruce.

'Bruce, I think I'm losing my mind, the walls are coming alive and I can see rainbows everywhere...'

I looked into his monkey-like face and he simply said, 'Mushrooms,' and burst out laughing.

Mushrooms? I thought, and then the penny dropped. For some reason this was the funniest thing I'd ever heard and we laughed uncontrollably until we were writhing on the floor with our eyes streaming. We were still there when nervous partygoers came to inform me the cops were here and wanted to see the householder out at the squad car immediately! Although deep shit, this was even funnier, and it was a full five minutes before I managed to stagger out to the car.

As I saw the cops sitting in their motor, my mood changed 180 degrees and the fear set in. There was something very, very sinister about that cop car, and as I got closer, I noticed that the bonnet seemed to be pulsing up and down slightly. In fact, the front end was bending towards me and the headlights, shit, they really looked like eyes, slanted yellow ones like a snake! Worst of all, what was that fucking growling noise coming from under the hood? Every time the bonnet raised a bit, I caught a glimpse of a reddish glow and what could only be razor-sharp teeth in there like those of a shark. I stopped dead in my tracks about ten feet away. There was no way out of it, the fucking cop car was going to eat me. Desperately trying to tell myself, 'It's not real it's not real,' I nervously shouted over the growling, 'Eh... Hello, officers, how can I help you?'

As I peered in at the cops, I was having trouble seeing their faces, there was just a kind of blur. A disembodied voice came from inside. 'You, sonny, get your fucking arse over here right now.'

In spite of my fear, I started forward, but as I got closer the images inside the car began to solidify and at last I could make out their faces. I did an emergency stop. Under the rim of their black-and-white checkered caps were bleached skulls; these guys were dead [it's strange that I have this recurring trip with cops; if I'm sufficiently out of my nut on LSD the cops are always dead-looking, it must mean something, but who knows what?].

'I said, get your fucking arse over here now,' screamed the cop, who by now was proper frothing.

'No way!' I replied. 'You're fucking dead!'

The cop paused, puzzled for a moment, trying to work this out. Had this little shit just threatened to kill him? Even fucked out of my my head, I realised he might take it badly.

'...I mean, I mean... you're dead right... I'm coming over now.'

Still puzzled, and not fully satisfied, the skull's eye sockets narrowed menacingly at me.

'Is there something fucking wrong with you, sonny? Are you soft in the head? If you just threatened me, you're going to be in a world of hurt very shortly, pal!' Then, seemingly remembering why he was here in the first place, he continued, 'Okay, we've had a list of complaints as long as your arm about this...' He paused while waving his hand across the scene of devastation that was the front of my house. '... This... disturbance... this... this—' words seemed to fail him '—this breach of the fucking peace. That's what it is, a breach of the fucking peace. I take it your parents aren't at home? Well, unless you want to spend the next twenty-four hours in a police cell then I suggest you close this party down right now. I'll give you five fucking minutes.' He held up a fleshless, bony hand. 'Five fucking minutes,' he repeated.

Now things were kind of going okay, I was just starting to think they might go away, when I heard a strange voice coming from behind me...

'Mushrooms... mushrooms.'

Was I imagining it? But no, there it was again.

'Mushrooms... mushrooms!'

And then it burst out laughing. It had to be Bruce hiding in the hedge just behind me. Obviously, he had lost the plot.

'MUSHROOMS... MUSHROOMS!' he repeated louder this time, loud enough for the cops to hear!

The cop leaned out, listening. 'Eh, what the fuck was that? IS SOMEBODY PLAYING SILLY BUGGERS WITH ME?'

It was all too much for my drug-addled tiny mind. I too shouted, 'MUSHROOMS... MUSHROOMS!' and ran back inside, creasing myself.

The last thing I heard from the cop was, 'You're in trouble now, son. We'll be back.' The car then took off with a screech of tyres.

Back in the house, Bruce had gone mad. He was clinging onto me making crazy noises; he looked even more like a monkey than usual and it all was too much for me, so I ran off to hide.

I woke up the next morning a very confused teenager in the cupboard under the stairs in the dark. Once I had extracted myself from the mops, vacuum cleaners and assorted shit, I went to stand up. A headache hit me like I had been coshed. Right away, I knew I was going to be sick. I rushed upstairs and threw myself onto my knees in front of the toilet bowl and started talking to God on the great white telephone.

'Oh God, oh God. Oh God, I'll never drink again.'

I'm sure you can imagine the scene, you've likely all been there yourselves. Finally, it stopped and I gathered myself and looked up. Judging by the state of the rest of the bathroom, it looked like God had had a busy night as I realised I was kneeling in a pile of half-digested raw carrots floating in a red wine sauce. That sent me puking again, dry-retching as there was nothing left in my stomach, a very painful and not very pleasant experience.

At last I had recovered enough to stagger downstairs and, weak with dehydration, I flung open the fridge door. The first thing that greeted me were two cans of special brew, undrunk from the night before. This nearly sent me puking again but I managed to push them to the side and pull out an ice-cold can of coke. Gulping it down, I started to feel half-human again and picking up a kitchen stool from where it had fallen on the floor, I sat down and surveyed the damage.

The place was fucked. Empty cans formed snowdrifts against the walls, smashed glasses and dishes were everywhere; it looked like someone had thrown a couple of hand grenades in through the front door. Reaching into my pocket, I pulled out a crumpled packet of cigarettes and lit one up (I wasn't allowed to smoke in the house, but what the hell, what house?). I was fifteen with my first psychedelic comedown pounding in my head and this seemed like the end of the world. My mother's words rung in my ears.

'Now, Keef, you won't have anyone in the house while we're away, will you?'

'Of course not, Mum.'

And from my stepdad, Howard, 'You better not, you little punk,' as he left.

Maybe I should kill myself? Or run away? These were my thoughts as I finished off the cigarette and gathered the courage to check out the rest of the house. It didn't take me long to find Bruce sprawled out half-naked on my parents' bed with what appeared to be a pair of girl's panties clutched in one hand. With difficulty, I roused him.

'Keef, where the fuck have you been?' he asked, yawning and wiping the sleep from his eyes.

'Err... I don't remember much after the cops left. Then I woke up in the cupboard under the stairs.'

'No wonder we couldn't find you and neither could the cops, man.'

'The cops?' I replied nervously.

'Yeah, loads of cops came and emptied the party, they were well pissed off too. They searched everywhere for you then kicked us all out into the street. But after they left, I managed to climb back in through your bedroom window and here we are.'

Bruce knew fine well how to get into my house, he'd watched me sneak out the same way many times in the middle of the night.

'Bruce, the place is fucked, and I'm fucked when my mum and Howard get back.'

'Nah, it isn't too bad. When do they get back anyway?'

'Sunday night,' I replied, getting the first tingles of fear.

'Sunday night? Chill out, man, it's only Saturday morning for fuck's sake, plenty of time...'

'Oh, and Bruce?'

'Yes?' he replied.

'What on earth are you doing with a pair of girl's pants in your hand?'

He looked down at them as if seeing them for the first time. 'Oh yeah,' he replied. Thinking back, 'there was this chick, I think she had too much of the mushroom tea and... well...'

'Fuck... mushroom tea.' I shook my head. 'Don't ever mention that shit again.'

We went downstairs.

'Okay, first things first,' he said, can of lager in hand as we sat in the wrecked kitchen. 'Get on the blower and get some people round here to help, that sluggard Muirhead for a start. It was that fucker who puked all over the walls in the hall. Also...' he reeled off a list of names and I got straight on it.

A few hours later and the place was starting to take shape, except for the smashed dishes, my mother's prized pot plant (smashed to smithereens), the massive stains on the carpets (not to mention the cigarette burns) and the overpowering stench of rotten booze and puke. But Bruce had a plan for almost everything and was even on the phone getting a specialist cleaner round to sort the carpets.

At last it was all done; the carpet cleaner had been paid with a cheque I had nicked from my mother's bureau and the place was not looking too bad.

'Okay,' said Bruce, looking around and rubbing his hands. 'Just leave the windows and doors open for the night to get rid of the smell and dump the empties.' All fifteen bin bags of them. 'And I think that's about it.'

Sunday night had arrived and I'd persuaded a reluctant Bruce to stay and give me moral support when they got back. We were nervously sitting in the back garden chain-smoking cigarettes.

'Keef, relax, man,' said Bruce, 'that party was fucking awesome and people will be taking about it for years to come.'

That brought a smile to my face. He was right, it had been a beauty, or at least the parts I remembered.

About eight p.m. they arrived, bustling into the house with their bags. I could already see my stepfather looking suspiciously around, seemingly surprised that the place was still here.

'So, had a good weekend?' I asked my mother.

'Yes, thank you, dear,' she replied before going into the kitchen and putting down her bags. 'And you, what have you been up to?'

I glanced sideways at Bruce. 'Nothing much, pretty quiet really.'

Then she spotted the plant, or lack of it. Bruce and I quickly split into the living room.

'Keith, where is my plant? The one in the crystal pot, you know the one your granny gave me before she died. Don't tell me...'

'Erm...' I called back to the kitchen, 'well, there was a bit of an accident. You see, I had a few friends round and...'

Just then, my stepdad burst into the living room and grabbed me, none too gently, by the neck. 'Keef, you little punk—' his favourite word for me '—I knew you couldn't be trusted, I told your mother she was crazy to leave you alone here. We go away for one weekend and you have a goddamn frat party!' He was always using stupid American phrases like 'frat party'.

Bruce chose this moment to desert me. 'I'll just go and make a cup of tea then. Anyone want one?' My stepdad ignored him as he scuttled off and began to squeeze a little tighter.

Just then the doorbell went and distracted him from his assault on me. I quickly brought my arm up with all my strength and struck him on the wrist, breaking his hold.

'I'll just get the door,' I croaked, ducking out and slipping away. I got to the door and opened it, only to find two cops standing there.

'You, you little shit.' said one of the cops angrily, reaching forward and grabbing my arm. 'Got ya.'

Although he no longer had a face belonging to the undead, I had no doubt that this was the cop from the party.

'Who's that at the door, dear?' my mother called from the kitchen where she was talking to Bruce as he made the tea. I didn't say anything.

'It's the police, ma'am,' a cop called past me. My mother and stepdad rushed to the door. 'Well, ma'am,' said the cop, pulling out his notebook. 'It's like this. After numerous complaints from local residents, who wish to remain nameless as they're scared of retribution from your son, we attended a disturbance here at the house.' He glanced down at his notebook.

'Disturbance?' my mother interrupted. 'What disturbance?'

'That's right, ma'am, a disturbance here on Friday night, a party that was completely out of control, people drinking in the street, loud music, a breach of the peace I believe were the words I used at the time,' he said, staring down at me.

'You little fucking punk...' I heard my stepfather mutter under his breath.

The cop continued, 'But unfortunately it's not the party that we're here about, it's another much more serious matter.' He paused and looked from face to face to let this sink in. 'Yes, a certain...' he looked down at his notebook for the name, 'young lady who we have reason to believe attended this event was found later at her home address by her mother, sitting naked in front of the washing machine having loaded it up with the contents of the dish rack and was attempting to spin dry them. We believe she had been administered some type of narcotic, possibly LSD, by a person or persons in these premises during the party earlier that night. And with a view to bringing charges, we're looking for a...' glancing down at his notebook again '...male, white, approximately five-foot-four, curly brown hair, who has features resembling those of a monkey, possibly the first name of Bruce.'

There was a crash from the kitchen as a tea cup smashed on the floor. 'Well,' I said, 'never heard of him.'

3

THE HOUSE AND GARAGE CLUB

Some people like to think they are party animals but my friends and I really were. Beat this: Tuesday – straight night at Bennett's nightclub for high-energy dance music; Wednesday – Cotton Club for funk, dance and soul; Thursday – no specific venue but we were always out; Friday – Fury Murray's for house, hip-hop and dance music; Saturday – Lucifer's for underground dance music; Sunday – Joe Paparazzi's for fresh house and underground dance. Now, you may have noticed a slight gap in this pattern: Monday night. There was nowhere to go on a Monday night in Glasgow. If you wanted to go out you had to go to Paisley, about ten miles away, to some shithole I forget the name of. Maybe the reason for no club on a Monday night was because no one goes out on a Monday night, but nevertheless I spotted this as a gap in the market and went to see Foster, the manager of Tin Pan Alley nightclub in the city centre, who had been letting me play warm-up sets every so often on a Saturday.

'Monday fucking night?' Foster nearly choked on his Lucozade.

He told me later that he didn't think we would last two weeks, but as they had nothing else on he thought, why not? But Foster hadn't counted on how much work myself and others could put in. We called the night 'The House and Garage Club' and when the PR campaign kicked in, there was hardly a space anywhere in the west end or city centre that didn't have a poster stuck on it and, after two weeks of flyering, people were sick to death of the sight of the things. But why would anyone want to go out on a Monday night? Well, £1 beers and 50p spirits was a good start, also add in the chance to hear underground house music you couldn't hear elsewhere and you had another. In saying that, no one was more surprised than me, except maybe Foster, when the place was packed out on the opening night and we were off.

How I came about possessing this underground music is another story.

I was in Tin Pan waiting to see Foster about another DJ set when I heard there was a superstar in the office. I waited downstairs for him. Tin Pan was closed at the time and the lights were very low so he must have got quite a shock when I bounded up to meet him out of the darkness.

'Marshall Jefferson? Hi, I've been waiting for you.' I offered my hand.

He jumped back, maybe thinking he was getting mugged, a life on the backstreets of Chicago must prepare you for anything. Recovering, he peered forward into the gloom.

'Yo, bro, how can I help you all?'

I offered my hand again and he took it this time, his huge black hand nearly crushing mine.

'Erm, I was wondering if you could sign this?' I produced a treasured copy of his track 'House Music (all night long)'. He seemed embarrassed but reluctantly signed it anyway and made to move off before I called him back.

'There is one more thing. I can't seem to find much of this style of music to buy in Glasgow. I'm just starting out as a DJ and this is the stuff I want to play.'

He stopped and considered me for the first time, paused in thought. 'Hmm, okay, dude, you go to Camden Market on a Saturday and on the bridge you'll find a friend of mine called Simon Slime. He'll sell you a tape with it all on. Look, guy, I'm in a bit of a hurry, so if that's it?'

'Wait,' I said. 'Camden Market?'

Marshall looked at me as if I was some hick hillbilly that lived in a cave. 'Yeah, man, Camden Market... London. Y'all heard of fucking London, yeah?'

I nodded dumbly.

As he left he turned to me and added, 'Hey, dude, good luck with the DJing.' Then he walked out.

Wow. I stood there awestruck clutching my signed record, autographed by a god of house music himself. That guy, along with Farley Jackmaster Funk, is one of the godfathers of house music and had been there from day one, playing at clubs like The Warehouse in Chicago. Not only had he wished me luck with my DJ career, but had pointed me in the direction of a source of new tunes that no one else had. Warm-up sets forgotten, I almost ran the 500 metres to Central Station to find out about the train times for London town.

* * *

Now, I'm keen on trains but I'm not so keen on tickets so I spent the journey dodging the ticket inspector and arrived in Euston station pretty knackered later that night. This was my first time in London unaccompanied and I realised that I knew no one, except for the name of Simon Slime of course, and as I stood there at the end of the platform in a strange city, watching the people rushing about on their missions, I thought... wicked, what an adventure.

I had just over £100 on me, and as it was only Friday night and I had no sleeping bag, I had to find somewhere to stay. I had been putting thought into this on the way down and had a plan.

'Hello, blah blah hotel, how can I help you?'

'Eh, yes, I certainly hope you can.'

The hand holding the receiver was mine, but the voice was that of a posh Scottish gent, obviously well off and pushed for time.

'My wife, son and I are planning a short trip to London and your hotel was recommended to me by a friend. I'd like to book a double room for myself and my wife and a single for the boy for a week.'

'That shouldn't be a problem, sir. What dates were you looking at?'

Now for the hook.

'Yes, well, that's the problem. My wife and I are still in Paris and won't be there until Saturday, but the boy arrives today. So, I was wondering if you could install him in his room and I'll sort it all out when I arrive?'

'Eh, hold on a minute, sir, I'll have to check that with the manager. How long did you say you wanted to stay again, sir?'

'A week, my man, a week. And don't take too long about it as I'm just about to go into a meeting.'

'Very good, sir...'

The receptionist rushed off. The hook was well and truly in the mouth, but would they bite? I crossed my fingers and waited.

'Sir? Hello, I've spoken to the manager and he sees no problem with that. What name is the booking to be under please, sir?'

Wow... hook, line and sinker.

'Erm, the name. Ah yes, Robinson, Mr Howard Robinson.'

Shit. I was so surprised it had worked that I hadn't sorted out a name and had given them my stepdad's name. Oops. Fuck it. Now this would never have worked in these more suspicious days, but way back in the late '80s it was a different matter.

Less than 2 hours later, I was lying on the bed in my three-star posh single room with an ensuite munching on an extra-large plate of club sandwiches, caning the minibar and watching TV, feeling very pleased with myself. Next morning, I would get up early, shower, enjoy a free breakfast and then head over to Camden Market, what could possibly go wrong?

BANG BANG BANG!

I turned over groaning and ignored it.

BANG BANG BANG.

'MR ROBINSON, THIS IS THE MANAGER. I MUST ASK YOU TO OPEN THE DOOR THIS INSTANT, WE'VE HAD COMPLAINTS!'

Shit. Mr Robinson. That was me! I forced open my eyes and sat up in bed surveying the room. Even with blurred vision and a pounding headache, I realised things were not good. It looked like a herd of wildebeest had been running amok in the place. Empty cans and bottles from the mini bar were scattered everywhere, the table lamp was overturned and smashed, half-empty plates on the floor and a river of puke led to the bathroom, not to mention the blaring TV.

I fell out of bed and tried to tidy up, but ended up just making it worse, so I staggered over to the door, took a deep breath and opened it a little while doing my best to block the view.

'What do you want?' I croaked, mouth like an ashtray. I looked at my watch. 'It's six thirty in the fucking morning!'

'Mr Robinson, we've had complaints. Guests have reported banging and crashing and the volume of the television, people are trying to sleep.'

I finally managed to focus on him: a small, fat and sweaty little creep. I looked at his name badge but unfortunately it did say manager.

'Okay, okay, I'll turn it down.' With this, I tried to shut the door in his face but he managed to get his foot between the door and frame and I was forced to reopen it.

'Mr Robinson, I really must insist on looking over the room. As I said, there have been reports of loud noises and as you haven't even paid for the room yet, I must insist...'

I bit my lip. There was going to be no easy way out of this one. He barged past me into the room and glanced around in horror at the mess of shattered glass and discarded bottles.

'THAT'S IT,' he screamed as he stormed back out of the room clutching the broken table lamp. 'I'm calling the police; this is criminal damage!'

'Fuck you, you slimy little git,' I shouted after him as he fled down the corridor.

Looking around, I noticed most of the guests were out of their rooms watching the unfolding drama. I smiled at them and went back in, slamming the door hard enough to crack the paintwork.

I gathered my few belongings and made to leave, then had second thoughts, headed for the fridge and scooped up what was left of the minibar, grabbed a towel and some toiletries and had a quick look around. Better hung for a sheep than a lamb as my granny used to say, although I reckon she was thinking more about eating too many biscuits from the cookie jar rather than ripping off hotels.

Still half-cut, I tried to stride purposefully down the corridor, occasionally bumping into the walls. Then I was stopped in my tracks by one guest who had come out of his room and was blocking my way.

'Now, listen here, young man,' he began, 'I heard what was said. The police are on their way and I suggest you return to your room.'

'And I suggest you return to yours... WHILE I STILL LET YOU!'

He scuttled back inside, probably to call the front desk. I reached the end of the hall. Lift to the front desk or the stairs? Not much of a choice really. I clattered down the stairs two at a time until I reached a fire door. 'Warning! Alarmed' the sign read. I kicked the panic bar and burst out onto the road, the alarm still ringing in my ears as I legged it up the road and onto the first bus I saw. Of course, the bus turned at the top of the road and headed back down past the hotel, giving me a good view of the guests emptying onto the pavement. I spotted the manager dude and sunk low in my seat; I didn't want to meet him again in a hurry.

My stomach turned with butterflies as I approached the bridge at Camden Market, trying to spot the tape vendor. There he was! Blond guy, skip cap, standing behind a small table stacked with cassette tapes.

'Simon Slime?' I asked and he nodded. 'I'm here for tapes of house music, what have you got?'

Slime reached down and quickly selected two tapes. 'That'll be a tenner, mate.'

'Hold on a sec, do they have the artists and track names on them?' Slime nodded, a man of few words indeed. I handed over the cash.

Talk about pivotal moments in life. Well, this was one. I rushed off with my treasure to the nearest bar, purchased a cold one, slotted the first tape into my Walkman and sat down to listen.

A couple of hours later, I had a list of tunes to acquire and headed off to Black Market Records in Soho to buy them.

Afterwards, I managed to skip the night train back up the road, which was a good thing as I had fuck all money left. And having made a good dent in the rest of the stolen minibar, I finally emerged bleary-eyed into the sunlight in Glasgow clutching my precious records.

And the rest as they say is history. The House and Garage Club continued in good health for more than a year, which was more than can be said for my personal life. I was soon in deep shit with the cops and it was time to leave town.

4

UP SHIT CREEK WITHOUT A PADDLE

Looking down the staircase, I saw one of Glasgow's finest running towards me. Oh shit, it's the cops! I legged it back into my room and locked the door. As there were so many separate bedsits in the house, I would only have a short time to think of something as they searched. I turned to Mad Dog who was sitting on the couch smoking a fat joint.

'Mate, for fuck's sake, put that out, the cops are in the house.'

Just as I said that, the door shook to the timbers as it was beaten on by a gloved fist.

BANG BANG. 'OPEN UP, IT'S THE POLICE.'

Shit, they already knew which room was mine! Mad Dog looked down at his joint and then at the large lump of dope on the table. His mouth was making O shapes like a fish. Again, the door was battered.

'ROBINSON, YOU SHIT, WE KNOW YOU'RE IN THERE. OPEN UP OR WE'LL FUCKING KICK IT IN.'

Mad Dog ran to the window and threw out the joint which still left him with the lump.

'Hey, Keef, it's your fucking hash,' he whispered and threw it in my direction.

Thanks a lot, I thought, as I caught it and looked around the tiny bedsit for somewhere to hide with it. Meanwhile, Mad Dog was trying to fit his huge frame into a small cupboard in the corner. I couldn't help but laugh as he squeezed himself in.

BANG BANG BANG. 'THIS IS YOUR LAST CHANCE. WE CAN HEAR YOU IN THERE.'

Realising there was no point in hiding, I turned my mind to escape. Running to the window, I threw it open and leaned out. Hmmm. It was quite a drop (maybe thirty feet) onto hard concrete, I'd break something for sure. I looked to the side and saw there was a ledge about six inches wide, maybe...

My thoughts were interrupted by a splintering noise as the door began to be kicked in. No choice left. I took a deep breath and out I went, straight onto the ledge and started rapidly inching my way along, body pressed against the wall. I just managed to slam the window shut as the bedsit door crashed in. I could hear them searching the flat so I got moving. It was scary shit but I was committed now, and looking along the ledge I could see that the drop was less a little further along and the concrete was replaced by grass and bushes. That was my target, but to reach it I had to move along the ledge another thirty feet or so. I got motoring, sure that my window would be thrust open any second and a cop's head would appear and I would be discovered. By now, I had reached the large plate glass window that covered the landing between the floors and as I worked my way across it I realised that I must be completely visible from the inside. I froze in place; I could see shadows inside on the stairs. Shit. Somehow they failed to see me and I let out a sigh of relief and continued on my way.

Now I was at the end of the building, that was as far as I could go. It was time to jump. I looked down at the drop, at least fifteen feet.

Butterflies rose in my belly. Maybe I could drop down using the ledge to hold onto. As I was considering this, I heard the noise I was dreading: the scrape as the window was dragged open. I jumped... and landed feet together with knees bent and executed a perfect parachute roll which took me into the cover of the bushes nearby. I lay there not moving a muscle, waiting for the cry of discovery. It never came and after what seemed like an age, the window slammed shut again.

I stayed in cover for a little longer, checking I was not injured and pulling some nasty thorns out of my flesh. Then I was up and running, vaulting the neighbour's wall down into the next garden and away I went. Five minutes later, I was at the bottom of the road behind some lockup garages and peered up to the house through a gap in a bush, my breath coming in gasps. There was quite a collection of cop vehicles outside: two cars, a van and a motorbike, and now some cops had started trying to get through the gate into the back garden. They must have sussed my escape route. I'd watched long enough – time to do one, so I shuffled backwards and away heading for the nearby canal. Shit. I realised they must want me pretty bad. How had it come to this? I was definitely up shit creek without a paddle...

There was no denying it, I'd been a bad lad. I'd stolen a car and 'wringered' it. Which meant I'd found a car the same as mine, same colour and everything but in better nick, taken it, changed the plates and numbers on it and then drove it about. Now, although this was not a very nice thing to do to the other owner, it was a crime that had so far gone unnoticed and would have remained so if Mad Dog had not entered into the equation. It was Mad Dog's job to take the original motor down to a friendly, ask-no-questions scrap yard to be crushed, but in his infinite wisdom he decided to take it to some waste ground for a rally beforehand. This ended with him being chased by the cops, crashing the motor and escaping on foot. The cops, of course, got the details of the owner of the car (me) and came up to my house. Imagine their surprise when they found an identical car parked right outside!

With friends like Mad Dog...

Then there was the magic mushroom drama. Not having taken magic mushrooms for a number of years, it was decided that we make a foray into the countryside to pick some as it was harvest time. Usually it takes a lot of effort to locate them but this time we stumbled on the field sent from the Hallucinogen Gods. There were thousands of them. So, we picked thousands and got them back to my bedsit and proceeded to brew them up into foul-tasting tea. I still don't know to this day why we took so many, but I reckon that Stefano, Mad Dog and myself had at least 300 each!

The results were unbelievable. After about twenty minutes, as I was still trying to ingest the foul brew, a fully formed rainbow fell out of the side of my mug. I started to feel really weird. Stefano split, saying he was going home, and I went into the bathroom to splash cold water on my face to try to straighten up (yeah, right!). As the cool water trickled down my chin, I rested my hands on the sink and looked into the mirror. Imagine my surprise when I found a horned devil with a flaming background staring back at me. I screamed and ran back into my bedroom, only to find Mad Dog crawling on all fours along the floor making noises like a dog, or maybe a goat. This freaked me out further and the only thing I could think of was to go to bed, fully clothed, boots and all, and hope it would all go away.

But of course it didn't, and by now Mad Dog was half on the bed growling and trying to bite me. I tried to reason with him but it was no good. Kicking him in the face, I threw the sheets off and escaped back into the bathroom, leaving him writhing on the floor making funny noises. In the mirror, the devil was still there and his lips were mouthing the solution to my problems… KILL HIM… KILL HIM! At the time, this seemed like the logical thing to do, so I went into the kitchen, selected the largest knife I could find and strode back into the bedroom to shut up Mad Dog for good.

Standing above him, my face distorted with anger, I raised the knife over my head *Psycho*-style and went to plunge it downwards into Mad Dog's prone form. At that instant, what remained of my sanity took hold and I pulled the blow to the right and the knife stabbed into the floorboards and was left stuck there, quivering. Rage took me and I attacked the bedroom door, somehow punching through the thick oak panels with my bare hands. If I couldn't kill him, I had to get out. I threw open the outside door and looked out but there was nothing there, everything was solid grey (I think this was my subconscious warning me not to go). Ignoring this, I left anyway, Mad Dog's barking still ringing in my ears as I fled. This was very, very unwise.

I wasn't going anywhere in particular, just away from the flat and the animal-impersonating Mad Dog. The only problem with this plan was that I was not running away from my problems but taking them with me, and I was definitely not fit for public consumption. Soon I began to have this mad trip where aliens or some shit had invaded Earth and crazy ivy-like plants were engulfing everything (sort of like *War of the Worlds* meets *Day of the Triffids*). Then it seemed that all the people were dying and had disappeared. I think this was brought on by an ambulance passing and the hour getting later, as of course I had no concept of time. As far as I'm aware, I just roamed the West End of Glasgow, doing God only knows what. One snippet I do remember is being followed by the cops near a place called the Pond Hotel. Looking inside the meat wagon, I could see the cops' faces were just ghastly skulls with red glowing eyes (a common trip of mine when it came to cops). I legged it as fast as I could and diving over a wall onto the railway, made my escape.

I remember walking along the railway and throwing my jacket, watch and skip cap away, why, I have no idea, but I walked for miles (lucky it was at night and there were no fucking trains!) and finally climbed the wall again to find myself in a near pitch dark field with two horses, one black and one white. For some reason, I identified the black one with evil and the white one with good. I started to chase the white horse around the place attempting to mount it so I could ride off or some shit. I think it was about this time that I decided that I was in my bed dreaming; a very, very dangerous way of thinking indeed. Next thing I knew I had abandoned the field and climbed onto the roof of a barn joined onto a farmhouse and was sitting on top of it, prising slates off and throwing them into the courtyard. A window opened and what must have been a very scared man confronted a large lunatic black guy mad on drugs as he demolished his barn roof.

To me, the guy just looked like another member of the living dead, his face a glowing skull.

'What the fuck do you think you're doing?' he shouted, still wiping the sleep from his eyes.

'I don't talk to dead people,' I replied and continued my strange work.

Another voice came from inside the window, probably his wife. 'Come back in, he's obviously lost his mind, I'm going to call the police.'

Now, if I'd had any idea what I was doing, that should have brought me to my senses and I would have beat a hasty retreat, but unfortunately, I still thought I was dreaming in my bed.

'YOU, YOU FUCKING NUTTER, GET DOWN OFF THAT ROOF IMMEDIATELY!' the cop shouted as he shone his flashlight in my eyes. He'd arrived without me realising.

I obliged him by running down the roof and jumping onto the cop car roof below and then began kicking and smashing the siren and light unit with my feet. The cops were not expecting this and they just stood there, gaping at me. If they hadn't expected that move, they definitely didn't expect the next as I jumped from the cop car and started to get stuck into them using the kickboxing I had been studying at a martial arts club on the southside. At first I had the upper hand, downing the first with a vicious side kick to the head. The next fell to a one-two combination to the body but alas there were four of them and finally as the element of surprise wore off, they subdued me.

I woke up in the back of the cop car trussed up like a chicken. Still thinking I was in my bed dreaming, I started to direct them to my house so they could drop me off.

Yeah, right...

Next morning, I opened my eyes, looked up and saw a strange dim white light above me. Where am I? I wondered, still not unduly worried. As I went to sit up, a massive shooting pain pierced through my head. What the fuck? I leaned gently forward and tried to take in my surroundings. Hmm. Dull painted bricks, small room, solid metal door – definitely not my flat then. But it did look familiar. Shiny metal toilet, strange smell of piss mixed with bleach, then it hit me harder than a copper's truncheon... Oh shit! I'm in jail. The broken memories of last night came flooding back; mushrooms, Mad Dog, madness, horses, climbing on the roof, police. *Oh shit...* attacking the cop car. Oh, my God... kickboxing with the cops.

But... but... I thought I was in my bed asleep...!

I jumped up in spite of the pain and started to batter on the door.

BANG... BANG... 'LET ME OUT... LET ME OUT... IT'S ALL A MISTAKE... LET ME OUT.'

Eventually a cop came, pushed aside the small metal grill, looked in, shrugged and said, 'Drugs,' then slammed it shut again.

Some time later, I was escorted, hand-cuffed, to a small room by the same cop as before, and upon entering, I locked eyes with a man in a crisp black suit sitting at the singular wooden table. I sat down on the chair opposite him and waited.

'Well, Mr Robinson,' began my solicitor as he read through my charge sheet and shook his head. 'I'm sorry to say but it looks like you will be taking a holiday at Her Majesty's pleasure, it would seem unavoidable.'

Oops.

'Erm, how long do you reckon I will do?' The five-million-pound question as far as I was concerned.

'Well, depending on the judge and how good a defence we put up, maybe eighteen months. So if I were you, I'd use the bail period you will receive to sort things out before prison.'

'Or I could choose that time to do a runner, so I'm off abroad. I'll contact you... if I return.'

And with that, I stood up and leaned over to shake his hand, already planning my next trip, far away from Glasgow and the juridical system.

5

THE BEACH AND TRUE LOVE

As we made the approach to Corfu airport, I couldn't help but notice through my window how foggy it was outside and, as the sun was just setting, it occurred to me this might be a little bit of a rough landing. My fears were confirmed when the pilot made an announcement.

'Ladies and gentlemen, this is your pilot speaking—' he got straight to the point --'due to the bad visibility, imminent darkness and the fact that Corfu airport is the only airport in Europe without landing assistance radar, please prepare for a bumpy landing. Thank you.'

There was a collective intake of breath around the plane, coupled with a tightening of seatbelts. I stared out of the window trying to see the ground as the plane came in steeply. Lower, lower and lower. I began to grip the arms of the seat. I looked at the girl sitting next to me, her face drained of blood, eyes wide open. I tried to smile then turned back to the window. Suddenly I saw the runway rushing towards us, shimmering through the fog; surely we were dropping far too fast? The pilot obviously thought so too and the engines screamed as I was thrown back in my seat and we overshot Corfu and clawed our way back into the sky. Nothing was said by the pilot for about fifteen minutes, then he announced that we would be stopping at Brindisi in Italy for more fuel and then we would try again.

The atmosphere on the plane was one of total terror as we made our next approach to Corfu some time later, but the landing was a safe one. And it was with much relief that I finally stood in the arrival hall to pick up my luggage. As I saw my kit come round on the conveyor belt, I knew I had brought too much stuff. A huge rucksack weighing a tonne, the largest yellow-and-black ghetto blaster you have ever seen and a massive box of records. It was after this trip I came up with my travelling mantra: before you leave, put all your stuff on the bed, cut it in half (not literally) and take more money. Try it, it works.

It was a pathetic sight as I moved in shifts with my stuff to the bus stands. There I encountered my second problem. I couldn't read Greek. Oops. I looked around at the signs on the buses trying to decipher them (I was trying to get to a place called Pelekas), but it was no use. I thought of getting a taxi but since I didn't know where my next funds were coming from, I rejected that. After a few tries, I finally found the correct bus and loaded my stuff into the belly boxes.

The journey to Pelekas was a nonevent as I could make out very little in the dark and fog. I remember the bus winding up and up what had to be a mini mountain which was strange as I had been told Pelekas had a beautiful beach. After about forty minutes we had arrived and soon I was standing in a little square in what appeared to be a small village in the mountains. All around me were bars and people drinking. I could hear many different languages being spoken and everyone seemed to be having a good time. I dragged my kit over to a low wall where loads of young people were drinking and sat down.

Well, I had made it, temporarily escaped justice (or, more truthfully, absconded) and arrived at what my friend had told me was the most happening party town in the Mediterranean. In my pocket was a letter of introduction to the local owner of a disco bar and all around me were party people. In normal circumstances, I would have been elated but sitting there, I realised that I wasn't on holiday and wasn't going home for a while. My friends and known comforts were all a long, long way away. I couldn't help feeling sorry for myself as I watched the revellers all around me talking, kissing and drinking. It seemed everyone knew everybody else but I was alone. I wasn't even me anymore as I had decided to leave my real name behind and take up a nickname, 'Krob'.

But I'm not big on self-pity and quickly binned it, composed myself and started to assess the situation. Okay, first thing: find out where the disco bar was and see if the owner could get me a room, I just had to dump this stuff. I looked at the letter and read off the name. Manu's Disco Bar, Pelekas. Hmmm, not very original. I looked around, not imagining I would spot it as the main road to my right took a sharp bend up the hill and away to the left, and judging by the amount of people heading that way, I suspected that Pelekas continued on for some distance.

Beside me on the wall was a couple drinking beers, arms around each other. I plucked up the courage and asked them for directions. 'Excuse me, I'm trying to find Manu's Disco Bar, have you any idea where it is?'

They turned towards me. The guy was about thirty and had blond quiffed hair with a red bandana tied around his neck and a patterned open shirt with a couple of gold chains. He looked like a pimp and definitely not British. The girl was about twenty and very fit, with shoulder-length blonde hair and a Penn State university top on (wild stab in the dark, American?). They looked at me and laughed out loud.

This was not the reply I was expecting and as my face turned red, I felt like asking them what the fuck they were laughing at. But the pimp guy just carried on pissing himself and started pointing to my left. I followed his finger and my eyes fell on a huge, brightly painted sign barely twenty feet away, which said... you guessed it... MANU'S DISCO BAR, PELEKAS.

I had to laugh along too, what a twat.

So...' said the pimp guy in accented English, 'are you new around here?'

I admitted it was true, very new, in fact brand new just out of the wrapper new, all of five minutes new.

The pimp introduced himself. 'Hi, I'm Roberto, and this is...' He turned to the girl beside him and gave her a gentle poke in the ribs. 'And I forgot your name...' The girl seemed outraged and looked at Roberto with her jaw dangling, unwrapping his arm from her shoulder. Roberto just smiled and gave me a sly wink.

'Hi, I'm Ke—Krob. From Glasgow, I'm a DJ.' (I only just managed to remember my new name.)

Roberto and I shook hands and he offered to get the drinks in. I asked for a beer and off he went still laughing and leaving me with the girl. It was a little awkward as she was clearly pissed off so I tried to break the ice.

'Eh, so, what is your name then?'

But she wasn't having any of it. 'That goddamn son of a bitch...' she began in that sing-song American high-pitched drawl that always ground my gears. 'That goddamn son of a bitch,' she repeated. 'He thinks he's so goddamn cool.' She turned to me. 'He picks me up at that fucking club, Coca Club or some shit, and gets me drunk, then takes me back to his room, fucks me, and the next goddamn night, he can't even remember my goddamn fucking name.'

Now this was slightly more information than I was expecting and it was hard to know what to say to it, so I said nothing and just smiled stupidly. She ranted on.

'Goddamn MOTHERFUCKING men, you're all the same.'

This was getting boring and I wished Roberto would come back as I was choking for a beer. I tried a different tack. 'So, you're a mother then?'

This went down like a lead parachute and with a 'FUCK YOU' she was off, just as Roberto returned with the drinks. I opened my mouth to explain but Roberto just shook his head and sat down, still smiling, and handed me my beer. As I greedily poured it down my parched throat, Roberto put one hand on my shoulder and waved his other dramatically across the square.

'No matter,' he said. 'Plenty more fish in the water.' I looked around, beer in hand, and had to agree with him, things were looking up already.

Roberto, who was Italian, explained a few things about Pelekas. In the '60s, hippies had come here and formed a commune on the beach and soon the place had a growing underground following as more and more travellers came each summer. As the rest of the island commercialised, Pelekas didn't because of the distance to the beach, which could only be accessed by a bumpy track, so it wasn't viable to build hotels down there. Now, Pelekas attracts travelling hippy types from all over the world and is one of the coolest places in Europe to spend the summer. Roberto claimed to have been coming here for ten years already and knew everyone in the town; also, the best clubs, restaurants and places to stay. He told me the place we were sitting now was called the Bench Bar and was where all the long-stay types met up before going on to the bars and clubs. Yet again, my uncanny knack of landing on my feet had come up spades.

Roberto offered to help me sort myself out. First stop was venturing inside Manu's Disco Bar. It was an open-plan sort of place with low walls, no windows and a huge canopy that covered both the inside and outside. We dragged my stuff inside and left it by a table and went up to the bar. Serving behind it was a blonde girl who looked more English than Greek. She must be Manu's girlfriend, Stella.

She obviously knew Roberto well and there was a lot of hellos, hugs and kissing, and before I knew it we both had cold beers in our hands. I liked this place already and a glance to my left revealed, hopefully, my new place of work; the DJ box. I explained my position, produced my letter and waited while she read it. It went better than I had ever hoped as it seemed she had already heard I was coming as my friend had phoned from Scotland. Wicked. She said that after a chat with Manu, the job should be mine. Manu would be back tomorrow apparently but I could move my stuff into a room above the bar till then at least. I could have kissed her, but I wasn't quite at home with continental customs yet so I vigorously shook her hand instead and Roberto helped me upstairs to the small room. It was no palace; it was tiny with beer crates packed in the corners, but it had a bed, its own small shower and toilet room and a balcony overlooking the square. Dumping my stuff, we headed back down to the bar to finish our beers. Roberto told me he would introduce me to the rest of the posse at the Bench Bar and then it would be time to party. Yes...

Next morning, I woke up in a strange bed, still fully dressed, wondering where the fuck I was. It all slid into place, Corfu, Pelekas, Manu's Disco Bar. I tried to lift my head...

BOOM.

The headache from hell hit me like a hand grenade. I staggered up and made my way over to a crate of Pepsi and grabbed one, using the side of the case to force the top off the glass bottle and gulped it down my dusty throat. I made my way out to the small balcony, pulled a crumpled pack of cigarettes from my pocket, sat down gingerly on the battered wicker chair, lit one up and looked out on the scene below. It was early and only the Greeks were up and about their business in the cool morning sun. I sat smoking and tried to remember the events of last night.

Roberto and I had headed back to the wall of the so-called Bench Bar and Roberto seemed to be right, he did know everybody. I was introduced to a dizzying array of people. My memory for names has always been shit so I just wore my usual smile and shook hands and tried to remember to use my new name. It was amazing how many different nationalities there were; Italian, Swedish, German, English, American, Kiwi, Spanish, even some from Israel. It was well beyond my experience, this really was an international melting pot, but luckily for me the common language was English and I spoke it, although I could tell many had a few problems with my Glasgow accent.

It seemed being a DJ out here held a lot of kudos and Roberto got as much credit from knowing me as I did him, and although technically I didn't even have the job yet, I was introduced as Krob, Manu's new DJ from the UK. Roberto and I got on well but I was getting a bit bored with his one-track mind; it seemed his only motivation was to bed as many chicks as he could in the shortest possible time. While this is an acceptable aim, there are other things to life, such as... hmmm... drinking and taking drugs. Hehe. As for the drugs, it seemed that they were a little thin on the ground and if you were caught even smoking a spliff you could expect a proper kicking from the cops and a long trip to what sounded like a medieval dungeon. But the drink was there in abundance and soon I was half-cut and relaxing with my new-found friends, thoughts of Glasgow, police and self-pity blown away like dust in a hurricane.

It seemed there was a set routine round these parts; meet at Bench Bar then start working your way up the hill to the nightclub, Coca Club, stopping at various bars on the way. By now, I was with a group of English lads from Leicester as well as Roberto and a few girls, so we headed off to the first bar on the corner. As we entered, I noticed a nod passed between Roberto and the barman, a hugely overweight Greek man with a bushy moustache. This was my first clue to Roberto's occupation, he was a sort of bar shepherd, touting business for the establishments in the town.

Soon we were moving on and up again. We reached the next bar and I went to enter, but Roberto quickly held me back. 'We don't go in there,' he told me and before I could ask why, we were off. I was having a great time and was getting on really well with the English lads, who were doing mad shit like having funnels of beer poured down their throats and dancing on the tables. By the time we finally arrived at the Coca Club, we were all pretty much worse for wear – well, I was anyway. Wide white stairs led down to a large white doorway with pillars either side. The building itself was also bright white with a huge red sign above the door, saying Coca Club in the style of the Coca Cola logo. Music boomed out. I gripped the metal railing a little unsteadily, stared up at the sign and let out a little laugh. The Coca Club by fuck? With a name like that, nobody was going to tell me there was no fucking drugs in this place, surely it was the cocaine club!

We staggered down the stairs and waited at the entrance as the doorman blocked our way. Looking past him, I could see what seemed like a sea of blonde-haired girls dancing inside. Roberto pushed to the front and handed over a sheaf of small cards with the Coca Club logo on the front; cool – guest passes. We breezed past the till and entered.

It was totally kicking, wild in fact, what a night, a blur of drinking and dancing. The music, while not up-to-date house music like I played in Glasgow, wasn't commercial holiday shit, instead it was an eclectic mixture of alternative stuff like the Cure, the Jam, The The, AC/DC, the Smiths, Nirvana, etc. (I NEED TO SORT OUT COCA CLUB PLAYLIST, I noted to myself.) Anyway, it was well good and there were an incredible amount of tall, fit blonde girls. In fact, I had noticed Pelekas seemed to be infested with them. I asked Roberto and was informed that this was a stop-off point for Swedish students as they travelled the Greek islands. Wow, what a fucking town! And it was in the Coca Club where I first met Juliet.

It seemed I had been right about the cocaine club... I mean Coca Club, and within the first hour Roberto, one of the Leicester boys and myself were in the tiny toilet filling our nostrils with shiny white powder. So much for the long stretch in jail. Feeling like a million dollars, I exited the cubicle and headed towards the bar and there she was.

Shoulder-length dark hair and a small black dress, body like a gymnast (which it turned out she was) and an angelic face with the cutest little ski jump nose. She stood out from the blonde Swedish posse like tits on a fish. I stopped at the DJ box to observe her for a bit. She was with another girl, or more like a woman, that looked very like her – must be her sister, I decided. There was no denying she was drop-dead gorgeous. But it wasn't just that, there was something special about her. The way she brushed her hair from her face and flicked it back into place with a tilt of her head, her smile and not to mention the long slim legs and *that dress*.

The huge quantities of booze and that line of cocaine had made me God's gift to women so I sauntered over to the bar to move in for the kill. Got to within a few feet, my bottle crashed and instead went to prop up the bar beside them. Shit.

As I ordered my drink, I sneaked some sidelong glances in her direction. She was looking back. I took the plunge. 'Hi, my name's Krob.' I looked into her big dark eyes and offered my hand.

'Nice to meet you, I'm Juliet,' she said, taking my head.

It was as easy as that. The small talk flowed. She was from Nuneaton, a town near Coventry, and having just finished school, she was here on holiday. I, of course, was a wanted criminal on the run from the police, with no secure job and an uncertain future, but I missed that bit out and told her the DJ stuff and how I was bored of Glasgow and had just decided to go travelling for a few years, first stop Pelekas. She seemed impressed with this and when I asked to be introduced to her sister I scored more points, it turned out it was her mother! She was very impressed and flattered at my error. Roberto started sniffing about giving them lecherous looks, but I ignored him.

After a few dances and more drinks, they said they should go as the little brother was alone sleeping at the pension (Greek for small hotel). I immediately offered to walk them home. I could tell the mother was impressed with this and I brassed it by taking Juliet's hand as we unsteadily climbed the steps to leave. The rush of cold air outside was the perfect tonic and as we walked back under the clear night sky and dazzling stars, hand in hand, everything seemed perfect. We arrived at the pension and my heart missed a beat when Juliet told her mother that she would be up in a minute. The mother had obviously decided I was the perfect gentleman and I even got a peck on the cheek as she left, telling Juliet not to be too long (i.e. not to go back to the Coca Club or my room).

Juliet and I sat on the steps smoking, chatting and then kissing. I couldn't believe my luck, there was no way that I was just going to walk away and let this girl go so I asked her if I could meet her for dinner the next night. We arranged to meet at the Bench Bar at eight p.m. She tried to leave about five times but kept coming back again to kiss me more. I thought of asking her if she wanted to come back to mine but something stopped me. Good things come to those who wait (one of my granny's many old sayings) and eventually she went in. I stood on the steps and watched her climb the stairs, and at the top she turned and blew me a kiss. Amazing.

I had a spring in my step as I bounced back up to the Coca Club, the words of The Police song 'Walking on the Moon' going through my head.

Walking back from your house

Walking on the moon

Back in the club, Roberto wanted to know all the details; had I banged her, was her sister up for it, where were they? He seemed very unimpressed when I told him the story. A few kisses and a dinner date was a total failure in his book and he headed off disappointed in me. I didn't give a fuck and went to the bar to get some hardcore shots to celebrate. A few tequila slammers with the Leicester lads and I was flying. After that things got a bit fuzzy, dancing on the tables outside on the balcony, a bit more cocaine, the place closing and getting tossed out by the doorman, running amok in the streets around the Bench Bar, more drinks there from the bar that never closes on the corner and then just before brain death, up the backstairs and out cold on the bed. Nice night.

* * *

The next morning, I was sitting mulling all this over when I heard a voice call up to me.

'Hey, Krob, you coming down for a coffee?'

Looking over the balcony, I saw Michael, one of the Leicester lads, down below. Coffee? Brilliant idea.

Sitting outside at a table at the cafe at the end of the road, we ordered our coffees and when they came, I took a large slurp and nearly spat it out on the floor.

'Aargh, what the fuck is that?'

Looking down into the cup, I saw it had a weird marble-like effect on the top and the taste was rough like it had grit in it. Michael just laughed. 'They drink Turkish-style coffee here; you'll get used to it.'

'No I fucking won't.' And with that, I got up to get a real coffee.

It turned out Michael was up early because he was working on a building site in the town; it was shit pay but enough to stay here for the season. He had invited his mates out for a two-week bender, so that explained the Leicester invasion. The rest of the lads were, of course, still in their beds. I made a mental note to invite my lot out as soon as possible, Norman Muirhead and Daddy Mac just had to see this place. Michael seemed like a good guy and it turned out he was a fan of house music too. I could see many a night propping up the bar in Manu's on the cards (providing I actually got the job, that is). Michael asked about the girl I had left with, it seemed I wasn't the only one that thought she was drop-dead gorgeous, en garde. Roll on eight o'clock! Michael left for work and I sat there with another coffee, nursing my hangover and watching the world go by.

There seemed to be a mixture of old-world types passing with donkeys loaded up with bundles of grass, wizened old ladies dressed in black and bent-backed old codgers muttering to themselves while smoking some hideous-smelling black tobacco. And then there were the new-school types on motorbikes or in 4x4s, smartly dressed, car stereos blaring – these must be people involved in the tourist industry, I decided.

My thoughts were broken by the arrival of a cop car. I was just taking a sip of my coffee as they cruised past when I froze, cup to lips, as they turned towards me, staring at me through large mirrored sunglasses, their unshaven, greasy, fat faces checking me right out. Jesus, these boys didn't look too friendly. It seemed like their bad vibes had darkened the day and I shivered as if a shadow had passed in front of the sun. Then they were gone and all returned to normal.

Hmmm. As the only black guy in the place, I stood right out, so I made another mental note to stay out of trouble.

By now, some tourists were up and about, looking like they were heading down to the beach. That was a great idea, but I had stuff to do, so I sat there keeping an eye out for Juliet but to no avail. Suddenly I noticed that the shutters were up at Manu's place, time to go get a job. I slurped down the rest of my coffee and headed over.

Sure enough, Manu and Stella were in there tidying up. Manu was obviously expecting me and stopped what he was doing to shake my hand. He didn't waste much time with bullshit and got right down to it. 'Okay, Krob,' he said, 'let's hear you play.'

Music to my ears. I ran upstairs and got my record box, hangover forgotten. Getting behind the decks, I saw with satisfaction that they were Technics and that they also had a decent Vestax mixer, better and better. Before I began, I had a look through the tunes that were already there; quite similar to the stuff I had heard last night at the Coca Club with a bit of shit holiday crap thrown in. Time to do my thing.

A few minutes later, I was cutting and mixing some of his records into my house tracks. You could see he was impressed; he had probably never seen or heard anything like it before. His girlfriend had already fetched a few of her friends from the square and they were all leaning over the DJ box checking out what I was doing. I played a few more mixes and then flicked the power to the deck off, letting the record slow to a stop while I cut the beat in and out. They all clapped and cheered and I smiled back with a big cheesy grin on my face.

'So...' I began, 'have I got the job?'

The look on Manu's face spoke a thousand words and soon we were toasting to my newfound employment with some hideous aniseed Greek aperitif called Ouzo (a drink I was to become intimate with in the following months). Everything was falling into place, it seemed Manu had been playing the tunes himself as the previous DJ was such a pisshead, he had been sacked at the end of last season (this must have been some feat judging by the drunks I had met so far!). So we were all happy. The deal was: free drinks, I could use the room upstairs to live in and I would get paid every week, not much by UK standards but fuck it, this place seemed like paradise. My only condition was to start tomorrow as I had my dinner date tonight. This was agreed and I went upstairs to unpack my stuff.

Spreading my things on the bed, I realised, not for the first time, that I had brought far too much kit. For example, did I really need a Rambo knife with a thirty-centimetre blade? Picking it up and pulling it from the sheaf I slashed the air back and forth, the gleaming blade sparkling in the sunshine as it whistled through the room. Fuck me, this baby would even impress the bad boys back in Glasgow. It was the kind of knife you could use to gut a bull elephant. Still, you never know. One thing that was definitely a good idea was the enormous ghetto blaster. Bright yellow and black with twin cassette decks and a ten-inch woofer, it looked and sounded the part. This was my insurance policy; if shit went down I planned to sell it and get out of dodge. But right now it had only one purpose, I went over to it and hit the play button. BOOM-TSS... BOOM-TSS... filled the room as I took a shower.

With my job sorted I was now free to hit the beach. I toyed with the idea of going to find out if Juliet was at her pension but I realised I didn't even know what room they were in. Anyway, best not to seem too keen, I would probably bump into them there.

I grabbed my towel and things and headed down. I had been told it was a long way and my sources weren't kidding. I was well hot and sweating before I even saw the sea, but it was worth it. Rounding a corner on the small dirt track, suddenly there it was, still a long way below but what a view. The sea was bright, bright blue, and from my vantage point I could see the whole coastline for miles. It seemed Pelekas beach was more like a massive crescent-shaped cove, maybe half a mile across, with golden sands and rocky outcrops guarding each end like giant weatherbeaten sentinels. My gaze was drawn out to sea where the water became a deeper blue and on to another coast, miles and miles away, shimmering in the sunlight. That must be Albania, the still-communist state, a secret country with sealed borders.

My excitement grew. I abandoned the view and almost started to run down the track. Suddenly I came across a hand-painted sign saying simply in English, *BEACH*. It pointed to a small path that led away from the road and into some olive trees. A shortcut surely, and a shaded one too, away from the heat of the road. Cooler now, I stepped up the pace and was soon running and jumping down the steep path. Eventually, out of breath, I cleared the trees and there it was, the beach. Just one more spurt would be enough. I sprinted forward through the sand, stopping only briefly to dump my stuff, then I was off again, the hot sand burning my bare feet as I ran. I reached the water, it splashed around me as I drove myself forward, deeper and deeper. Finally, when I knew I would fall, I dived in, a perfect entry, shallow and long with hardly a splash. Ecstatic, I disappeared into the cool water, letting my dive take me forward and back up, reappearing and shouting, 'YEAH... FUCKING... YEAH!', while jumping up and down and waving my arms about like a madman.

As you can tell, I like the beach, always have, always will.

Finally sated, I realised I needed a drink. My hangover combined with the trek to the beach had left my mouth drier than an Arab's sandal and I exited the water, collected my things and headed for the nearest bar/restaurant only fifty metres away.

I sat at a table smoking a cigarette, cradling an ice-cold Pepsi and, with my shades on, checked out the beach. You would have to be sexually crippled or have a pathological hatred of fit topless blondes not to be affected by it. The talent was unbelievable, but there was something missing, and it took me a few minutes to put my finger on it. Then it hit me; there were no families or old people. I realised it must be the trek down here. This place was perfect. The only stain on this perfection, to me anyway, was the two naked suntanned Greek men playing a form of table tennis at the edge of the water with wooden bats, their hairy arses and peckers on display. Well, you can't have everything.

Then I remembered Juliet, finished my drink and went for a wander. I didn't find her but instead came across some of the Leicester lads and the rest of the day was spent drinking beer, swimming, talking shit and, of course, checking out the girls.

Evening arrived and it was time to get back up the road. It turned out that you didn't have to walk after all. There were two battered old open-back trucks crammed with punters that did the run for a few drachmas. As we slowly wound up the hill, the sun was starting to get low in the sky and the red glow that spread from the mountains painted the landscape. It was breathtaking.

Jumping off the back of the transport in the square, I headed straight to my room to get washed and polished for my date. Twenty minutes later, there I was standing in front of the bathroom mirror in my best gear, looking good, or so I thought but now I know better. There is a Facebook site called 'Pelekas Bench Bar' and I have browsed it, finding some photos of me. Cringeworthy stuff, what the fuck was I wearing? A hideous top with *Fiori* written on it, which I now know means flower in Italian, and a red bandana to boot. Still, the cutoff denims and the canvas shoes weren't too bad, I suppose. Anyway, I digress, so long as you think you look good, that's what matters, it's eighty per cent confidence. If you're confident then you carry it off even if you do look like a twat. Standing there admiring myself, I realised I didn't have a clue what restaurant to go to or anything. Oops. I went downstairs to see Stella; she was bound to have some ideas.

Perched at the end of the bar, cold beer and cigarette in hand, I got some advice and with Stella's help soon had it all planned out. She was going to lend me her scooter and I would drive Juliet up past Coca Club to the Sunset Bar restaurant. This was a place where (as the name suggests) you went to view the sunset but as it was now nearly dark, it would be quiet and apparently it served the best food around. After scoff, back down to Manu's, then the Bench Bar and finally to Coca Club. I was starting to really like Stella, she seemed to have sussed that I liked this girl and thought the whole wine and dine thing was sweet. I already felt relaxed in Stella's company and knew that I was making a good friend.

Looking at my watch I saw it was already 7.50 p.m. Stella told me to get my skates on, gave me a final beer and shoved me out the door. Sitting on the wall, I started to get a little nervous. What if she didn't turn up? I kept looking up at the corner. But I was worrying about nothing as by 8.05 p.m. I spotted her coming, but unfortunately tagging along was the mother and little brother. This was defo not in the fucking plan! I stood up when they arrived and tried to hide my disappointment. Juliet looked just as stunning as last night, even without my beer goggles. Stella had said to make sure that I kissed her on the cheek when she arrived as it's the custom here. When in Rome (or Greece)... I kissed her and the mother and then started to wonder how all four of us were going to fit on one scooter? The mother must have sussed me out and quickly said her goodbyes and headed off with the little brother. I breathed a sigh of relief and bold as brass put an arm around Juliet and headed into Manu's. Stella was right on it and soon we had a quiet table on the balcony and with a wink she was off to fetch some cocktails.

Conversation flowed with no awkward silences and while we talked I just looked at Juliet, amazed at how gorgeous she was. I explained the plan and went over to the bar to get the scooter keys.

'Here they are,' Stella said as she handed them across. 'Krob, you be careful, don't crash my baby.' Stella looked over to where Juliet was sitting. 'And you be nice to that girl, she's very sweet, just promise to treat her right.'

I looked over too. Yes, very, very sweet. I promised and took the keys.

The scooter was maybe not the manliest of rides as it was bright fucking pink but beggars can't be choosers. It started the first time and we were off. I noticed Michael and Roberto sitting at the Bench Bar and gave them a toot on the horn, trying to keep the big cheesy grin off my face. They waved as we left them behind and accelerated up the hill, weaving through the tourists. We passed the Coca Club and left the town for the open road. I opened the throttle and the little bike responded admirably. As the speed increased I noticed Juliet move closer and tightly wrap her hands round my waist.

As we sat with glasses of wine checking the menu, I secretly thanked Stella for her help, this place was perfect. Our table was on the balcony looking to the west where the sunset would have been. The sky was still red on the horizon but the moon was rising high and looked huge compared to the one back in the UK. Stars were beginning to come out high above, soft music was playing on the stereo and we almost had the place to ourselves.

We were sitting there listening to Phil Collins's 'In the Air Tonight', looking into each other's eyes. I leaned over and kissed her and we were still kissing when the waiter came to take the order. I was falling for this girl big time.

Back at Manu's, we sat with that well-stuffed feeling sipping Southern Comfort and lemonade. I felt guilty just sitting there while Manu played the tunes, so I volunteered to spin for half an hour. The place was busy and I soon had the dance floor heaving. I looked up at Juliet and felt a flash of anger as guess who was sitting next to her? The incorrigible Roberto sniffing around. I caught myself... fucking hell, was that jealousy I could detect? After all, he was only chatting to her. I finished up my set quick style and headed back over. I gave her a peck on the cheek and almost nudged Roberto off the seat as I pushed in.

'What's happening, gorgeous?' I asked, ignoring him.

'Oh, nothing really,' she replied. 'Roberto here was just telling me a group of them are going down to the beach later in his friend's jeep for a nighttime swim.'

'Oh, was he really?' It wasn't a question. I gave him a firm nudge in the ribs with my elbow.

He seemed shocked, I don't think he was used to being treated like that. Well, he had a lot to learn about me then! 'So... Roberto, you're inviting *us* for a trip to the beach then?'

He recovered quickly. 'Eh... yes, yes. You both come then... after Coca Club. Okay, I'd better go now.'

I nodded and he left. We watched him go. 'He seems like a nice guy?' commented Juliet.

'Hmm,' I replied, 'yes... lovely.'

I won't bore you with the Bench Bar and the Coca Club. Basically the same shit, different night, except I got talking to the owner this time and got him to promise to give me a set at the club which was cool as fuck. By the end, I was slow dancing to cheesy tunes with the best of them, which in that place was basically a grope-a-thon. Oh dear. Then it was outside and into the jeep. I could see Juliet was a little worried when she saw the driver stagger out of the club and then fall into the driver's seat. She wasn't the only one. In my mind, I could picture the jeep as it plunged off the road in the dark, rolling over and over down the steep slope then blowing up in a ball of flame, just like in the movies. We decided that if his driving was out of order through the town, we'd jump out and walk the rest.

This was forgotten about as Michael came out clutching a crate of beer and some Swedish girl and jumped aboard. I was glad he was coming along as I got on well with him. The trip down the track was pretty scary really, including a few close calls with the edge, but it was worth it once we were on the beach, drinking and smoking under the stars. I noticed that Roberto kept well away and we sat chatting with Michael and his Swedish bird who turned out to be training to be a nuclear physicist, which was a bit weird. Anyway, it wasn't long before we were stripping off our clothes and heading to the water. There was no way I was taking off my boxer shorts as the sight of a topless Juliet was severely affecting me. I don't know if you've ever been late-night skinny dipping before, but if not you should definitely try it, preferably pissed up with some mates. It's wicked. Even more wicked is moving away from that group a little with your gorgeous, sexy-as-fuck partner for a bit of fun. We stood waist-deep in the water, our arms wrapped around each other. I rose to the occasion and wanted to just rip her pants off and bang her right there and then and had to make a conscious effort to contain myself. After all, there were a lot of people there, what if I got knocked back? Plus, I had no condoms and I'd never even had sex in the water before, was it even possible?

On the trip up in the jeep we were totally shattered. Juliet was well pissed and kept falling asleep on me. I had to hold her tight to stop her being catapulted out of the car. I got them to drop us off at her pension, by which time I was basically carrying her. It occurred to me that maybe this was the condition Roberto aimed for before going back to his. Lucky for Juliet, I'm a bit of a gentleman and I managed to get her to point me in the right direction to her room and we staggered up the stairs. I wasn't looking forward to this, guaranteed the mother was up waiting for her darling daughter to get home. I almost decided to dump her at the doorway and bolt, but no, I had taken her out, I would return her.

I checked the door... cool... it was open... I tried to be quiet going in but we must have made enough noise to wake the dead as we crashed about the apartment, we defo woke the mother anyway. She hit the lights and as I stood there squinting into the bright glare, supporting her pissed-up daughter, I could see she was none too pleased.

'I think you'd better leave,' was all she said.

I tried to reply with some lame excuse, but as I slurred bullshit, I realised that Juliet wasn't the only one who was pissed up, so I placed her gently on the couch, kissed her on the cheek and beat a hasty retreat. I heard the door slam behind me as I bounced off the corridor walls on my way out.

The next morning, I was sitting in the cafe again, hiding behind my shades and nursing another hangover, wondering whether I should venture up to Juliet's and face the music or just sit there and feel like shit. As I considered my options, she came around the corner. Unfortunately, mother and kid brother were in tow too, but they hadn't spotted me yet and were busy looking at Manu's shuttered and bolted-up bar. Maybe I should just stay low. It was too early in the morning to get shouted at and with my hangover there was the risk I would just end up telling the mum to fuck off.

Too late. They had spotted me.

They came up to my table. I looked up at Juliet amazed that she still looked as beautiful hungover first thing in the morning as she did last night. I wanted to give her a kiss, but instead stood up and tried to pretend nothing had happened.

'Morning,' I began brightly. 'Can I get you two a tea or coffee? And what about you, wee guy, do you want a Pepsi?'

We all sat down and Juliet croaked that she just wanted water, the mum wanted nothing (a bad sign, I thought) and little bro, a Pepsi, of course. I ordered and waited for the shit storm.

Her mum took a deep breath and began. 'About last night...' Here it comes, I thought. '...I just wanted to say that I'm sorry if I seemed a little ungrateful last night. It was because I was worried. But Juliet's a big girl now, old enough to make her own decisions, and after all, we are on holiday, and on reflection I don't think she could be in better hands than yours. You took her to dinner, out dancing, even to the beach at night, and you looked after her and brought her back safely. I'm almost jealous, I can't remember the last time her father and I went skinny dipping!'

'Mum! Shut up!' Juliet was getting embarrassed

I was lost for words and must have looked it. I glanced from Juliet to her mum, and finally little bro, who was staring at me as he sucked the life out of his Pepsi. I randomly thought that maybe he wasn't the full shilling.

'Erm... yeah, right, are you sure you wouldn't like a coffee?'

'No, no,' she replied, 'we'll be off and leave you two alone for a bit. Then we'll come back and we'll all go to the beach?'

'Eh... yes,' I replied, 'that would be lovely.'

Her mum gave Juliet a kiss and left with the little bro.

Juliet sighed with relief and came to sit beside me, slumping onto my shoulder. 'Aaargh... I feel like death warmed up,' she complained. 'That was some night last night... what I can remember, that is.'

'Yes,' I agreed, running my fingers through her hair. 'Last night was wicked.'

Suddenly, she sat up. 'Oh no... I think I'm going to be sick...'

Strangely enough, I think it was at this moment that I realised I was falling in love with this girl, just as I ran into the bar and grabbed a small plastic bin and gave it to her and gently stroked the back of her neck as she threw up into it. I noticed that some guy and his woman were staring at us in disgust so I ripped off my shades and asked them, 'What the fuck do you think you're looking at?'

Angry black man with a Glasgwegian accent in the area? They quickly moved on and I tended to Juliet.

Dictionary: *Love – an intense feeling of tenderness and compassion. A passionate feeling of romantic desire and sexual attraction.*

It doesn't quite do it justice by half, does it? Let me try.

Love – an overpowering feeling of the need for someone, characterised by inability to think of anything else, feelings of jealousy, protectiveness, butterflies in stomach, urge to shag them stupid, blind faith in everything they say and do and the improbable belief that this is forever. Probably caused by chemical imbalances in the brain brought on by the genetic need to reproduce and protect the offspring with a suitable mate.

Anyway, it's a rollercoaster and I had a season ticket. It's unfortunate that I had never heard the term holiday romance... Oops! Oh well, I was young.

The following meetup was the good time. We were inseparable, joined at the hip. Probably sickening to those on the outside, except Stella who thought it was sweet and also the mum who thought the sun shone out of my ass. Inseparable for the next ten days until Juliet was due to go back to the UK at any rate. That was the elephant in the room that was never discussed.

Instead of using Stella's scooter all the time, we rented one of our own and were mobile. Up and down to the beach at will, we even ventured out away from Pelekas to the south of the island to try some other beaches and bars, but let me tell you as far as Corfu is concerned, Pelekas is king. We had what became a ritual, every evening just before sundown we would drive up to the sunset restaurant and watch the sun go down, and it was there that the relationship upped a gear.

Juliet squeezed my hand. I was staring into the dripping red sky. 'Look at me,' she said.

'What... sorry?' I was lost in space.

'Look at me,' she said again. 'There's something I want to tell you.' That got my attention. 'Krob... I think... I think that I love you.'

I looked back at her and got all warm and fuzzy inside. 'Yes, babes... I love you too.'

'B-But I'm leaving in five days...' I noticed there was a tear in her eye as she leaned closer, almost whispering now. 'I don't want to go home, I want to stay here with you.'

I sighed. 'I don't want you to go either.'

The elephant in the room was now rampaging about smashing up the furniture and trumpeting loud enough to shatter the fucking windows. I just held her close and wiped away the tears, turning my head so she couldn't see I was crying too. Finally, she collected herself and spoke.

'Krob?'

'Yes?'

'Tonight I want to go down to the beach and go skinny dipping again...' She paused, sat back and smiled. '...just the two of us this time.'

Oh yeah... this was it, wild thing all night long. Good things come to those who wait.

The sense of anticipation was almost unbearable, it felt like electricity was flowing between us. We drove back to Manu's where I played my set, but it seemed to go on forever. At last it was finished. I couldn't stand it any longer.

'Look, babes... let's not go to Coca Club or the Bench bar... Let's go straight to the beach, yeah?'

I got a big kiss and a yes. I went up to Stella to see if I could get a bottle of wine. I got one and was about to walk away when she called me back.

'Krob,' she said. 'You might be needing one of these.' She had a bottle opener in one hand and two glasses in the other. Was it so obvious? I asked for a bag too.

Well... sex in the water is possible after all and it was amazing; consummating a relationship with someone who had just told you they loved you in such circumstances was truly mind-blowing, and afterwards I went to fetch the bottle of wine and we stayed in the sea sipping it from the glasses and cuddling. The stars and moon were out and the Mediterranean was glassy smooth, only tiny ripples lapping against the shore. I felt more content and at peace with myself than I ever had before. The anger that always bubbled below my surface seemed to have floated away and I was calm. I didn't want it ever to end.

Eventually, I realised Juliet was shivering so we left the water, dressed and headed back up the track – we were late to meet her mum. Back at Manu's I returned the bag to Stella. Now I'd always thought it was just bullshit that girls and boys glow and give off some weird aura after top sex, but when Stella smiled and looked mischievously at me and I noticed Juliet's mum was regarding us very suspiciously as well, Maybe it's true after all.

Anyway, something had changed, this girl was mine now, and it felt good. But in the back of my mind a shadow of darkness was growing, like the first sign of a storm gathering.

6

ULTRAVIOLENCE AND A WEDDING

Time flew by as the days counted down and suddenly it was D-Day. All their stuff was packed and there was only thirty minutes till the taxi arrived to take them to the airport. We split on the bike for one last drink at Manu's. The mood was dark and we sat in silence. I stared into my drink. Finally, I spoke. 'Well, this is it then.' A stupid and blindingly obvious thing to say but also unfortunately totally true.

'No, it's not,' Juliet started. 'As soon as I get back I'll get a job and save up and come back here...'

I looked over at her, assessing her. She meant it all right but it's an easy thing to say now, sitting here, but back in Blighty... who knows? I said nothing.

She looked back at me with a hard look on her face I had never seen before.

'Maybe you don't know me as well as you think.' I raised an eyebrow at this and she continued. 'I'll be fucking back here if it's the last thing I fucking do... And another thing, you better fucking wait for me.' She slammed her drink down on the table. Stella looked up from the glass she was cleaning.

I couldn't suppress my smile. 'Wait for you, babes? I'm missing you already.'

'You'd better be. If I find out I'm just some holiday romance, it'll be my dad that comes over here to wring your neck.'

Holiday romance? I let the concept wash over me, then rejected it. 'Juliet, I think my neck's pretty safe.'

The taxi was loaded and I was standing there doing the small talk with the mum – *goodbye, how nice it was to meet you, you must come to England to visit, hasn't it been nice*? – I hate goodbyes, especially long, drawn-out ones.

Saying goodbye to Juliet was a nightmare; kisses, cuddles and tears. Then they were gone, the taxi lifting a cloud from the dusty road as it sped off. I did the obligatory watch-while waving-till-out-of-sight thing and then headed to Manu's, ordered a double Jack Daniel's and coke and slammed it down on a table, shades on and staring straight ahead.

'Krob? Sorry, love,' Stella called out from behind the bar.

Stella really was an all right girl. I turned and managed to smile back thinly. 'Thanks, but I'll live.'

And I went back to staring straight ahead, anger inexplicably rising inside. Why is the wrong track always fucking playing at times like this? It's one of those things that really makes me wonder about this reality. At that moment it was 'Drive' by The Cars, the lyrics ringing true: 'Who's going to pay attention to your dreams? / Who's going to drive you home tonight?' Fuck off.

Next thing I knew, Michael and his nuclear physicist Swedish bird came and sat beside me.

'Hey, Krob, Juliet left then?' Michael asked. I just nodded darkly. I didn't feel much like chatting at that moment. 'Look, man, we're really sorry, she was a top girl, but listen, we've got a plan.'

'Plan?' I lifted my sunglasses from my eyes.

'Yes, a plan,' he continued, 'we're going out to a new nightclub across the island this evening. Why not come with us and drown your sorrows?'

'Sorry, I can't... I'm working here tonight,' I replied

'No, you're not. I've cleared it with Manu, you've got the night off.'

I looked over at Manu, he nodded. It was then I realised I had some really good friends in Pelekas. I thought for a few seconds. 'Erm, yeah, why not? Thanks, guys.'

So, it was back in the jeep with the motley crew: Roberto, his driver, Michael, the Swedish nuclear physicist and some added randoms. Stereo blaring, we wound our way down out of the hills, through Corfu town and to the south of the island. It's much more commercial down there, proper two-week holiday shit, English breakfasts and Guinness. I mean, why people want that shit when they're away from home beats me, surely you travel to experience new stuff, not just Blighty with some sunshine? Anyway, we were tooting the horn at hot chicks and drinking beers from a cool box in the bag. Everyone was having a good time, except me; I played the part but inside the darkness was gathering.

The club was basically a shitter: shit music, shit people, shit decor, shit lights, shit system, but it had one thing going for it – free booze. It was the whole reason we were there. Roberto knew the owner, and as this was opening night he had a pocket full of free drink vouchers which he handed out.

Drown my sorrows? I was having a good try. One ticket got you one Jack Daniel's or two Ouzos... So, Ouzos it was then. Now there's something very wrong with Ouzo, especially if you can be a bit volatile like myself and especially, *especially* if the love of your life has just split back to the UK. I know how it starts, my brow furrows and my eyebrows start to bunch in, I ball and un-ball my right fist. That's how it starts, but how it finishes, I never know. I caught myself and calmed the fuck down. We were all seated on this naff pink couch thing and Roberto was talking to some English tourist chick so I talked to her friend who wasn't bad-looking at all, short, spiky blonde hair, quite small and thin, cropped top showing off a tanned stomach and a short red kind of hockey skirt and shiny trainers. It was a forgettable kind of conversation and my heart wasn't in it but the chick seemed happy enough, so on it went... Blah, blah, blah... now the DJ was playing the fucking conga and the idiot punters had formed a snake and were embarrassing themselves by weaving their way around the club. Oh, for a machinegun to put them out of their misery.

I don't start trouble, I hate to throw the first punch, always better to let them do it, so then you've got right on your side and you can go to town, but when I want to I'm a masterclass at making sure they fling that punch, kick or bottle. Trouble finds those that look for it and by now I'd had shit loads of who-the-fuck-are-you-looking-at stares. The stage was set.

As it turned out, I didn't have to do a thing. I was watching Michael dance with the physicist when some Neanderthal English guy came up and felt her ass, Michael pushed him away and the guy punched him in the face and Michael went down. This was more than enough excuse; attack my friend, would you? Bad move, motherfucker!

I jumped up, sending drinks flying, and using the railing around the dance floor as a springboard, got my whole body airborne and smashed the guy right on the kisser. With my entire weight behind it, the guy didn't just go down, he flew backwards across the dancefloor and right into a table, spilling drinks all over the punters who sat there. I know it's not good to glorify violence but this was a punch to be proud of; I'll never throw another one like that one. Everyone froze for a second. Then the place erupted. Proper Vesuvius style.

The guys looked down at their drink-soaked clothes, stood up, vaulted the table and started towards me. The friends of the guy I'd sparked out moved in too and a group of Greeks that were on the lookout for trouble weighed in as well. The three mobs that were trying to reach me crashed into each other on the dancefloor and fists and feet started flying. A guy came into me from the side and cracked me in the face but soon regretted it as he punched like a little girl's blouse. He desperately tried to get away as I pummelled him. He sank into the melee around us. Meanwhile, the fight had spread, it seemed the whole club was battling Hollywood bar-room brawl style. Oh shit, what the fuck had I done? The music went off and I could hear the smashing of bottles.

Not everyone had forgotten about me unfortunately, and I could see three guys fighting through the crowd towards me and one was fucking massive; he was wading through the punters by simply pushing people to the side with his huge arms. Oops, time to get to fuck. I started for the door. I nearly made it too, then I heard a cry of, 'THERE HE IS!'.

Some big greasy motherfucker tackled me from the side and we went down. I struggled like a madman to get him off, throwing punches, knees, elbows, anything, I just had to get back on my feet. An elbow caught him in the face; I heard a crack and I felt his grip loosen. I staggered upright, just in time to get smashed to the floor by the mob. I curled into a ball and tried to protect my head as the blows rained in. It was nasty business and I think I lost consciousness for a few seconds. As far as I could make out, the mob started to fight amongst themselves because next thing I remember I was crawling through their legs as the madness went on above me.

As I got to the edge, I felt a girl's arm reach under mine and help me up. It was the blonde girl I had been talking to earlier. 'Quick,' she said, 'come with me, you've got to get out of here.'

I didn't need a second telling and with legs still like jelly, I staggered out the front door, face down as she supported me. Outside, the cold hit me. My head started to clear. I wondered where the others were and started to look around me.

'No, no.' The blonde girl was pulling on my arm. 'We've got to go, you don't understand, these are some dangerous people! Quick, quick, this way!'

She was leading me across the car park and towards a low wall when I heard a commotion behind me. Looking round, I saw the English guys I had been fighting with (including the one I had punched) running out of the club towards me. But they weren't after me; they were trying to escape from a group of Greeks with bottles and fucking baseball bats! Time to go. We got over the wall just as a cop car screeched round the corner. Then we were running, behind a building over another wall, across some waste ground and, finally breathless, we sat on a wall at the end of a driveway to catch our breath. The girl was still with me. In gasps, we talked it over.

'Fuck me,' said one of the English guys, 'those guys mean fucking business!'

'Yeah. Last week, I saw that same group of Greeks put some guys in the hospital. They hang around bars and clubs waiting for trouble. I think they're in with the cops too,' explained the girl.

I saw the guy I had punched. His left eye was nearly swollen shut. 'Shit, man,' I said to him, 'sorry about that, but you punched my mate and touched up his girlfriend.'

'Yeah, mate, sorry. I was just pissed up, being an arsehole, so I deserved it. But fuck me, you can throw a punch. It felt like being hit by a bus!'

'You caught me on a bad night, that's all,' I replied and we shook hands.

'Do you think it's wise to stay in this town now after this?' one of the English guys asked.

'No way,' replied the girl, 'you want to get as far away as possible. These guys won't give up.'

'Well, where I'm staying is fucking great, a town up north called Pelekas. It's wicked, not commercial like this dump. You could come there,' I offered.

'Pelekas you say? Sounds gre—'

Suddenly, there was a screeching of tyres as a car skidded to a halt at the end of the driveway. We all looked around. Before it had even come to a halt, three big Greeks jumped out with baseball bats. I could hear another vehicle approaching fast too. Oh shit, we split in all directions. The girl and I jumped the wall and started running. But one of us had not been quick enough and I could hear the sickening thuds of bats on flesh and screaming as we ran.

'Quick,' said the girl, 'my apartment's just round the corner. You can hide there.'

Next thing, I was lying on her bed as she looked at my injuries. 'God, they really did a job on you,' she commented as she dabbed at my face with hot water and cotton wool.

Till then, I hadn't really thought about it. Getting a kicking doesn't really hurt at the time, the adrenaline blocks it out but as that wore off, it was starting to hurt big time, and now it was my eye that was swelling shut.

'Why are you doing this?' I asked her.

'Doing what?' she replied

'Helping me. I mean, you don't even know me. All you know is that I started a massive bar brawl.'

'Well, for one thing you didn't start it...'

'I suppose so,' I agreed.

'And for another thing, I saw what those guys did last week. They nearly killed that poor lad. Apparently, he's in a coma in hospital.'

'Shit. That could have been me. Thanks.'

'Oh, and one last thing, you're pretty cute as well.' With that, she gave me a kiss on the lips.

I broke it off quickly. 'Ouch, that hurt. But wait, I don't even know your name.'

'Anna,' she replied.

'I'm Krob. And as for cute, I doubt it now. Can you pass me that mirror?'

Anna passed me a small hand mirror that was on the bedside table and I had a look. It wasn't actually that bad. Okay, my left eye was swollen shut, I had a cut lip and there were some nasty-looking bumps on my head, but I was still in one piece, if a little groggy. The worst pain was my ribs; they had taken a proper pounding but they didn't feel broken. Anna gave me some paracetamol and a massive glass of straight whisky to wash it down with. She also had some weed and rolled a fat spliff.

Maybe that was enough to explain what happened next. She unbuttoned my jeans and slipped her hand down the front of my boxer shorts. Before I knew what was happening, she was on top of me, pulling her pants to the side and sliding me inside her.

Yeah, I know, only hours before I was crying into my beer about Juliet. For fuck's sake, she had only left in the taxi less than twelve hours ago. Maybe she hadn't even arrived home yet. But this girl had just rescued me from deep shit and probably the cop station, so it would be rude not to.

Afterwards, as I lay back on the bed with Anna in my arms and smoking a cigarette, I felt guilty as hell. Then there was a bang at the door. We both looked at each other thinking the same thing. The cops, or even worse, the baseball bat-wielding Greeks!

'Shh,' said Anna, finger to her lips as she got quietly up, slipped her top and pants on and went over to the door.

'Who is it?' I admit it, I was shitting it!

A low voice came from behind the door. 'Anna, is Krob there?'

Phew, I would recognise that voice anywhere, it was Roberto. Once he and Anna's mate were safely inside, they wasted no time in bringing me up to date. 'Krob, we must leave this town. The police and those mad Greeks are everywhere searching for you. They want to kill you. We must go now; the jeep is out the back.'

I was up in a flash, injuries forgotten. I gave Anna a quick kiss on the lips – at which Roberto raised an eyebrow – and we headed for the door.

'Where was that place you said you were staying at?' asked Anna as she pulled me back for another kiss.

'Pelekas, it's up north,' I explained, and we left.

Creeping down the stairs, we poked our heads out of the doorway. It looked clear. The jeep started as soon as they saw us and I got down as low as I could behind the seats as we got the fuck out of Dodge.

We were well outside the town before I finally got back up and looked around. Michael was sporting a busted nose and I was pretty fucked up but we were alive and free. I reached into the cool box for some beers and next thing we were laughing, drinking and standing up in the seats, shouting, 'FUCK YOU, FUCK YOU,' while giving the finger to that shitty town.

Back in Pelekas the next day, it was a late start and it was after lunch by the time I was sitting in the cafe with Michael, nursing another hangover and a sore face. We were both wearing sunglasses to hide the damage. Michael was looking at me and laughing. I tried to laugh back but it hurt too much.

'What's so fucking funny anyway?' I asked, starting to get worried.

'Well,' he replied, 'there are so many bumps and bruises on your head that you look like you've been hit repeatedly in the face with a shovel.'

'Great!' I tried to smile again but my jaw wouldn't let me. I lifted my T-shirt instead. 'You think that's bad, check this out.'

Michael leaned in for a look. 'Ouch!'

My ribs were covered in bruises, one in particular was huge and bright purple and blue; it felt like someone was stabbing me in the chest with an ice pick every time I breathed.

'Jesus, do you think they're broken?' he asked, sitting back.

'Nah, just badly bruised, I think.'

'You sure? Maybe you need to go to the hospital.'

'Even if I did, there's nothing they could do. I did something similar skiing a few seasons ago. I just need to rest them.'

'Hmm.' Michael didn't look totally convinced.

'Anyway, I'm more worried about this.' I showed him my hand which was badly swollen with cuts on the knuckles. He leaned in again. 'Now that might be broken,' I pointed out, 'and anyway, you don't look so hot yourself.'

His nose was so swollen that he had bent the supports on his sunglasses to fit them over his nose.

'Lift your shades a second. Yeah, two black eyes, that's usually caused by a broken nose. Are you sure *you* don't have to go to the hospital yourself?'

Now it was his turn to look worried. Revenge is sweet. We both started laughing.

Fuck the pain.

'Okay, I'm off to get a neat whisky as my ribs are killing me. You want one?' He nodded. Returning with the drinks, I asked a question that had been on my mind. 'So, do you think there'll be any comeback from last night?'

Michael thought for a second. 'Well, Roberto's pretty worried that they'll connect him with us and come to Pelekas. Helga, too.'

'Shit, I hadn't thought of that!'

We both sat in silence imagining carloads of tooled-up Greeks cruising the streets of Pelekas. I changed the subject. 'Speaking of Helga, where is she?'

'Helga?' Michael laughed again. 'She's still in bed, maybe with alcohol poisoning. She can't say much anyway as she was knocking lumps out of some girl at the club too, proper banging her head off the floor and everything.'

'No way,' I laughed, 'so our nuclear physicist has a bit of the Viking in her after all.'

'It's particle physicist,' said Helga, appearing from nowhere. 'And yes, I do have the spirit of my Viking ancestors flowing in my veins.' She sat down and caught me looking at her. She was also wearing large wraparound glasses, and was that the outline of a bruise I could make out? 'Before you ask, yes, the little bitch did get me with a lucky one, but not so lucky for her. She paid big, very big.'

But my mind had moved to something else. 'Oh shit, I just thought of something. I told that girl Anna and the lads that we stay in Pelekas. Shit, they even know my name.'

'Oh shit indeed,' replied Michael, biting his lip.

A few days passed and it seemed to blow over but Stella had been none too pleased, warning me that it wasn't good having the

DJ looking like a victim out of a horror movie. I just shrugged; where I'm from, shit like that just happens and she didn't seem impressed either when I showed her my busted hand and said, 'You should see the other guy'. Manu said nothing about it and I was starting to see who wore the trousers in their relationship.

Yeah, we were the talk of the town for a few days and I definitely got some funny looks spinning in the Coca Club, but as the damage subsided, it was soon forgotten, that is until about a week later when a guy and a girl walked into Manu's. I recognised them immediately. Colin (still sporting the black eye I had given him) and Anna, the little blonde chick. Colin had a large bag with him. They saw me and walked straight up to the DJ box. I had a quick look left and right, but they seemed to be alone. We had parted on good terms but you never know and as for Anna, this was a memory I was trying to blank out, locking the guilt down somewhere near Australia. After all, I had been phoning Juliet almost every day and she was already saving to come back out. They were all smiles.

'Hi, mate,' said Colin, offering his hand.

'Hi,' I replied, warily shaking his hand. 'Look, I'm a bit busy just now, why don't you get yourselves a drink and sit down, I finish in about twenty minutes.'

I tried to ignore Anna, but it was impossible not to notice how fit she was. As an afterthought, I added, 'Make sure you say you know me at the bar so you get a shot from the good bottle.'

Yes, I knew all about this trick as I had helped Stella fill up the empty good bottles with cheap shit a few times but there was always one good bottle at the end of the bar.

As I played, I kept looking up and catching Anna's eye and she was constantly looking over at me. At one point, she blew me a kiss, I glanced over to see if Stella had noticed. Shit, she had and she looked none too pleased. I tried to tell myself that it's my fucking life and I'll do what I want. I finished my set, grabbed a beer and headed over. The story they told was not a good one. The guy that had been caught by the Greeks was in deep shit.

'Yeah, man, he's still in fucking hospital. What a mess, even his own mother wouldn't recognise him,' said Colin. Anna nodded in agreement.

'Shit,' I replied, shaking my head, 'that's not good.' It was hard to get the sounds of his screams as the bats had pummeled his flesh out of my mind.

'And it gets worse,' added Anna, 'the Greeks are looking for you as well. They've been asking questions all around town. The guy you were fighting with on the floor needs an operation to reset his cheekbone.'

I swallowed hard and a slightly sick feeling rose in my gut. I remembered my elbow to his face well. 'But do they know about Pelekas? That I stay here?'

Anna shook her head. 'Not as far as I know, and we haven't said anything.'

Well, that was one thing. Colin cut in... 'In fact, I was hoping to move here.' He patted his rucksack. 'If it's as good as you say. My mates are splitting back to the UK as soon as the guy gets out of hospital, and there's no fucking way I'm staying in that town alone.' I told him he could stay at mine.

Much later, after the normal tour of town, and as every night is Saturday night in Pelekas, we were on the beach.

'Wow,' said Colin, sitting in the sand and sipping from a beer. 'This place is fucking paradise.'

I was thinking much the same thing as I sat with my arm around Anna. I had told her all about Juliet and she said she didn't care and she was going back to the UK in a few days anyway. A no-strings-attached shag with a fit blonde girl who was cool as fuck? Don't mind if I do.

Soon, we headed off into the dark with a blanket.

Life went on, but call me paranoid, I took some precautions in case carloads of Greeks arrived to put me in the hospital – or worse! The DJ box in Manu's was against the back wall, and to the left was a large window leading to a balcony where beer barrels were kept. I often used it as a shortcut to my room. I took to keeping money and my passport in a pouch tied round my waist and the plan was to bail out the window, run along the balcony, drop down onto the deck and run for the bushes, where in a clearing a small way in, I had hidden my Rambo knife under a tree. Maybe not foolproof, but at least I had a plan so it made me feel better inside.

One night I was playing at Manu's when Michael came running in. One look at his face and I knew something was very wrong. 'Krob... it's the Greeks, they're here in the town asking about a black English DJ! I'll take over the decks, GO, GO, they're at the Bench Bar!'

I needed no second warning and was out of there like shit off a shovel, scrambling along the balcony, over the edge and into the bushes. It took me a few minutes to find the tree and my hands were shaking as I unsheathed the massive knife, the silver blade glittering in the moonlight as I crept back to the edge of the undergrowth to look for signs of pursuit. There were none.

I waited for what seemed like ages (it probably was ages), until eventually Michael appeared at the balcony and whispered down that they had gone. I climbed back up.

'You're sure they've gone?' I asked nervously.

'Yeah, man. They had a quick look in here and then fucked off. I saw them climb back in a jeep and split town.'

'Phew.' I felt the tension leave me in huge waves. 'I need a fucking drink!'

After that night, they never came back, and Michael, Colin, Roberto and I became a tight unit living the good life in Pelekas to the max. For a while, nothing much of note happened until two of my friends, Johnny Mac and Norman Muirhead, arrived on a two-weeker to visit me. I had promised them a holiday to remember and they weren't disappointed.

When I was in Camp Bastion in Afghanistan waiting to be sent to the frontline and I was on Facebook chatting with Norman who now lives in Australia. We were talking about the Pelekas Bench Bar page.

'Norry, do you remember that holiday in Pelekas?' I asked.

'Remember it? How the fuck could I forget it! I had to spend two weeks in hospital afterwards recovering!'

'Oh yeah. Hehe.'

'Krob, do u remember the fucking orgy in the half-built rooms we were staying in?'

'OMG. That's right, with Tanya and that Danish chick, Klithard or some shit like that, she was hot. I remember her leaning over the balcony and saying it's such a nice view from here and we were all sitting down behind her looking up that tiny minidress she used to wear and you said, not as good as the view from here.'

'Haha, that's right, XXX Klithard, her boyfriend hated me and no wonder. Remember what she used to say? Are you coming to the beach, Norman?'

'Yeah, haha.'

'I blew it with her after I started the bar brawl with those Italians in the Coca Club just as we were about to go skinny dipping at the beach.'

'In fact, is that not the night you told the old Greek guy to fuck himself and Greece? He gathered a lynch mob and I was sure they were going to kill us!'

'Yeah, the old bastard. He had kicked us out of our rooms because of the complaints.'

'Wasn't that our third set of digs? After that, all we could get was the half-finished building site place with no windows or doors.'

'Yeah, but it was either that or live in the trees down by the beach.'

'Those rooms were the pits. I remember waking up one morning to find Johnny Mac sitting up in bed talking to the flies: "Please, god, can't you leave me alone just for a minute".'

'Fuck me, that was some two weeks!'

'Hell yeah, best holiday I ever had. Hey, Keef, do you fancy coming over to Oz if you live through Afghan? It's wicked here and I've got a Honda CBR 600 to raze about on, how about it?'

'No problem, Norman, I'd love it.'

The boys were out at the beginning of July and after they left, things returned to normal. Well, almost. I'll never forget coming out of Coca Club to see a guy fall at least thirty feet off a wall into a skip filled with rubble, bounce out and splatter on the road. He must have been so pissed his body didn't tense up and he escaped with only superficial cuts and bruises! Speaking of the Coca Club, I was doing really well there and had moved from a half-hour warm-up set at the beginning of the night to a forty-five-minute proper set in the middle. Using the same formula as Manu's – mixing house music into the indie stuff they played – I had the place proper bouncing.

Rave on... Almost.

I didn't see as much of Roberto anymore as I found out he had a dark side. I finally went into the bar we never went in and got talking to the owner. It turned out Roberto's chick-pulling antics had a secondary purpose. After he had shagged the life out of them and they had passed out, he would creep around the rest of the pension trying the room doors. If one was open he would stagger in pretending to be legless and fall about the place making loads of noise. If the occupants woke up, he would say sorry, wrong room and move on. If they didn't, which was highly likely as Pelekas drowned in an ocean of booze every night, then he would rob them blind; cameras, money, you name it. Not very nice. Well, that explained why the fucker always had money. Anyway, the owner had caught Roberto and given him a right kicking but no cops got involved as people in Pelekas didn't phone the cops, it had a bad reputation around the island as the druggy town. The owner seemed an okay guy and when he saw my ghetto blaster he offered to buy it from me at the end of the season, an offer I kept in mind.

I confronted Roberto with this information and after a struggle, he admitted it, even telling me he had a guy in Corfu Town who fenced the stuff for him. I think he misjudged me, maybe he thought I would think it was cool or want in. I mean, I'm hardly squeaky clean myself, but robbing off your own kind, who are probably as skint as yourself, is a step too far. I kept a bit of distance from him after that.

Next highlight was the return of Juliet, and although I had not exactly been faithful, I had kept in touch and when she returned for two weeks and I met her at the airport, it was loved up to the max time again.

We had a wicked time, even having a fake wedding on the beach which was attended by half of Pelekas. We were still fucked from the night before. Stella and co had taken Juliet on a hen night. I remember seeing Juliet in the bar that never closes, lying on her back on a table having booze funnelled into her mouth while the place cheered. My stag do was much the same; we already went pretty crazy every night anyway so you can imagine what it was like when we really let loose.

For the big day, I borrowed a jacket and tie and Juliet wore only French underwear and a net curtain borrowed from my room as a veil. The priest was the lecherous Roberto. In his hand he held a silver tray and instead of the usual vows, I had to promise to faithfully service the bride every night! A promise I tried to make good on almost immediately. By this time, we were both leathered again on

JD and had to be rescued from drowning in the sea, but not before we had shagged in the water, and this wasn't in the middle of the night in the dark but in broad daylight! Jesus, the wedding car, a pink convertible VW Beetle, got stuck in the sand trying to leave the beach and it took ages to dig it out. Finally, we were off and spent the night in a room at the sunset restaurant. A night unfortunately I remember little about, but I do remember being sick as a dog with alcohol poisoning the next day.

When Juliet left again, I was gutted for the second time. I've often wondered what would have happened if she had stayed, would we be still together, would we have kids, etc? But it wasn't to be.

I was pretty upset and when Michael asked me jokingly if I wanted to go to a club across the island to drown my sorrows, I declined. They say you can have too much of a good thing and it's true, by mid-August I had decided it was time to split. Michael and Colin had gone already and it just wasn't the same. I took my ghetto blaster to the forbidden bar and got the equivalent of £100 for it, not bad, and that coupled with my savings meant I could leave Pelekas behind. The plan was to travel to Switzerland and get a job picking fruit.

The goodbyes were heavy, but finally it was over and I got on the bus to Corfu Town and boarded a ferry for Italy. Now comes the bit I'd been dreading. To get out of Scotland, I had done a pretty bad thing; I had stolen a cheque from my mother and cashed it at the bank to help fund my trip. Not my finest hour. This meant that I had not contacted her in all the time I had been away. In fact, no one had a number for me at all. My mother had decided it was time I came home and had sent my mate Bruce out to fetch me back with the money for a flight. He arrived the day after I had left. Unfortunately, he loved Pelekas too and got a job there. If he hadn't he would almost certainly be alive today, because two seasons later he died in a horrific motorbike crash pissed up on Jack Daniel's. I still miss him today.

The job in Switzerland didn't come off so I skipped trains all the way to Calais and even managed free passage on the ferry to Dover! Eventually, I reached Juliet's house in Nuneaton but not to the welcome I expected. Her old boy took an instant dislike to me and would only let me stay one night in the fucking garage! I quickly left town and headed to Michael's place in Leicester not far away. He sorted me out a job on a building site. I still managed to have many adventures including sleeping rough and having my leg busted up with a hammer by a psychotic workmate who had just got out the nick for biting off someone's ear in a bar brawl! Anyway, it was over a year before I finally returned to Glasgow.

I returned to my hometown and decided to hand myself in to the cops, but not with the thought of spending too much time in jail though. I had a plan, but would it work?

Two weeks later, there I was, with my lawyer, at the local police station. The next day I was brought from the bowels of Glasgow Sheriff Court to face the music and was remanded in custody for reports. This couldn't be helped, after all I had skipped bail. As I was under twenty-one, I was to be taken to a young offenders' institution called Longriggend for my three-week 'lie down', as it's called. But first I would have to spend the night in the notorious Barlinnie prison, or *the big hoose* as it's not so fondly known as, in Glasgow's east end. Bar-L was properly medieval at the time, and sitting in my little holding box, looking at the cold bowl of congealed shit that passed for food and waiting to be processed into the prison population was not the greatest moment of my life. Next morning, I emerged from my cell to slop out (a beautiful process involving taking your shit pail to tip it out as there were no toilets in the cells at that time). Luckily, my anal virginity remained intact and I was shipped to the YO.

The next three weeks felt more like three months as I crossed the days off on the wall like a prison movie, I had no idea that time could go so slowly. It was quite a rough place, and at night you could hear screams coming from the cells at the end of the corridor as the block hardman bullied his cellmate while the screws did nothing. I, however, got on well with my cellmate and learned skills like how to pass a lit newspaper through the heating pipe so the neighbours could get a light.

Unfortunately, I was moved to a cell opposite the bully and one night he tried to get my new cellmate to 'fire into the black bastard!'. The poor wee guy was shitting it as I was much bigger than him and he called back, 'I cannae dae it, the big man's all right.' This infuriated the bully and he promised me he would chib me the next morning by crushing the metal waste paper bin into a weapon. This seemed like a good idea so I crushed my bin into a weapon as well and in the morning when the cell doors opened I waited but fuck all happened.

At last it was court day. I had asked family and friends to come as it makes a good impression and was well pleased with the turnout. I too had made an effort and had on a shirt, tie, proper shoes and trousers. The lawyer was well primed with my story.

The judge addressed my lawyer, saying, 'Well, looking through the extensive list of offences, including a count of police assault, which this court views very seriously, I am leaning towards a custodial sentence. Unless you have something to say in mitigation?'

'Yes, your honour...' started my lawyer, 'While I do understand your position and the seriousness of the charges that my client has pleaded guilty to, I ask you to consider other options... My client was hanging around with a bad crowd at the time and became involved in drink and drugs. After he committed these offences he realised the error of his ways and quit Scotland for Greece where he held down a proper job, entered into a stable relationship—' (If only he knew.) '—and cleaned up his act. Now he has returned to Scotland to face up to his responsibilities and throws himself on the mercy of the court.'

A brilliant speech and I would have clapped if it had been allowed, but instead I tried to look as sorry as I could. The judge stared at me, then my crying mother and then at the case papers on his desk. Time stopped. I held my breath.

The judge finally raised his head. 'After looking carefully at this case, taking into account that the defendant handed himself in and pleaded guilty at the first opportunity, I can't see how justice would be served by locking him away. Instead. I have decided on a £600 fine, a two-year ban from driving and he will be bound over for good behaviour for a year.' He looked at me. 'Mr Robinson, you have been given a second chance, but if you are ever brought before this court again, then the full force of the law will fall upon you... Next case please.'

Life has good moments and bad moments and this was a very good moment as I walked free from court to pick up the strands of my life.

After my court experience and miraculous second chance, I kept pretty quiet for a while, even getting a proper job as a barman in a trendy cafe bar called Nico's in Glasgow's city centre. In the day, it was arty types munching croissants and sipping cappuccinos but at night, it was heaving with clubbers fitting in a beer before heading out. All in all, a pretty cool place. I also got the job as resident DJ in the function suite called Reds upstairs.

The most eventful thing to happen there has to be when I DJ'd for the deaf. Yes, you heard right, the deaf – and not just hard of hearing, these people couldn't hear shit, but they could feel the beat and danced away happily until there was a fight and a guy got bottled! I was very surprised, as for some reason I didn't think the deaf behaved like that.

I stopped the music while the doorman sorted it out. Usually when you kill the music in circumstances like that, the place erupts as the punters discuss what just happened. Not this time, total silence as the deaf communicated in sign language! It seems the sign for being bottled is the same as in spoken tongue, which amused me to no end. Soon the mess was cleaned up and we continued, but incredibly that wasn't the end of the matter and for the first time since we opened we had to close early as a bar brawl broke out. I watched incredulously as the deaf punters knocked the shit out of each other. Eventually, the cops had to be called and some of the deaf were arrested. As they were led away, I couldn't help but wonder how you read them their rights. Anyway, I have a healthy respect for deaf people now and I suppose it was just my ignorance and prejudice that made me think they weren't just like the rest of us.

The function suite, however, was not where I wanted to go musically, and the final straw came when some pissed-up punter put his jacket through the hatch for the DJ box (the DJ box was in the fucking kitchen!), saying he thought it was the cloakroom. I started looking for another job after that.

My search for alternative employment was brought forward a little when I was sacked. The night manageress's boyfriend was stealing vast quantities of alcohol from the bar and the manager, Tommy, was doing a Sherlock Holmes trying to track down the culprit, as I found out one night as I was taking out the bags of empties. I placed them with the other rubbish as normal and went to go back inside but as I turned, I was sure I could hear someone creeping about behind the bins so I pretended to close the back door and hid watching. Sure enough a human shape emerged and started going through the bags, it was Tommy. I shouted, 'GOTCHA!', and Tommy jumped about two feet in the air.

After that, he was always quickly pulling open doors to catch people unawares and see what they were up to. Unfortunately, this led to me being captured dividing up a bit of hash in two for some of the staff. Oops. I quickly hid my hands behind my back.

'What's in your hands?' demanded Tommy.

'Eh, two bits of hash.' And that was that.

Luckily, I hadn't been neglecting my record buying and had been spending all my DJ wages on banging techno to add to my slower house collection and now I just needed somewhere to play it. I went about persuading the owner of Joe Paparazzi's nightclub that I could do a better job than his Friday night DJ (which wouldn't be hard) and introduce a rave sound to his nightclub. Gino had known me since the days I was a punter at Fresh, the club that had started it all for me and he gave me a go. I designed a colour flyer with a picture of some sci-fi eclipse on the front and promises of banging rave techno and hard house and we were off.

Joe's was a well-designed nightclub. In the past, it had been an old cinema and had many different levels and balconies that looked down on the dance floor. It had Glasgow's best laser system, a lighting rig that lowered over the dance floor and a massive screen and projector. It was perfect, and was soon packed out with punters buckled on acid, the new drug ecstasy and cocaine. They would gather on the lowest level just outside the toilets and wait for the acid to come up, then when I raised the lighting rig, hit the smoke machine and the lasers, they would pour onto the dance floor and remain there cutting shapes till the wee hours.

I loved that job; the place was thumping and every week we would go back to mine for an after-party. Very messy, I can tell you. It was during this period that I organised a birthday party in a warehouse unit. Everything was coming together; music, drugs, flyer design, warehouse parties, knowledge of where to hire generators and vans. The seeds were sown, and it was nearly harvest time.

7

SADDAM'S BUNKER

We were all at Tin Pan Alley nightclub on Mitchell Street in Glasgow's city centre on Hogmanay of 1990, quite happily drinking the cheap booze and dancing the night away when the music suddenly stopped and the lights came on. What was wrong? Was there a fire? Had someone been stabbed? I looked at my watch, cool, only three a.m., plenty of time left. The clubs had been closing at six a.m. for a whole year now because Glasgow was a city of European 1990s culture and... oh no! It was now no longer 1990, it was 1991! And with typical Glasgow bluntness, the closing times reverted to the normal three a.m. What a bitch! People booed and jeered but to no avail.

Within ten minutes, we were all out on the street facing the facts. It was cold, wet and we had nowhere to go. I took as many people as I could back to my pad on Wilton Street to subject the long-suffering neighbours to another night of mayhem.

'Well, the problem is...' I was explaining the situation to my mates, beer in hand, sitting in the living room. '...that people are used to going on till six. They've got money left, no drugs left, they're expecting to still be able to party, and now it's all ruined.'

They nodded in agreement and I got up and went for a piss. I was standing there pissing when it hit me. Of course! I ran back through while doing up my zip. 'Guys, guys, I've got a plan! Let's do a fucking after-party!'

Now it was easier to shout AFTER-PARTY than to make it happen. Most of my mates probably thought I was just blowing off at the mouth but the idea stuck in my head and much later I was lying in bed with my then-girlfriend Louise still banging on about it.

'But, Louise, it is possible. All we need is a venue, like an old warehouse, some speakers, make up some flyers, buy booze to run a bar...'

'Yes, darling,' she replied, sounding tired. 'Look, we'll talk about it in the morning. Good night.' And with that, she rolled over and went to sleep. But I couldn't sleep and got up and found a pen and paper and sat at the kitchen table with a cup of tea and made a list.

A few days passed and things had moved forward. I had done a birthday party last year for a friend so it was an easy matter to find out the cost of renting the rig and the lights and the rental guy said that any weekend in January would be fine as that is a quiet month event-wise. I already had decks and a mixer. Also a generator would be needed, again easy, a plant hire shop was just up the road. The bar was to be bought from a cash and carry, an Asian mate who owned a corner shop would supply the card. The only thing left was to set the date, make a flyer, rent a van and... oh yeah, the small matter of a venue! We had used an industrial unit for the birthday party last year but that was no longer available. We drove around and looked at a few empty warehouses but they all seemed... very well locked up.

We were all sitting up at mine, smoking dope and drinking beer, discussing this very matter when Johnny Mac suddenly stood up. 'Wait a minute, what about the tunnels?' We all looked at him blankly.

'The tunnels? What tunnels?' I replied, none the wiser.

'Keef... I thought you of all people would remember the tunnels.' I looked at him even more blankly, prompting him to continue. 'The abandoned railway tunnels! Remember we used to use them when we were kids to move our motorbikes around the west end so we wouldn't get huckled by the coppers.'

Then I remembered. 'Oh, those tunnels! Yeah, there's one running right under Byres Road. In fact, there's an old station down there. Wait a minute, what about the one under Otago Street beside Kelvingrove underground, that's defo still open, I walk past it all the time.'

It might have been two in the morning but for some reason there was no time to lose, so we grabbed a couple of torches and, as always, I also took a metal pole.

'Well, you never know who you might meet down there,' I said as John looked at the metal bar questioningly, and we jumped in John's motor and headed down there.

The entrance to the tunnel was pitch black and even I had to admit it wasn't very welcoming. Louise and Smudge weren't very keen but when I asked if they'd rather wait behind in the dark with no torch in the shadows beside a very dodgy path by the river, they soon followed.

'No one will come to a party in here,' Smudge said as the torch beam fell on a huge rat that scuttled away, squeaking into the darkness.

As we stepped into the yawning entrance over piles of empty beer cans, I noticed Louise's fingernails were digging into my arm. I have never been scared of the dark, maybe something to do with being brought up in the country, I don't know, and Johnny Mac's not really scared of anything, so we continued on in.

After going 150 metres or so, we started to get pretty used to it. The floor of the tunnel, although not completely flat, was made up of small stones and no trouble to walk on and as we penetrated further, the biting cold outside had gone and we noticed that the temperature inside was much pleasanter.

We stopped for a proper look around. The tunnel was about thirty feet wide and forty feet high, in an arched shape, made from red bricks, dry, and surely the sound couldn't penetrate through so much solid rock above? I was satisfied, we had a venue.

Back at the flat, there was a noticeable rise in the level of excitement. The others could see that this maybe wasn't pie in the sky after all. We had run club nights before, I played banging tunes, we had a venue, so it was RAVE ON. One thing remained, what on earth would we call it? Many names were suggested.

'What about tunnel party?' Smudge suggested... but there already was a nightclub named The Tunnel so it might confuse people.

'The underground,' suggested Louise.

Not bad, but just not quite what I was looking for. I went off for a piss. It's strange but I seem to come up with my best ideas when I'm pissing; maybe it's something to do with the hypnotic tinkling noise, or the relief of flushing the bladder, fuck knows, but anyway, I was in there pissing and could faintly hear the TV droning in the other room. It was BBC news.

'...and I'm here in Kuwait with the third Armoured Division...' This was all we had heard for weeks as the allies stepped up the propaganda campaign for the coming war with Saddam Hussain. '...as we wait for the inevitable order to invade Iraq, Operation Desert Storm...'

That was it!

Operation Desert Storm... Saddam's bunker rave. I ran back through... with piss dripping down my trousers.

'Guys... guys, I've got it.'

Next stop, flyers, not a drama as I had made loads of successful club flyers for Joe Paparazzi's and Tin Pan Alley. This was in the days before Photoshop so it was cut and paste with scissors and Letraset time, but before long I had an acceptable original. In the centre was a map of how to get to the tunnel entrance, up top was 'Operation Desert Storm' and the date, small pictures of fighter jets, Saddam's face, a CND peace symbol, an emblem from the 2000AD comic strip, Rogue Trooper, in the corners and at the bottom the words 'Saddam's Bunker – Death or Glory'. I used a font called stencil, you know, the military stamp-style writing, and as I handed it over to the printers ordering 500 in blue card, I felt it was a job well done.

That weekend we hit clubland; Sub Club on Jamaica Street as well as Tin Pan Alley and the Arches. We didn't want to hand out the flyers with the map on it so we resorted to word of mouth. I made a mental note to get pre-flyers made just with the date and name for next time... next time? Well, maybe I was getting a little ahead of myself there, but people seemed genuinely interested and when the clubs closed at three a.m. again, we could tell the ravers wanted it to be now, not next weekend.

At last, the night of the rave arrived. The rental van was packed with the rig, lights, bar, tables, decks, generator and cables, and we had also made a quick backdrop on a sheet with a cartoon of Saddam on it with 'Saddam's Bunker' written underneath.

I was nervous to say the least and checked and rechecked everything. Did we have spare batteries for the torches? What about change for the bar? Change... shit, we needed change for the door as well, as a £3 entry was being levied. With these last-minute hitches solved, we headed down to the tunnel entrance at about ten p.m. and ran into our first problem. The fucking van wouldn't fit down the path to the tunnel entrance. This was a major problem as it would mean carrying the kit from the car park one hundred metres to the tunnel, not to mention the one hundred metres down the tunnel unobserved. I could see some people wanted to sack it off but I gathered the willing – Johnny Mac, Louise and Smudge – and we started to unload and the rest soon joined in. The sweat was pouring off us by the time we had the kit into the tunnel entrance, and not just from the work, that path is well used, especially at ten on the weekend, and not just by Joe Public, the cops often used it too. A lot of people saw us but in Glasgow sometimes it pays not to ask any questions and it went without a hitch. The next flit down the tunnel was just as hard physically but we were out of sight and the pressure was off. Thirty minutes later, it was a very tired group of people that were leaning against the equipment smoking cigarettes and breaking out a few beers from the bar stock.

We posted a lookout on the tunnel entrance and started setting up. We were all buzzing and not just from the forthcoming gig. A couple of grams of Charlie were dished out and it's amazing how much quicker shit gets done then; people were whistling and chatting away as they threw up the rig and set up the decks, etc, and BOOM, it was done. The place looked cool as fuck. If we could just pull this off, it was going to be talked about for a long time to come.

All that remained was a quick sound check. I started the generator, powered up the amps, put on a tune and...

BOOM, BOOM, TSS... BOOM, BOOM, TSS.

It fucking worked! We all went crazy, jumping around the tunnel like mad people, until Smudge, who was on lookout duty, came running down the tunnel. 'For fuck's sake, turn that off! You can hear it as plain as day in the fucking car park, man.'

Oops, I hadn't thought of that! Of course, the sound would travel down the tunnel like a wave... this was very bad news. There was nothing for it but to turn the rig around and face it in the other direction off into the darkness. The tunnel continued all the way to the Western Infirmary, maybe a mile or more away; that was far enough to protect us from discovery.

As planned, some would wait with the gear while myself and a few others would hit the clubs with the flyers. I chose the Sub Club, my favourite place and the trendiest underground-style venue in town. The interest was phenomenal. An after-party in a railway tunnel in the west end! The news spread like wildfire and soon I had no flyers left and was having to ask people to share them. Even the boss, Tony McCrimmon, was coming, this was looking good. At about two a.m., I headed back to the west end, scared shitless that the event had been rumbled while I was away, but my fears were groundless and all was as I had left it. Now there was nothing to do except wait for the ravers.

I wasn't disappointed. By 3:10 a.m., three taxis and cars had arrived at the bridge and people were pouring out. 'Where is it? Where is it?' they asked, running down the steps to get in there in case it got busted.

I've always thought it's a good sign when people are running to get to your gig. By five a.m., there must have been hundreds in there and I abandoned my post on the bridge and headed in.

As soon as I entered the tunnel, I could hear the dull thump of the bassline. Moving further forward, I started to see the lights flashing in the distance silhouetting Louise and some others who had set up the table for taking the money bang in the middle of the tunnel. Giving Louise a kiss, I asked her how it was going.

'Well, dear, there are loads down there but getting the money off them was a little more difficult. Most just ran past us without paying!'

Another lesson learned the hard way; if you want the cash, you have to control the entrance so they file past one at a time! Anyway, fuck it, I headed into the rave.

It surpassed my wildest expectations. The ravers were going mad, jumping to the beat as one and screaming and whistling every time the kick drum dropped out. Yes, we had fucking done it. I pushed my way through the masses to the bar and got a beer. I was just in time; the beers were running out already! I made another mental note; buy shitloads more stock for the bar next time. Wiping the sweat off my hands, I racked up another line of Charlie and headed to the DJ area to play my set. I've always been a good DJ and had been practising my set for weeks. Soon the place was going even crazier than before and I was lost in the beats, cutting and scratching for Scotland.

I had been playing for over an hour and was in my own world when Smudge came up and tapped me on the shoulder. At first I waved him away and carried on but when he tapped me again, more insistently this time, I turned around and, looking at his face, realised that something was very wrong.

'KEEF... KEEF!' He struggled to be heard above the music. 'THE FUCKING COPS ARE ALL OVER THE CAR PARK. THEY HAVEN'T FOUND US YET BUT THEY WILL.'

Shit, not good. 'How many of them are there?' I asked.

'All of them, I think,' he replied, and I got a sinking feeling in my stomach.

'Okay, Smudge, tell Louise to grab the door and bar money and go back to the flat with it. Tell her I'll meet her there later.'

Smudge just looked at me. I could tell he was thinking that I would be very lucky to walk away from this one, but he did as I asked and disappeared into the darkness. It was hard to concentrate on my set without constantly glancing up to stare back down the tunnel and it wasn't long before I looked up and my worst fears were realised. What seemed like hundreds of little lights bobbed up and down, growing larger as they came closer. It looked like they had found us then. Soon the ravers noticed them too and I could see people frantically getting drugs out of their pockets and sniffing, popping or simply throwing them on the floor.

By the time the cops had reached us, the ravers were clearing out big time and there was a near stampede as people left, tipping over tables and speakers as they legged it. As I looked around the tunnel, I got a sinking feeling as I realised it was just me with about fifty of Strathclyde Police's finest, all from the local cop shop. It was a dead cert that some of them would know me. I couldn't believe that every fucker, even my mates, had done a runner and left me on my own to take the blame. There I was, standing in the dark with all the kit and surrounded by cops with basically my dick in my hand.

The head cop swept his torch beam across the scene, finishing by shining it directly in my face. 'Well, I never, if it isn't Mr Robinson. I don't know what's been going on down here, but I know one thing, you're for the tin pail, laddie!'

I tried some bullshit. 'But I'm just the DJ! The organiser, a guy called Tom, left just as you arrived. Maybe you saw him, tall guy with a big dog? I'm sure he'll be back soon to explain everything...' Yeah, right.

'Okay,' replied the cop, unconvinced, 'I'm sure he will. But if everyone else has done a runner, then why are you still here?'

A fucking good question, I thought. 'Err, well, some of the equipment is mine, like the turntables.'

'And the rest of the stuff? Is that yours?' the cop motioned with his hand to the speakers and lights now mostly lying strewn on the tunnel floor.

'Well, err, not really... but kind of.' Shit, this wasn't going well, they were bound to find out that the stuff was all rented in my name. 'You see, it's rented,' I tried to explain.

'By who?' the cop demanded.

I was pissing against the wind here and decided to say nothing.

'Well, speak up, Robinson, cat got your tongue?'

I just looked at the floor and continued to say nothing.

'Right, that's it.' The cop reached for his notebook. 'I'm arresting you on suspicion of...' He turned to his mate and asked, 'What are we arresting him for?'

'Breach of the peace?' the other cop suggested.

'That'll do for a start. I'm arresting you for a breach of the peace... anything you say will be taken down in evidence and may be used against you in a court of law.'

But as his mate reached forward with the cuffs, he held him back. 'No, not yet... first get him to carry this shit down the tunnel and into the van!'

When the cops realised it was going to take all night for me alone to carry the equipment down the tunnel, they lent a hand and after they had thrown the kit into the meat wagons, they cuffed me and threw me in after it none too gently. As the cop van pulled away, I could see Smudge and a few others standing, watching from the car park.

Much later that morning, I was brought up from the cells to an interview room.

'Okay, let's go over this one more time, Mr Robinson. So, this guy Tom contacts you at which bar again?' The cop said and looked down at his notes. He was trying to trip me up but I had fabricated my yarn well.

'I've told you all this already, Curlers on Byres Road.'

'...and conveniently, you don't know his second name, his address or his telephone number?'

'That's right, officer,' I replied.

He banged his fist on the desk. 'And you expect us to believe this crock of shit? Just admit you organised the event and you'll be out of here in an hour.'

Yeah, right, I thought. 'Officer, I don't really care what you believe, I'm not saying another word till my lawyer gets here.'

The cop sat back in his seat with his arms folded behind his head and stared straight at me. 'Yeah, your lawyer is outside now and he's causing a lot of trouble. We're wondering how a two-bit piece of shit like you got such a good lawyer anyway?'

I just smiled.

'Okay, you're free to go. But don't think we won't be keeping an eye on you from now on. And if you pull another stunt like that tunnel party, you'll be in it way past your neck, understand? Now get out of my sight.'

I wasn't arguing and before he could change his mind I was off, collected my possessions from the charge desk and, after a few words with my lawyer, I walked out of the police station a free man. Some of my mates were outside so they hadn't totally abandoned me, but I can't say I was very pleased. At least Louise and Johnny Mac had a good excuse. I had asked her to take the cash up the road and Johnny Mac had gone with her, and they were there to pick me up but the others, just leaving me there to face the music, was not cool.

We got into John Mac's motor and he asked me, 'So, Keef, what are you going to do now?'

'Well, John,' I replied, lighting up a cigarette, 'start looking for another venue, I reckon.'

And with that, Desert Storm was born.

8

THE GRAHAMS

The Grahams (name changed for legal reasons) were mates of mine in Glasgow and you would have to say they were at the dodgy end of the spectrum. If my hippy mate, John O, was at the peace, love and light end of the list, then they were at the other end, the dark side end. Their names were Shuggy and Jace. Shuggy was of medium height with dark hair, a pretty cool guy, good-looking in a roguish way and was the brains of the duo but with a bit of a vicious streak. Jace, although the older brother, tended to go along with his younger sibling's plans most of the time. Anyway, here's a little story to introduce them into this tale...

I rang the bell at the Grahams' second-floor flat in Anniesland and was standing there waiting when the door was thrust open to reveal Jace in a state of agitation.

'Keef, quick get in!' Jace grabbed me by the jacket and dragged me inside.

'Fuck's sake, Jace!' I replied as I was bundled into the flat. 'What the fuck is going—'

He put his finger to his lips. 'Shh, you've got to see this... follow me.'

I followed him into the living room where Shuggy was crouched by the window peering out. Turning, Shuggy noticed me and told me to get down. Soon the three of us were kneeling there looking out onto the main road.

'What are we looking for?' I asked, scanning the street.

'It's the fire-in,' replied Jace, giggling insanely.

'The fire-in?' I asked, puzzled.

'Yeah, Keef,' Shuggy explained, 'you know that bampot we get to run around for us... Chris.'

Ah, the fire-in... he was talking about the poor lad that was desperately trying to join their little criminal cabal. He thought he was in there but in reality he was being used and abused. They would get him to do their dirty work for them and if they couldn't persuade him with words, a bit of violence usually did the trick. I don't think he was very big in the brain's suit. The saying 'the weak shall inherit the shit' came to mind.

'What's he going to do?' I asked, properly interested now.

'He's going to hold up the fucking building society across the road, that's what,' replied Shuggy as Jace added another insane cackle.

'WHAT?' I asked in disbelief.

'Shh, here he comes now!' said Shuggy

I looked down, and sure enough there was the fire-in getting out of a red VW Golf right outside the building society. In his hand was a black holdall. The car sped off leaving him standing on the pavement.

'No fucking way,' I said, shaking my head.

'Yes, fucking way, and he fucking better do it too if he knows what's good for him,' said Shuggy, an icy and malevolent tone creeping into his voice.

But I wasn't so sure. He was hardly rushing in there with guns blazing. Instead, he was pacing about outside, obviously having second thoughts but still looking dodgy as fuck!

'Oh no, he's going to bottle it,' observed Jace.

'No, he's fucking not,' stated Shuggy, and it seemed he was right because the fire-in had taken a black balaclava out of his pocket and was pulling it over his head.

'Oh, my God!' was the best I could come up with.

Now the fire-in was properly into gear. The holdall was unzipped and in his hand he had a sawn-off shotgun. With a quick glance left and right, he opened the door and rushed inside.

For a few moments we were speechless, but as we watched events unfold through the building society window, the excitement grew.

'Fucking hell, Shuggy, he's doing it, man!' I cried out. 'He's got the shooter out and he's pointing it at the clerk!' Then it occurred to me... 'Jesus, is that thing loaded, Shuggy?'

Shuggy was leaning over, intent on the scene below. 'Of course not, Keef. For fuck's sake, you think I'd give that halfwit a loaded shotgun?'

Things in the building society were already starting to go tits up. The fire-in wasn't controlling the situation very well. He had forgotten to herd the customers into a corner, so as he approached the counter they were piling out the door behind him in all directions shouting and screaming. People in the street were turning to see what was happening. Oops.

'Shit, this isn't looking too good,' I observed

'No, he's still got time,' insisted Shuggy, silently urging him on. 'Come on, for fuck's sake, hurry up, you halfwit!'

But the halfwit was having problems. He couldn't seem to convince the staff to part with the cash and it was only when he climbed on the counter and put the shotgun to the head of the terrified clerk that she started to hand over bundles of notes. Seconds ticked by as he fumbled the money into the bag. I noticed we weren't the only people watching what was going on; a hysterical woman, obviously an escaped customer, was deep in conversation with a passer-by, pointing frantically into the building society, no doubt explaining every detail. Finally, halfwit got his shit together and burst out the door, still holding the gun and bag and started legging it up the street towards the red Golf double-parked about one hundred metres up the road. It was then I noticed he wasn't wearing any gloves.

'Fuck's sake, Shuggy, that nugget's not wearing any gloves, what about the forensics?'

But forensics was the least of his worries. As he ran, a crowd, led by a pretty big, muscle-bound, have-a-go hero, was in hot pursuit and gaining fast. He dodged and weaved, swinging the cash bag at the guy's head. We held our breath. He sidestepped between two parked cars and threw the shotgun and cash in through the passenger window of the Golf then dived in after it head-first. The last view I had of him was with the have-a-go hero locked onto his legs as the Golf spun its wheels with smoke pouring from beneath the tyres. People were trying to force open the car doors, it was touch and go. At last, the car started to move, leaving the crowd behind. The hero clung on for a few seconds then fell, nearly getting his legs run over by the fleeing car, and as the golf screeched around the corner with its engine screaming, we could already hear police sirens wailing in the distance. I could see a guy writing the registration of the car on his hand.

Back in the flat, we let out a collective sigh of relief.

'Oh, my God,' I said, slowly shaking my head, 'that was un-fucking-believable!' Then something occurred to me. 'So I take it that car was stolen then?'

I sat dumbfounded as they explained the so-called plan. Finally, I said, 'So, run that past me again. You're trying to tell me that the red Golf is not stolen but belongs to Jace's seventeen-year-old private schoolie girlfriend? You're pulling my fucking leg.'

But they weren't, it was really true, even officer dibble would have no problems solving this crime, and they would quickly connect girl to boy, boy to flat and... I was out of there, fast.

'Guys, I'm gone before the door comes off its hinges. If I were you, I'd do the same thing. See ya.' And with that, I split double time for my car and away.

Surprisingly, the girl blabbed and swapped her comfortable existence of private school, nice house and a bright future for a shared cell in the local women's prison, Cornton Vale. The fire-in was duly caught and locked away for a long time too; after all it was armed fucking robbery, no matter how inept a job. The Grahams, however, although interviewed, managed to slip the net and were never charged. Very bad lads, but also very lucky.

Now Desert Storm parties had been going along very nicely, thank you; the tunnels, the castle and a couple of warehouses were no problem. That was until we rented a warehouse on the Southside from a well-known Glasgow motorcycle gang. Maybe I should have seen it coming, as the parties got bigger and more talked about, it was inevitable that people would come who weren't the fluffy pill-popping ravers that we were used to. Machete-wielding maniacs like to party as well and they chose this event to turn up for some fun! It's at times like these it can be useful to have some dodgy friends about, cue the Grahams.

When I went for the meeting with the bikers at their gang hut/bar, I had no idea what to expect, certainly not the massive Nazi swastika flag with a blood-red background hanging above the bar that greeted me as I came through the door. The head biker, Dave, must have read the expression on my face and put his massive arm (nearly as wide as my leg) comfortingly around my shoulder and told me not to worry as he said, 'It was only Pakis we hated'... Great, that made me feel a whole lot better. I had Asian mates, what the fuck was I going to put on the flyer? 'Sorry, no Pakistanis... due to racist biker gang.' Anyway, I sat down, they brought me a cold beer and we negotiated a price for the warehouse. They assured me that they all hated rave music and would not be attending the event themselves which was good news, and in the end, I sat and talked with them for a few more beers and even a couple of games of pool. I like extreme people and these guys were that and more. Hours later and half-cut, I left, warehouse in the bag and the mission accomplished.

Some events go smoothly like clockwork, everything just falls into place, a great time had by all, rave on, but some don't, and what can go wrong does go wrong. This event was one of the latter; it was cursed from the word go. In fact, it stressed me out so much that after the gig I noticed that a clump of my hair had turned grey almost overnight. This was the gig from hell.

I had just picked up the 2,500 flyers, 1,000 A3 posters, 500 laminated tickets and fifty laminated guest passes from the printers and was back at my pad proudly showing them off to the rest of the posse. I really had outdone myself this time, these things looked properly professional and I was busy telling them so when Smudge, who had been staring intently at one of the flyers. interrupted...

'Keef, they look cool as fuck...but where is uknown?'

'Uknown? Smudge, what the fuck are you on about,' I replied, a little pissed off to be cut off in mid-flow.

'Destination uknown... it says it right here,' Smudge said, pointing at the flyer.

'Smudge, it's destination unknown, you knobber.'

'No, it's not... look.' And he passed over the flyer.

Snatching it off him I looked at it. *Desert Storm sound system,*

Afterparty, Destination... UKNOWN.

'Oh fuck! Bollocks!' I flung the bundle of flyers at the wall and stormed out to the kitchen to get a cold beer. The bad vibes had begun.

It was too late to change the publicity – too late and too expensive. So, for the next two weeks, I had to look at *destination uknown* every time I handed out a flyer or pasted up a poster. But it seemed people saw what they expected to see and few noticed except me.

At last, the night of the rave arrived. We had booked two coaches, one at the Arches nightclub and one round the corner at Tin Pan Alley, to take the bulk of the ravers to the gig. Interest was high, tickets had sold well, the rave was already set up and now the clubs were emptying onto the street. What could possibly go wrong?

My friend Norman Muirhead was organising the Tin Pan coach while I sorted the Arches one. I looked at my watch – 3:15 a.m. – okay, I had ordered the coaches for three a.m. so they were only fifteen minutes late. Then it was 3:30 a.m., shit, where were they? The ravers were getting restless. It was an extra £5 a head to get the coach and most had already paid me to ensure they got a seat. Worse still, in my paranoia about being robbed, I had given Stefano my cash and sent him round to Tin Pan to collect the rest from Norman so mass refunds were out of the question. I got on my mobile to the bus company.

'...our working hours are eight a.m. to five p.m. Monday to Friday and...' Shit, an answering machine, so I hung up, cursing the company, the drivers, their mothers, the lot. Which, of course, accomplished nothing. It was time for action.

I took a deep breath and shouted above the crowd: 'YOUR ATTENTION PLEASE! If you could all remain here while I run round to Tin Pan Alley and see if the coaches have gone there by mistake.' I pointed to Smudge. 'Smudge will stay here and answer any questions you have.' And with that, I legged it, glancing behind me to see the crowd gathering round Smudge and looking none too happy.

Running round to Tin Pan, I could feel the butterflies in my stomach working overtime. Please, God, let the buses be here. I rounded the corner and SHIT, no buses, just a large crowd and poor Norman all alone.

Norman spotted me and started straight over with a guy right on his shoulder.

'Norman, I don't know what's happening, the buses just haven't—'

'Keef,' Norman interrupted me, 'Keef, I don't give a fuck about that. See the guy behind me?' I nodded. 'He's got a fucking gun in my back and if you don't give him a fuckin refund right now, he's going to shoot me.'

Now, Norman is usually a joker but one look into his bulging eyes and sweaty complexion told me this was no joke. I fumbled into my pocket and thrust some crumpled notes into the gunman's free hand and he fucked off, shoving a pistol down the front of his pants and leaving me with a very relieved Norman.

Norman was just catching his breath and starting to explain his tale of the punter from hell when a commotion began behind us. Turning, we saw a fight break out among the waiting ravers and this was no schoolground slap around but a proper full-on scrap: fists, feet and heads flying in, girls screaming, and since this was Glasgow, it was only a matter of... *bang, smash*... the first beer bottle went over some unlucky punter's head. Then the unmistakable glint of streetlights flashing on cold, hard steel.

The crowd scattered as at least three knifemen tried to corner one guy. This was looking nasty. But the guy was fast on his feet ducking, doubling back and twisting away from the vicious thrusts and slashes. Somehow, he got into his vehicle unharmed and locked the doors. His attackers began to try to smash the windows with the butts of their knives while kicking the wing mirrors off. Norman and I stood transfixed. The car started, engine revving insanely. People in front jumped out of the way. But the guy inside was panicking and instead of pulling forwards he selected the wrong gear and lurched back in reverse, running over one of the knifeman's girlfriends, crushing her beneath the wheels. If I'd thought the knifemen were going at it before, now they were going totally insane. Trying to topple the car over and smash the windows with beer bottles. The back window went in just as the guy pulled off and ran over the girl's leg for a second time.

I just looked at Norman. 'Oh, my God.'

Now, normally I would have come forward to help the girl but not this time, fuck that, I'd probably just end up getting stabbed for my trouble and if I didn't sort out the transport to the rave toot sweet, we'd all be getting stabbed anyhow. I had to beg Norman to stay where he was while I ran back round to the Arches. It was now four a.m.

'Please, God, let the buses be there, please, God, let the buses be there.' I repeated out loud to myself as I ran, heart racing, blood pounding in my head, stomach doing loop-de-loops. Anyone that saw me must have thought I had gone mad, which maybe I had. As I approached, I willed the buses into being and turned the corner...

But there were no buses outside the Arches. Oh shit! It was all too much for me and I collapsed to my knees and started vomiting onto the pavement.

As I reached the dregs of my stomach and the inevitable diced carrots started to spray out, I had a moment of clarity and an idea. Of course! The fucking truck! We had rented a 7.5 tonne box truck to cart the kit over to the warehouse and, due to my car having broken down, I had brought the thing into town. I could pile people into that and take them to the gig, illegal and dangerous, yes, but definitely possible. I struggled to my feet, coughing and wiping sick from my face and staggered to where the crowd had Smudge surrounded, shouting abuse and pushing at him. Again, I took a deep breath...

'LISTEN, FOLKS, I HAVE NEWS ABOUT THE TRANSPORT TO THE RAVE—' The mob immediately abandoned Smudge and headed in my direction. '—The buses will not be coming.' This was probably the wrong thing to say and it was a full thirty seconds before I could make myself heard again as I backed away, palms up.

'PLEASE, PLEASE, LISTEN TO ME. The buses may not be coming but instead you're going to travel in the back of that truck.' I pointed over at the 7.5 tonner parked across the road. All heads turned towards it and, before they could react, I took my moment. 'Now, I'm just going to Tin Pan Alley to get the rest of the ravers and as before, Smudge here will answer any of your questions, THANK YOU.'

I threw Smudge the truck keys and he gave me a dirty look as I ran off back to Tin Pan and left him to face the music.

Back at Tin Pan, the ravers were too busy with the aftermath of the fight and the injured girl to have killed, cooked and eaten Norman just yet, in fact an ambulance had just arrived and the injured girl was being loaded inside.

Minutes later, we had marched the ravers back to the Arches and arrived to find that Smudge had managed to load most of the crowd into the back of the truck where they seemed quite happy. Due to the transparent roof panels, it was quite light inside and they were sitting chatting, skinning up, popping pills and snorting lines, like sitting in a truck in the early hours of the morning was quite the thing. For the first time that night, I felt some of the tension drain away, maybe we might make it after all. Once we had started getting the Tin Pan mob inside, sitting was out of the question, there was standing room only. The ravers were packed in like sardines, but somehow we got them in and as I closed the shutter, I had a last view of countless pairs of trainers, then click, I locked the catch. I had a quick look around and couldn't see any cops. So far, so good.

Norman, Smudge and I walked round to the front and got in. I started her up and began to pull away; she was really sluggish and at the first corner past the lights, I thought she might tip over as the suspension bottomed right out. This was well sketchy, well overloaded and well illegal, but fuck it, we were on the way and it was only a fifteen-minute drive to the rave. A smile spread across my face as I stared straight ahead into the night, gripping the wheel for grim death. Norman shattered my moment.

'Keef, did you see who got in the back?'

I turned to him for a second, wondering where he was going with this. 'Just the ravers, no?'

'But Keef, you must remember the machete maniacs from Tin Pan? They're in there too!'

Oops! I fought back images of mad slashers carving up the ravers in the back. 'But Norman, not all three of them? Surely after your girlfriend was crushed by a car, you would at least go with her to the hospital?'

Norman raised an eyebrow. 'Well, I definitely recognised one of them getting in the back, the small ratty-looking one in the tracksuit. The other two? I'm not so sure,' he replied

I just sighed and shook my head. Why was nothing in life ever easy? A quick glance in the wing mirror confirmed this. 'Guys, the fucking cops are behind us.'

Fear gripped the cab, especially on the driver's part I can tell you. Machete maniacs were forgotten for now. At the very least, the judge would set fire to my driving licence in front of me, at worst, a spell in correctional facilities beckoned. Norman and Smudge looked at me as you would a condemned man, which was not very helpful.

Another glance back. Yeah, they were still there, and since we were the only vehicle on the road, it was hard to imagine that they weren't taking an interest. It's always difficult to decide how to respond when the cops are behind you, especially if you're committing a crime. I mean, you should just drive normally, but what is normally? The limit was thirty mph, but hugging the limit is suspicious, and going over it is a reason to be pulled over, hell, just driving a truck at four a.m. on a Sunday morning is suspicious enough.

The road widened and slowly, the cops began to overtake. I wiped my sweaty palms on my trousers and stared straight ahead, trying to ignore them. They pulled up beside the cab and I could feel them staring in at me, but what could I do? I looked down and smiled. They didn't smile back. The cop in the passenger seat began to wind down his window. This was it, pulled! I started to wonder what I had on me. Flyers and tickets to the rave, maybe a bit of hash. Oh yeah, and about a hundred people in the back of the truck... shit.

The blue lights went on. Here we go. I looked down again and the cop was on his radio. I started searching my pockets for the hash and stuffing flyers and tickets under the seat. Then something amazing happened, the cops U-turned and sped off in the other direction with the siren on, lights strobing, and heading to another call!

Norman looked over at me with wonder written all over his face. 'Keef, you have the luck of the devil.' He shook his head as he fumbled for something in his pockets. 'Here, do you want a cigarette?'

I could see Norman's hand shaking a little as I took the cigarette and light he offered, and I was amazed to see my hands were also shaking, the stress was getting to me.

Luck of the devil? Yeah, that was right enough.

The turn for the warehouse was approaching, it couldn't come soon enough for us, I can tell you. A last glance in the wing mirrors confirmed we were not being followed so I pulled in through the gate and into the yard of the warehouse, stopped out of sight in the shadows and jumped out, dying to get the keys out of the ignition and my ass away from the driver's seat. The car park was already pretty packed with cars and I could hear the familiar thump, thump of the rave booming out from the building.

For the second time that night, countless pairs of trainers greeted me as I pulled up the shutter. I had to jump aside as the ravers poured out of the back, and by the looks on their faces, it maybe hadn't been a very pleasant trip. Their comments confirmed this:

'Where the fuck are we?'

'I thought I was going to die!'

'I couldn't breathe.'

'I was getting crushed.'

'I want my fucking money back!'

I couldn't be bothered arguing with them, we were here and we were alive and by tomorrow they would be talking about it as if it was the most exciting journey of their lives.

'THE RAVE IS THIS WAY,' I shouted above the crowd and pointing to the door, I strode forwards. 'Come on, Smudge, Norman, let's get in there before the rush.'

As we entered past the first set of swing doors, I was pleased to see two tables had been strategically placed across the hall leaving a narrow zig-zag path for the ravers to thread their way though, past Webby and Balfy (the doormen) and on to Louise at the till. I smiled. It meant we had a fair chance of actually getting some cash off them!

The crowd was right behind us, so I only had time for a quick hello to Webby and Balfy, a kiss for Louise and a promise to bring them some drinks from the bar before diving in. Inside the warehouse the rave was pumping, strobes pulsing, rig banging. It was hard to tell how many ravers were in there but there were at least 400 people and they were bouncing up and down, waving their hands in the air and whistling and screaming every time the beat paused. Sorted. I expertly weaved my way through the crowd and reached the bar, leaving Norman and Smudge far behind. I really, really needed a drink.

I greedily downed a cold can of Stella, crushed the can, dumped it back on the bar and headed to do my rounds, planning to stop back and collect the drinks for Louise, etc. on the return journey. First stop, the generator, for some reason other members of Desert Storm were allergic to filling the geny and it always fell to me. Taking my mini-Maglite torch from my pocket, I slid along the wall past the punters into what passed for our backstage area. The usual suspects were behind the decks, playing tunes and sniffing lines. I swerved away from them and into the darkness before they could notice me and trap me into conversation; I had work to do. Following the main power line back, I got to the generator, banging my shin on a concrete post on the way, the usual excruciating pain and another scar to add to my collection. I reached the generator and took off the filler cap and shone the torch inside; as I suspected it was nearly empty. Putting the Maglite between my teeth, I grabbed the jerry can and filled her up. Cool, that should keep the tunes on for four more hours or so.

Satisfied, I moved back to the DJ area, time to check the rig. Every DJ I have ever met turns up the sound system as he or she plays their set, they just can't help it. Our rig was pretty basic at that point, just the internal 3k system in the van and a few satellite boxes on the edges, not really enough for an event this size, so it was hard to blame the DJ for turning it up. Sure enough, I arrived at the decks to find the amps and mixer well in the red and the sound distorting. A quick EQ on the mixer, turning the amps back a few clicks and all was running in the green again, perfect. Time for a quick chat and line of Charlie with the lads.

Pleasantries dispensed with and nose refreshed, it was time to check on the door, so back to the bar to collect the drinks then somehow get through the crowd without spilling them. Torch on and using the elbows is my preferred method. I arrived there to find Webby pushing past me.

'That's it, Keef, I fucking quit!' With that, he threw his torch on the table and plunged into the rave.

I stood there staring after him with drinks in hand, then put them down on the table and turned to Louise and Balfy.

'What the fuck is up with him?' I asked, noticing the pale look on Louise's face.

Louise paused for a moment to collect herself, I had a bad feeling about this. 'Shit, Keef, some nutter wouldn't pay his fiver and when Webby tried to stop him from getting past, he pulled a blade, I thought he was going to stab him!'

Suddenly it all came flooding back. Shit, I'd forgotten to tell them about our friend. Webby was a nice guy, but tackling knife-wielding maniacs was not his scene. I could imagine it all; man won't pay, Webby tells him to get on his bike, man pulls knife, Webby looks at guest list.

'Ah yes, here it is, madman with huge machete, yes, you're down, in you go,' I couldn't blame him for buggering off.

'And even worse,' Louise continued, 'he waved the knife around... it nearly took my head off, and he began shouting, "I'm in charge here now... nobody sells any drugs in here except me!".'

My eyes narrowed and I felt blood rushing to my head. Oh, did he really? Threatening the staff and my girlfriend? Fuck this guy. And I could think of a few dealers who might not be too impressed either.

'You guys must have had a good look at this fuckwit. I think he's the same dude that was involved in some shit outside Tin Pan earlier.

Skinny, quite small, white, spotty little rat in a tracksuit, huge machete?'

They both nodded.

'Okay,' I told them, 'let's fold up this door now, I reckon that's most of them in anyway. Louise, here's the keys for the truck so stash the cash under the seat. But be subtle, like. Balfy, can you go with her please?'

They nodded again. Louise was already stuffing notes into the cash box from her bum bag.

'I'm going to see if I can sort this guy out,' I said.

Louise must have seen this look on my face before and she looked worried. 'Keef, please be careful, that guy's a nutter.'

I gave her a hug and a kiss. 'Of course I'll be careful.'

I turned back into the warehouse, I could feel her eyes following me but I didn't turn back.

Right, where is this little rat? I said to myself as I scanned the dance floor. On second thought, maybe I should get some backup first. Where are the Grahams?

Then I spotted our track-suited friend but he didn't look so tough now. He was staggering from side to side, his left hand was held against the side of his face and blood was pouring through his fingers and running down his arm, splashing on his tracksuit and onto the floor of the warehouse. He had obviously been slashed.

I had mixed emotions; the Glasgow call of 'haud yer face together, wee man!' came to mind. I mean, this guy really was a chief penis, but I've never been into knives, and don't carry one as I doubt I've got the bottle to use it. If you're going to pull a weapon out, then you should use it right away, not wave it about, get it taken off you and then get done with it yourself. I wondered if that was what had happened to our man here?

I considered it for another few moments. Firstly, I really should help him, in spite of the fact he was an arsehole, just because it was the right thing to do. Secondly, people were starting to notice him, it really didn't look good for Desert Storm to have slashed-up punters roaming around the rave (cold, I know, but true). And lastly, what if he died? That would really bring the shit down on everybody. The best plan was to patch him up, get him the fuck out of there and to a hospital as soon as possible, but not by ambulance as that would attract the cops for sure.

Action time. I moved in towards him and was surprised to meet Shuggy Graham and a few of his mates standing a few paces away watching our bleeding friend intently. My suspicious mind started doing overtime.

'Shuggy, I was just coming to find you as we were having a spot of bother at the door. Some prick with a machete... but it seems someone's beaten me to him?' I said pointing over at the bleeding tracksuit-clad man, while levelling my gaze at Shuggy.

'Yeah, we've already met,' Shuggy replied. I left it at that.

'Look, we need to get him the fuck out of here, people are starting to notice, and if the cops get called... I'll go and get the first aid kit. Can you guys move him over there out of sight? I'll be back in a minute.'

I couldn't help but notice, as I moved off, that man was none too happy to see Shuggy and his pals, and even less happy to be dragged off into the dark part of the warehouse by them. I got a sudden fear and upped my pace, reaching the decks in record time, grabbed the first aid kit and legged it back. But it seemed my fears were groundless. Shuggy had even got a chair for him and the guy was sitting there calmly (well, as calm as you can be when half your face is hanging off), probably in shock.

Getting Shuggy to hold the torch, I put on some surgical gloves, unpacked some lint pads from the kit and showed them to the man.

He seemed to get the idea, and let me peel his hand away from the injury. I mopped up the blood and had a look. He had a nasty slash running about four inches from just below his left eye down nearly to his chin. This guy needed medical treatment. I did what I could: a quick pass with an antiseptic wipe, another mop with more lint, then some butterfly stitches to try to hold it together and finally a large pad held on with surgical tape. Once done, I replaced his hand back over it. Good as new... not!

Peeling off the bloody gloves and throwing them away into a corner, I lit up a cigarette and turned to Shuggy. 'Okay, what about transport to a hospital? We can't just leave him here.'

'Yeah, Keef, don't worry, I've sorted it. There's a van waiting for him out the back.'

I raised an eyebrow. Shuggy was being unusually helpful.

We got the guy to his feet and led him to the back door, where sure enough a battered-looking, blood-red transit van was waiting. The back doors swung open as we approached, the engine started and I could see two big-looking characters already inside. As the tracksuit man was being bundled in, I put my hand on Shuggy's shoulder. 'Shuggy, you guys are taking him to a hospital, aren't you?'

Shuggy just smiled. 'Don't you worry, Keef, we'll take care of him.'

The doors closed and the van sped off. Hmm, that's exactly what I was worried about! I stood watching the van disappear round the corner, biting my lip, wondering what the fuck I had just let happen.

I remained there for a few minutes, just staring straight ahead, alone with my thoughts. What the fuck was going on? When we did the first tunnel party, everything was so fluffy. I could never have imagined in my darkest dreams that a few months later, mates would have guns in their backs, threatened with machetes and people getting slashed in the party. If someone close to me got badly hurt,

I couldn't handle it.

Maybe this should be the last party?

With these thoughts and a heavy heart, I turned and trudged back inside to the rave. As soon as I entered, my mood changed, my head started rocking to the beat, my fingers clicking as I looked down the warehouse. The crowd was silhouetted against the strobe lights bouncing up and down as the multi-coloured fans of light from the moonflowers scanned across them, dancing over their heads. The beat paused for a second and then the ravers roared as it dropped in again. You could almost taste the energy in the air, crackling like electricity. Fuck the machete posse, this was the rave and the rave must go on! Where there's a will, there's a way, and I definitely had the will so the way would be found. With energy levels recharged past the max, I strode forward and headed for the decks. I had a shit load of new banging tunes and it was time to play my set.

The decks were mounted in the back of the Storm van as usual so you stood behind and played them through the back doors. I fished my record box out, got the Maglite between my teeth and started leafing through the tunes, every so often selecting one and turning it to the side so it stuck up clear from the rest. Once I had a good fifteen tunes ready to go, I pulled out my first selection and placed it on the free turntable and opened a beer, lit a cigarette and waited. There would be no beat-mixing this tune in; I would wait for the track that was on to wrap up then bang mine on.

As the last chorus started to fade, I killed the lights and hit start on the deck. The turntable spun up to full speed and the melodic beginning of the track filtered out through the crowd, echoing back eerily off the warehouse walls. The crowd whistled, yelled and clapped in total darkness. Then the beat kicked in... thump, thump, thump. I hit the lights and the strobes and moonflowers exploded across the dance floor; the crowd went mental. Yeah, man, this is what it's all about, this is what makes it all worth it.

The next track I beat-mixed in; the process of mixing may sound easy but is in actual fact very difficult (as anyone who has tried will tell you). To put it as basically as possible, the turntable will let you speed up and slow down the record eight per cent either way, so coupled with the other deck, that gives you sixteen per cent to play with. The plan is, one record is playing (the one the ravers are listening to) and the other one only you can hear on the headphones. You drop it in and decide if it's faster or slower, adjusting the speeds to match and when you are happy, you mix it in by using the crossfader which lets the crowd hear the two records together, then you (hopefully) seamlessly fade the old one out. Hey presto, a perfect mix.

If you're really good, you can create a new tune from the two tracks by using a mix of EQ (equalisation – e.g. dropping in and out the bass and treble) and rapid use of the crossfader to cut out beats and drop in basslines. That's what I do. Somehow, I can open my mind and let the energy of the rave inside. My hands, the records, the mixer all become one. There is no conscious thought of what to do next, the music just flows. You might think this is bullshit but I know it's true, because when I try to make a recording when not at the rave, I can't replicate it to the same standard. Without the primal energy of the crowd to feed off, it just can't be done. Well, not in my case anyway.

So, basslines were pumping, the crowd was jumping and I was in the zone. There is some video footage of this event and you can clearly see the people going insane. In spite of all the shit that had gone down, this was one kicking rave, at least until the cops turned up.

I'd been playing for about an hour when Smudge tapped me on the shoulder. I brushed him off but he was insistent.

'WHAT THE FUCK IS IT, MAN? CAN'T YOU SEE I'M FUCKING MIXING!'

I screamed at him above the music.

'KEEF, IT'S THE COPS AT THE DOOR,' he shouted back.

Bollocks. 'HOW MANY OF THEM?'

'EH, ALL OF THEM, I THINK.'

Terminator 2 quote... haha, Smudge.

'WHAT DO THEY WANT?' Stupid question. Maybe they want to let the rave go on another twenty-four hours or so? Yeah, right.

'THEY WANT TO SEE THE ORGANISER.'

Brilliant. Just what I needed. The way my luck was going, I would be instantly arrested and all the gear taken.

I got Smudge to take over on the decks and headed to the door with a heavy heart. Nearing the warehouse entrance, I could see loads of Glasgow's finest crowding round Louise and a few others. A fat and ugly cop was shining a torch in their faces and shouting.

'I DON'T GIVE A FUCK WHAT YOU SAY, IF YOU DON'T FIND ME THE ORGANISER IN THE NEXT TWO FUCKING MINUTES, I'M GOING TO JAIL YOU ALL FOR OBSTRUCTION AND...' The usual blah, blah, blah.

To tell you the truth, I couldn't be bothered with this asshole. Usually, I can be pretty cooperative but not tonight; tonight, I was feeling uncooperative to the extreme. I just wanted to turn tail and head back into the rave, sniff some more coke, drink a beer and check out the chicks. For all of two seconds, I considered this course of action. But what could I do? With a sigh, I reluctantly started forward for my Spartacus moment.

'Hi, I'm the one you're looking for, I'm the organiser.'

Fat Cop and his buddies abandoned the others and surrounded me. Great. Fat Cop ripped a notebook and pen out of his jacket pocket and focused his piggy eyes on me, 'So, you're the organiser, are you?' he stated pointlessly.

'I just said that, didn't I?'

'Don't you get cheeky with me, sonny Jim.' Fat Cop's face was reddening as he wagged a sweaty digit in my direction. I hoped that maybe he'd have a heart attack. 'Okay, Mr Organiser,' he started, his pen poised, 'what's your full name, address and date of birth?'

I gave my details and Fat Cop radioed them in. While we stood waiting for the results from the police computer, the interrogation continued. 'So, what are you doing here?'

Jesus, this guy was no Sherlock Holmes! 'Eh, having a party, officer.' A few of my mates laughed.

'Yes, I can see that, but I want to know why. Who gave you permission to use these premises, have you got an entertainment licence, ID?'

'Which one first?' I answered

'Eh?'

'The why, the who, the licence or the ID?' I clarified for him.

'Just answer the fucking questions, smartass.'

'Sorry, could you repeat them again?' I said and smiled back at him.

Fat Cop's eyes narrowed. 'Look, sonny, you're in big trouble here. Any more lip and I'll fuckin' nick you right now.' He was proper frothing.

'Arrest me? But why? It's not a crime to have a party,' I replied innocently.

'I'll be the judge of that,' he growled. 'And what about the drugs, eh? Next, you'll be telling me that no one's taking illegal drugs in there. I know what these parties are like, these RAVE parties.' He said the word rave like it was a satanic ritual.

Typically, just at that moment the doors swung open and out staggered a sweaty raver, eyes like saucers, sweat dripping onto his soaking hoody, face gurning and with a line of drool running down his chin. Everyone turned to look.

'There, there.' He pointed, looking pleased with himself. 'That waster, that's exactly what I'm talking about.'

Sweaty raver, who was obviously going outside for some much-needed fresh air, spotted the cops and somewhere in his drug-addled brain sensed danger and a signal was sent to his feet to make a quick 180-degree turn and head back inside. Unfortunately, the signal failed to reach the rest of his body which just kept going. He fell arse over tits and into the wall. The cops looked down at him in disgust as he picked himself up and half-crawled back inside. Fat Cop shot me a telling stare, daring me to deny the obvious. I gave it a go anyway.

'That dude has probably just had a few too many lagers at the bar, that's all.' Shit, I'd mentioned the bar word and I regretted it instantly. Fat Cop was all over me like a rash.

'Bar? Did you say bar? Well, there's a crime for a start, the Licensing Scotland Act 19 clearly states—'

I interrupted him mid-flow. 'Yes, we have a bar but we don't take money. We sell raffle tickets and the winners receive a drink.'

'Eh? A bar's a bar and no licence means you're in big trouble.' Fat Cop smiled revealing a set of discoloured teeth and a waft of bad breath.

'No, no,' I replied, 'this bar's a raffle; you buy a ticket and every ticket's a winner. You get the picture, all totally legal.' Now it was my turn to smile, revealing a set of pearly white gnashers and mint-fresh breath. Fat Cop stopped smiling; he must have spotted my pearly whites, reminding him of his own dental problems. My smile widened.

'Raffle tickets?' he repeated. It was almost painful to watch the slow ticking happening in Fat Cop's brain as he tried to take this in.

I got on the front foot. 'Anyway, there will be no alcohol left by now.' I glanced over at Louise, who took the hint and headed off inside to make it happen. 'But maybe we could sort you out some jelly donuts.' The colour drained from Fat Cop's face. Shit! Did I really just say that?

Apart from the intolerably loud rave music pumping from inside, you could have heard a pin drop. Fat Cop reached towards his baton and stepped forward. At that moment, another cop walked in from outside; he had some silver braid on his cap. Fat Cop stepped back but his stare remained fixed on me, his fists clenching and then unclenching then clenching again.

Silver Braid spoke. 'I take it that's Robinson?' he continued without waiting for an answer, 'well, he's on file but no warrants. I can't really be bothered with him or this bullshit.' He turned to me. 'Right, Robinson, pack your kit and get to fuck. You've got ten minutes or it's the tin pail, understand?'

I chanced my arm. 'How about thirty minutes, officer?'

'Look, pal, this isn't a Chinese restaurant! Ten fucking minutes!'

'Okay, twenty minutes then.' I had nothing to lose.

Silver Braid considered this for a moment. 'Hmm, you've got fifteen.' He turned to leave but stopped. 'But if I have to come back here—'

'—it's the tin pail,' I finished for him.

'That's right, the tin pail. Okay, boys, let's go.' Silver Braid stormed out.

Fat Cop grabbed me by the hooded top and drew me close, his stinking breath nearly choking me. 'There'll be another time, smartass. Your cards are marked!' He released me and I went inside.

I prised a reluctant Smudge away from the decks and pressed the stop button mid-tune. Howls and boos of discontent rose from the dance floor. I grabbed the mic and cleared my throat. 'Ladies and gentlemen, your attention please. As you may be aware, the police have arrived.' More boos and jeers. 'But they have allowed us to continue for another fifte—sorry, twenty minutes.' Cue massive cheers. I selected my most banging tune and slapped it on and the place went crazy. I nearly added, 'Glasgow posse, wave your machetes in the air, wave them like you just don't care', but I stopped myself just in time.

With the help of Smudge and Louise, we packed up the gear and got out of there with no minutes to spare. The cops had already left, apart from Fat Cop who hovered, checking his watch to time us, and we drove off in the van, all remaining ravers left on the street. They could find their own ways back.

Sunday night was the debrief at my flat. Everyone was there, gathered around the kitchen table, with a few additions such as Shuggy Graham. People were not happy, some were for killing Desert Storm off completely! Well, after all, Norman had nearly been shot, Webby nearly stabbed, the buses hadn't turned up, the machete maniac had been slashed and we got busted by the cops; all in all, not a good night's work.

'Look,' said Webby, 'I'm just not up for it anymore, Keef. I don't care what you say, no rave is worth being stabbed for.'

'...or shot,' added Norman.

'And yet again, after paying the wages, we only just broke even,' said Louise, looking up from the pad of figures she had been poring over and brushing her long blonde hair from her eyes.

I looked around from face to face and said, 'It's okay, I've got a plan.'

They all sat back and waited quietly to hear what I had to say. I cleared my throat. 'My plan is this: we are not set up to deal with the pond scum that arrive at the gigs these days. In the beginning, it was basically just all our mates that turned up to Desert Storm parties, but as it has got so much bigger, more and more dodgies are coming, especially later on as people are drifting back to schemes around Glasgow and other non-clubbers are hearing about the gig and coming down. Now, I for one couldn't handle it if one of you got fucked up by these idiots, so I suggest its time to fight back. We hire the biggest, hardest doormen we can find, people who no one will fuck with, stick them on the front of the warehouse and solve all our problems in one fell swoop.'

'But who will we get to do it?' Smudge interrupted

'I was just getting to that. That's why Shuggy is here. Shuggy knows the doormen that do the Savoy in Sauchiehall Street. He assures me that these guys are badass and that for £200 they'll do the door. So, what do you think?'

We all talked it over but there was little to say against it. On the surface, it allayed all our fears, and if these guys couldn't hack it, well, it was them in the firing line, not us. The only one who didn't seem convinced was Mad Dog.

'So, Keef, what are the names of these guys?' Mad Dog asked.

'Err, the names? I don't know.' I turned to Shuggy.

'The head doorman is called Danny T,' Shuggy replied.

This meant nothing to me. But it did to Mad Dog.

'T as in...?' He paused, shocked. 'Are you fucking crazy, Keef?' I thought that was a bit rich coming from Mad Dog. He continued. 'Keef, these guys are proper nut jobs. They are one of the hardest families in Glasgow.'

But I wasn't to be dissuaded. 'Perfect then, nobody will fuck about with us, will they?'

Mad Dog was still shaking his head. 'Keef, please don't do this, you'll open a whirlpool of darkness and you won't be able to close it again!'

But with everyone else in favour despite, or perhaps in spite of what Mad Dog said, the plan went forward and we had our doormen ready for the next rave.

9

THE WHIRLPOOL OF DARKNESS

Shuggy and I drove down to meet with the new doorman at Danny's house in darkest Govan, one of the best-known and hardest council housing estates in Glasgow. Parking my BMW outside, I depressed the key fob to activate the central locking, but as we walked away, I stopped and looked back. Shit, I had forgotten to remove the security front panel of the stereo and was about to start back when Shuggy stopped me.

'Keef, don't worry about yer motor, no fucker will touch it parked ootside Danny's hoose.'

I must admit I was a little nervous as we walked up the driveway and I had to wipe my sweating hands on my trousers, much to Shuggy's amusement.

We rang the bell and it was answered by a tall, athletically built guy with short dark hair in his early twenties. He smiled when he saw Shuggy and ushered us inside.

The living room was pretty normal looking; tidy and lived in, no sign of madness in here (except maybe the samurai sword mounted on the fireplace). We sat down and Danny called through to the kitchen and ordered up some brews. He sat in the chair across from me, leaned forward, folded his arms and stared straight into my eyes. It was a powerful stare that was hard to hold but I did my best. Danny got straight to the point.

'So, you must be Keef?' I nodded and he continued, 'Shuggy here tells me you've been having some problems at your raves?' We got to talking and drinking.

Much later that night as we staggered back to the car, high on coke and far too pissed to drive, I couldn't see what all the fuss had been about. This guy Danny was a good guy, for fuck's sake, he had already saved my black ass from some nut job down at the local bar/club and I had only known him a matter of hours.

After we had agreed a deal at his house, we headed out to the local boozer to drink to it. The place didn't look that inviting; a battered-looking two-storey brick building standing on its own in some rubbish-strewn waste ground, metal shutters still down even though it was the middle of the afternoon. The sign outside was hanging off and it was impossible to make out the name, but if it had been called the Flying Tumbler I wouldn't have been surprised. If I hadn't been with Danny and Shuggy I would have thought twice (maybe three times) about going inside, I couldn't imagine they get many strange black punters rocking up, in fact I reckon they didn't get many strangers in there at all!

Once inside, the whole place turned round to check us out. I got some pretty nasty looks from some pretty nasty-looking people but once Danny had introduced me at the bar all was cool and the drinkers went back to their pints. It seemed he knew them all and it wasn't long before we were relaxed and sitting at a table with a few chicks downing Jack Daniel's. Danny seemed like a pretty easy-going, friendly sort of guy and it wasn't long before he had bought a wrap of coke and we were sniffing fat lines in the toilet. As the night went on, the locals took to me and I was soon shaking my thing with the rest of them on the small dance floor. A little blonde chick in particular took an interest in me and we were chatting away like old friends.

My only mistake was on the pool table. I'm pretty good at pool and had beaten all comers when a guy with a huge slash mark across his face came up, he was next on. He didn't seem so friendly. I broke off and potted two balls, and he growled as I continued to sink them double-time. But I was too busy chatting to the blonde chick to feel the rising tension, or notice that loads of the punters had gathered round who had suddenly taken an interest in my pool skills. I got onto the black, which meant that my opponent hadn't potted a ball, in fact he hadn't even had a shot. If I potted the black now, I would granny him, the ultimate humiliation on a pool table. As I bent over my cue and sunk the last ball, I glanced up in triumph, but one look at his face and I realised that maybe this hadn't been such a good idea.

He was not a happy man, he was so angry he could hardly get his words out. I had embarrassed him in front of the whole pub. Looking again at him, he looked like one hard bastard, well-built, in his forties and covered in homemade tattoos (including a very noticeable swallow on his hand meaning he had done bird (i.e. time in jail) and wanted everyone to know about it. It was almost one hundred per cent he had a blade on him, in fact, probably a huge machete stashed in his jacket as well. But right now, it looked like the pool cue was his weapon of choice.

'You taking the fucking piss, you black bastard?' he growled in a low menacing voice.

Oh shit, a racist as well. It was far, far too late to take back the winning shot so I stepped to the side keeping the pool table between us and held on tightly to my cue.

Danny saved the day, he came up and put a protective arm around me and asked what was going on. The guy wilted and fucked off. Danny then suggested gently that maybe that was enough pool for tonight. I didn't argue.

As Shuggy and I drove up the road, the coke taking the edge off the Jack Daniel's so at least we were going in a straight line, I was thinking about the effect that the new doorman would have on the next gig, a wry smile on my face.

'What you laughing at, Keef?' Shuggy inquired.

'Oh, just thinking of the looks on the faces of the plastic hard men from clubland when they turn up at the next Storm gig and find Danny and co on the door, bit of a shock, eh?'

'You better believe it,' replied Shuggy

I did.

The next gig was in an industrial unit somewhere to the east of Glasgow. Rutherglen, I think. The venue wasn't anything special, just a big shed with a high roof and corrugated metal sides. I was standing at the door with Louise when Danny and the boys turned up. They were with Willie Ross, a friend of Shuggy's, and as they strode across the car park, they looked like something out of Reservoir Dogs, suited up with black ties or open shirts and striding towards us. Danny had a large black sports holdall with him which he handed to me, telling me to put it behind the till. It was much heavier than I expected and I had to brace myself as I leaned over and placed it down beside Louise's legs. She looked at it questioningly; I just smiled and told her better not to ask.

The ravers started to arrive but instead of the usual melee as they tried to force their way past the door without paying or threatening poor Webby and co with knives, they were faced with Danny. This wasn't the jovial Danny from the bar a few weeks before (he was gone) but a deadly serious, no-nonsense, hardcore Danny, who seemed to have grown even larger than his six-foot-one frame as he prowled the doorway like a cat. They stopped in their tracks. I couldn't suppress a smile as I observed things from behind the till.

He soon had the ravers all in a nice neat line with their money out ready and waiting to go in. I could see familiar faces, people that were usually troublemakers, eyes to the floor and shuffling forward. I turned to Webby and nudged him with my elbow.

'Told you this would work.' He had to agree.

Suddenly, Danny grabbed someone out of the queue and threw him roughly against the wall. He must have recognised him. 'Empty your pockets and give me your blade,' said Danny, who wasn't playing and as two more of his boys closed in, the punter meekly handed over a nasty-looking kitchen knife.

'You'll get it back at the end,' Danny informed him and pushed him back into the queue. I heard a guy murmur to his mate, 'Fuck's sake, that's Danny T.'

As far as I was concerned, it was my 'mission accomplished' moment and our days of trouble were firmly in the past, and when one of the doormen came up to me and asked what to do with a raver that had tried to climb in over the fire door, it massaged my ego to no end.

It was the ravers' fault it had come to this (or the bad element among them anyway) I told myself. Push had come to shove, and we were pushing. Rave on, happy days.

It was at this gig that I noticed the first Desert Storm graffiti: Desert Storm Tour of Destruction, 1992. It was written on the wall in spray-paint, cool! The rest of the gig was only memorable because of the lack of trouble and the incredible amount of money we made. Everyone was paid, everyone was happy and I even invited Danny and his family back to my place for an after, afterparty, which was kicking. As it finally wound up on the Sunday night and they left, we all shook hands looking forward to the next gig. As I shut the door, happy as I'd ever been I reckon, and with a bright future ahead of us all, I thought, what could possibly go wrong? Whirlpool of darkness? Go fuck yourself!

The next Desert Storm rave was a beauty. We were becoming pretty professional in our organisation, and I in particular had honed the venue part of it to a tee. I searched Glasgow for a warehouse till I found one near Govan shipbuilders on the Clydeside. It ticked all the boxes; perfect size (10,000 square feet), no neighbours to complain about the noise, easy access for vehicles, secluded off-road parking and although it was for rent, it had been vandalised.

A quick call to the letting agent and here was my blag:

'Hello, DTZ letting agents, how can I help you?'

'Err, hi, my name is Keef Robinson from Desert Storm Entertainments and I've been looking at your property near Govan shipbuilders. I've noticed it's been empty for quite a while and when I looked yesterday, there has been quite a lot of vandalism since my last visit.'

'Yes, yes, bloody kids. We're having loads of trouble down there, smashed windows, the locks broken and so on. Are you thinking of renting it?' the agent asked hopefully.

I already knew about the broken locks as I was the one that had broken them.

'Well, not a long-term rental as such, but I'm looking for a venue to do some filming for a music video and I was wondering if you would let me use it for the weekend and in return we will board up the windows, secure the doors again and give the place a general tidy. As you know, it's a bit of a mess.'

I could almost hear the agent's mind ticking. 'So, you would fix the windows and doors, tidy up the place and all you want to do is some filming?'

'Yes, that's right.'

Venue in the bag and warehouse keys in my pocket, it was time to do a fire plan. This involves satisfying the fire brigade that it's safe to hold an event in a building. One of the cops' main ways of closing down gigs is fire safety. First, I would draw a plan of the warehouse and mark on it where I was going to put the exit signs, fire extinguishers, emergency lights and buckets of sand, toilets, etc, then kit it out as marked. There are quite a few regulations you must adhere to. For instance, you must be able to move thirty feet in a straight direction from the fire exits before hitting an obstruction, each exit must be marked by a green exit light, you must have a way of sounding an alarm in the event of an emergency (air horn in my case), and many more, but I had been studying the regulations thoroughly and was confident I could impress a fire officer enough on the day to get a pass.

The fire inspection was duly passed and all that remained was a phone call to the cops to tell them that there would be some noise at the venue due to filming that would take place over that weekend and could they please mark it in the desk sergeant's book. So, when the cops arrive on the night asking what the fuck is going on, I could tell them to phone the station and check the book, after which they would usually chill out and help with the parking. The cops would also ask if the place had been cleared by the fire brigade, which it had. I'd give them the number and the fire officer's name and bingo, it's rave on. This plan was used by us again and again with only one drawback. You could only do a rave in each cop district once, for obvious reasons.

Meanwhile in the background, we had pulled out all the stops to make this one a big one. I had involved a guy called Bradley from a traveller family that I worked for in clubland, so funds weren't a problem. I had arranged to rent a much more powerful sound system, stage, and lights including a laser. We went all out on the flyers and posters, covering the whole city over a period of four weeks. We had tickets for sale in all the record stores and clothes shops and I had arranged with Slam (the biggest club promoters in Glasgow) that I could promote inside their gigs and officially run buses from outside their club at the Arches, instead of round the corner like before. The die was cast, we could all feel that this was going to be a good one.

The gig didn't disappoint; it was massive, our biggest yet. The ravers were crammed in and pressing against the stage. The green laser formed huge tunnels and walls of green light as it cut through the fog from the smoke machine, as 1,500 ravers danced the night away. The cops only came for a brief visit; I told them the filming was finished and this was the after party, so they went away satisfied and the rave continued until the Sunday afternoon, the winding-up strangely coinciding with the bar stock running out! The only slight blemish on an otherwise perfect night was finding one of Danny's doormen running an illicit half-price entry system at one of the fire doors. I talked with Danny and he promised to sort it out and the doorman would never work at Desert Storm again. Sorted.

After this rave, confidence was sky-high and the future looked so bright I told my friends to buy dark sunglasses so they could look at it! The next event had to be something special so I racked my brains for something totally different. After a couple of weeks of driving hundreds of miles around the Glasgow area drawing blanks, I was in the toilet pissing when I had my eureka moment yet again. I ran out of the bog and into the living room, piss dribbling down my leg.

'Smudge, Smudge, I've got it, I've got it! We'll have the next Desert Storm at the castle in Renfrew, you know, the Monkey House?'

Smudge didn't have a clue but Johnny Mac did. We both knew

the place well. A deserted mansion/castle in the countryside with a huge walled courtyard surrounded by acres and acres of unkempt gardens. We had found a secret way in through an unlocked window years ago and it had been the scene of many a picnic date organised by the Mac and I to impress chicks over the years. But then Mac thought our chances were slim.

'Yeah, right, Keef, nice idea and perfect place, but there is no fucking way they're going to give you the keys for that joint, never.'

That sounded like a challenge to me and I love a challenge. Over a month later, as I stood with the manager of Monkey House Estates, Mr Tonner, (not a relative of Bruce Tonner) staring from a huge ornate window on the main staircase and looking down onto the 800 or so sweaty ravers bouncing in the courtyard. I turned to him and said, 'Well, Mr Tonner, I reckon that's the one hundred or so people in now, don't you think?'

'Oh, my God! Oh, my God, what have I done?' The manager's face was ashen as he looked out over the crowd for the first time. He was sweating and had to loosen his tie before continuing. 'But... but... Mr Robinson, this wasn't what we agreed at all! You promised me a maximum of eighty persons would attend the filming of a music video!'

'Eighty, one hundred, let's not quibble over numbers. It's all going brilliantly, don't you think?'

'Mr Robinson, I may have been an idiot to have been taken in by you and your associate Mr. Mitchell, but I'm not blind. There must be hundreds out there. I'm going to lose my job over this... this... this...' words failed him, so I helped him out.

'Rave party, I think that's the phrase you're looking for, Mr Tonner.'

Six weeks earlier, Bradley and I had turned up at the Monkey House Restaurant, attached to Formakin House, where the trust's office was located. Parking Bradley's red Porsche right outside the office window, we headed inside, clutching important-looking coloured files and dressed to the nines. Mr Tonner soon fell under our spell and the cops and fire brigade quickly after. Bradley, who always thinks bigger, booked the famous Andy Weatherall as the star DJ (he wanted him to land in the grounds by fucking helicopter for God's sake, but I managed to persuade him out of it due to cost) and the rest just fell into place. On the night of the rave, the buses leaving the town centre after the clubs were packed and even though the gig was nearly twenty miles away (by far the furthest we had attempted yet), the rumours of castle courtyards and famous DJs coupled with our growing rep ensured a packed-out venue. My main worry was the weather as an outside gig in the West of Scotland is a sketchy thing to say the least but luckily the weather was perfect.

Again, there was only one thing that tarnished the dazzling silver techno shine off things a little: why did 800 ravers x £10 not equal £8,000? We didn't take much more than £5,000 all-in, even factoring in the bar money! Something was amiss. I thought long and hard about it. Which motherfucker had their dirty thieving, sticky fucking paws in the cookie jar?

But Sherlock Holmes had to take a back seat as fate was about to throw open the door to the Whirlpool of Darkness.

A sea change had overtaken the doormen in the last few months; when I had first met them, they were smart looking, suits, jackets, proper trousers, shiny shoes, but now you could hardly recognise them. They had become ravers with hooded tops, jeans, trainers, skip caps, and more worryingly, they could now be found in many of Glasgow's trendy nightclubs mad on ecstasy having it on the dance floor. This had never been part of my plan. While I was becoming pretty good friends with Danny (he's a nice guy if you're his mate; generous, friendly, a gentleman, a good friend but a bad enemy) and even though I went out with him and his friends for nights out here and there, little alarm bells in my head warned me not to get too close. The warning signs were there.

One Wednesday night, I arrived at Reds nightclub for a few drinks and a boogie, and I was just about to go in when I noticed the pavement outside was covered in blood – and I don't mean a few drops, I'm talking a fucking lot of claret here. Puzzled but not unduly worried, I went inside, and as I reached the dancefloor, I saw Danny heading towards me. I was about to greet him with a how's it going and slap on the back when I noticed the look on his face. The jovial Danny smile had gone, replaced with a darkness. I pulled up and the greeting died on my lips, something was wrong, very wrong. He pulled me close and raised his voice over the music. His face was twisted and contorted. I stared into his eyes, they were like bottomless pits, I looked in through this window to his soul and shivered. I knew that violence had been done.

'Keef, Keef it was amazing, I done him right over, what a rush. He thought he was a hard cunt but we showed him, dragged him into the fire escape, haha, slashed him again and again, slashed that fucker proper, proper style.'

Danny made a slashing motion with his hands and pulled the first few inches of a huge machete out of a scabbard in his trousers for me to see, before sliding it back.

Oh shit.

'Who? Danny, who was it? Who?' I insisted. I knew most of the people in the fucking nightclub, but it was hard to get through to him, he was on another planet, high on adrenalin and no doubt coke, beer, and fuck knows what else. I grabbed him by the shoulders. 'DANNY, WHO? THE NAME!'

Finally, he answered. 'Who? Eh, some fucker called Tommy, I think. Tall bastard with dark curly hair.'

Oh, my God.

'Tommy? Not Tommy Flanagan?'

'Flanagan, yeah, that's right,' replied Danny.

Dark thoughts flashed through my mind. Oh no, not Tommy, that's my mate, I run club nights with him. Fuck, this is my fault, I got these people involved in the rave scene. What have I done? Mad Dog was right! The Whirlpool of Darkness!

Tommy had survived the slashing but I felt too guilty to visit him in hospital. I reckoned I would be one of the last people he would want to see. Tommy's scars are truly horrific and cover his face on both sides from cheek to chin. Nasty fucking business.

Tommy disappeared off the scene and I didn't see him out in Glasgow ever again. So, imagine my surprise when I was in the cinema watching the movie *Braveheart* and who should appear on the silver screen sporting his scars but Tommy, playing a Scottish hardman whose woman is about to be taken by the English overlord. In fact, he's in the film the whole way through, strutting his stuff with Mel fucking Gibson no less! He also went on to have a major role in *Sons of Anarchy* playing Filip 'Chibs' Telford. Cool, you just can't keep people like Tommy down. He took a setback that might have broken most normal people and turned it to his advantage, big time. Fair play.

As for me, I had a Desert Storm party run that weekend. This event was to be held about twenty-five miles outside Glasgow. Bradley and I had rented a marquee tent and we were pitching it in the grounds of a burnt-out hotel at the side of Loch Lomond, a beautiful spot to the north of Glasgow. But my heart wasn't in it. I kept thinking back to what had happened to Tommy. I had told no one what I had seen and it was eating me up inside. The others couldn't understand what was wrong with me, my usual energy and 120 per cent commitment were lacking and we coasted towards the weekend on autopilot. It reminded me of something that had happened in Glasgow a few years before. A girl had been stabbed to death in an under-18s club in the city centre called Heaven (ironic, eh?). It got a lot of press coverage at the time but not as much coverage as when the club promoter put up a poster round town the next week, saying, 'You don't have to die to go to heaven'. Surely it was only a matter of time before someone got killed at a Desert Storm event? Something had to be done.

I don't remember much about the Loch Lomond gig except that some fucker decided to cut a hole in the back of a tent and half the people got in for nothing meaning we lost money. But it made no difference to me, my mind was made up. This was the end.

Desert Storm was finished.

10

THE UNIT AND THE MACHETE WARRIOR

After a few months of inactivity and feeling sorry for myself (pathetic, I hate self-pity), I started to get the rave itch again. There was no way to restart Desert Storm again as the same problems would just come back to haunt me. So, what to do?

The solution required some lateral thinking. Not my strongest skill. I'm great when there's a plan, full power straight ahead, blasting obstacles out of my way. But reversing and going around? Not so good.

The lease was about to expire on my latest West End flat and there was no way the landlord was going to renew it, hardly surprising since I don't make the best neighbour (unless of course you like weekly all-night parties, constant noise and weirdo's coming and going at all times of the night and day). I was getting bored of the frequent house flits and was driving into town along the Clydeside Expressway mulling over this very problem when I noticed a 'to let' sign on some railway arches. Before I had really considered what I was doing, I had left the expressway and was round the back of the railway peering through the gates into the arches. Then I remembered I wasn't in the rave business anymore and with a sigh I turned and was about to get back in the car when the germ of an idea started to grow in my mind.

The premises consisted of two arches, both very clean and modern-looking. The first was really only half an arch with an office at the back and the front half was secure parking with a gate at the front covering the whole arch. The other arch had a large sliding concertina door on the front and through the small plate window on one panel, I could see that inside it was brand new... hmm.

The first arch would make an ideal living space and the second arch, well, what about a fucking illegal nightclub?

I looked around the area; very, very quiet, most of the other arches seemed unoccupied and there were no houses to be seen. The other side was the expressway. Even the access road was a dead-end. This place really was in the arse-end of nowhere. Fate was also taking a hand. Just that morning, I had been looking into a government initiative for starting new businesses. They would pay your first three months' rent on premises and give you £50 a week for a year.

Next thing, I was jumping up and down, doing spins and shouting 'yeah, yeah, fucking yeah'. Grabbing my mobile, I dialled the number for British Rail Rentals.

'Hello, British Rail property services, how can I help you?'

'Err, my name is Keef Robinson from Desert Storm Entertainments and I'm interested in renting some arches off you.'

The poor guy, like many before and after, had no idea what he was about to get himself into. If he had known he would have hung up straight away and called the cops.

BOOM, BOOM, TSSST... BOOM, BOOM, TSSST.

The dance floor in the main arch was full and the bar was doing a brisk business. Hot chicks in spray-on tops and miniskirts were dancing on top of the speakers and bar. In the other arch, ravers were sniffing lines off the bog cistern while I was in the office counting the money with my girlfriend, Louise. I leaned back in my executive chair and let out a huge cloud of smoke from the enormous skunk spliff in my hand.

'Line of coke, dear?' she asked, brushing her long blond hair from her face and bending over the desk, her fantastically long legs seeming to go on forever.

'Don't mind if I do,' I replied brushing the piles of cash to the side to make room as my other hand slipped slowly up her skirt. Ha, ha, this was the life! Rave on.

We called the place The Unit, not very original I know, but the name Desert Storm was not to be used. A break from the past and hopefully the previous troubles was required and it worked. The doormen heard about the unit and asked if there was work there. They were politely told that it was a small place and we were fine, thank you very much.

Things went well, very well in fact. I lived there, my friends hung out there, and every two weeks or so, we had a party with minimum publicity. But somehow, word spread and we were never short on ravers. Money was made, people were happy.

It was quite a strange place to live. You would come out at night to skateboard to the all-night garage for supplies and there would be some hooker bent over the boot of a car getting it from a punter. Luckily, I'm not scared of the dark or of being alone, although I wasn't alone much as the place was usually a hub of activity. I was selling a bit of dope at the time for extra pennies and that meant there was a constant stream of punters in the evening which kept me busy, but if I had known what this would lead to, I would have knocked it right on the head there and then.

We were all in Unit one evening, Smudge, John O, Simmy, etc., when the door to the warehouse received a heavy knock. I was playing

Nintendo at the time, Mortal Kombat, frantically working the joypad with my fingers, battling away against the character Sub Zero, a ninja-style warrior all in black, his head covered by a black bandana... I turned from the game.

'Hey, Smudge, can you get the door, I'm playing a game.'

Smudge reluctantly got up and headed towards the door. As an afterthought I added,

'Hey, Smudge, we're not expecting anyone, make sure you check the spy hole before you unlock it.'

After all, we were in a warehouse in the middle of nowhere. I returned to my game...

'Yeah, yeah,' replied Smudge as he reached the doorway.

Next thing I knew, there was a crash followed by a shriek and a tall dark figure burst into the room. At first, I couldn't believe my eyes. Sub Zero from the video game was now standing in the fucking warehouse! I looked dumbly from the screen and back to the room, my hands still tapping at the controls. But no, I wasn't hallucinating, he really was there. Dressed in black paramilitary army gear with a toolbelt with various knives, etc. hanging off it and what appeared to be a sawed-off shotgun sticking out the front of his trousers. Not to mention a black SAS-style balaclava on his head and to top it off the largest meanest-looking machete I had ever seen. Enter the Machete Warrior. Oops.

I turned to Smudge, an accusing look on my face. Someone hadn't checked the fucking spy hole like they had been told to. Smudge just looked at the ground. But there was no time for these thoughts. Quick as a flash, Sub Zero lifted his machete high in the air and chopped it down on a small wooden box on the table, cleaving it in two.

'ALL RIGHT, GIRLS, WHERE'S THE FUCKING DRUGS AND MONEY!'

Everyone in the room froze. Wow. Now that's how you make

an entrance. I had flinched backwards as Sub Zero had raised his machete, thinking my time had come and I was just getting used to the fact that I was still in one piece when Sub Zero turned the point of the blade in my direction, the wicked-looking tip hovering just under my chin.

'YOU, GET UP. FUCKING MONEY AND DRUGS, NOW! ARE YOU FUCKING DEAF OR HAVE YOU JUST GOT A DEATH WISH? MOVE IT!'

Sub Zero had obviously done this before. Control the situation, well there was no doubt who was in charge. Don't give them time to think, like to think about the fact that there was only one of him and about ten of us. One young guy, a sixteen-year-old skater, was taking advantage of the fact that Sub Zero couldn't look all ways at once and was slowly working his way along the wall towards the door and freedom. Unfortunately, Sub Zero had eyes in the back of his head and, quick as a cat, turned and went to slap the lad on the head with the flat of the machete blade. but the boy moved and the blade caught him square on, causing a nasty wound that splashed out blood which immediately covered the wall.

Oh, my God. I jumped up as he raised the blade again and grabbed his arm.

'No, no leave him alone, I'll give you the fucking stuff! Leave him alone!'

I grappled for the knife. Sub Zero turned and elbowed me hard in the face then slapped me with the blade, cutting me behind the left ear. I fell back in a heap as he towered over me.

I learned a lot about myself that day. I'm one stubborn motherfucker for a start. There was quite a lot of hash and money in the office at the time, but there was no way he was getting that. The trick was to get rid of him as fast as possible with the least bloodshed and with the smallest possible amount of gear.

The Skater Boy had been in to buy a small bit of hash and the main lump [about 30 grams] was still softening on the heater. A good start. I picked myself up, holding my hand to my bleeding head and with Sub Zero covering me with the blade. I headed over to the heater and picked up the hash.

'There, there, take it, that's all we've got just now, take it.' [Yeah, right, there was another 500 grams and a grand in cash in the stash.]

Sub Zero took a rucksack off his back and placed the small lump in there. Hmm. I couldn't help thinking that this guy was expecting more. My mind started to tick. How had he known about...? My thoughts were interrupted as Sub Zero smashed the massive blade onto the table again. Skater Boy flinched on the floor where he was lying in a rapidly growing pool of blood, obviously expecting another cut.

'THAT CAN'T BE IT FUCKING ALL. ARE YOU'S TAKIN' THE PISS? WHERE'S THE CASH?' Sub Zero banged the table again to emphasise the point.

I reached over for the desk drawer.

'YOU! OPEN THAT DRAWER REALLY SLOWLY.'

I held up my hands, palms outstretched. 'Cool, man, it's cool. You said you wanted the money, it's in here,' I said then returned to opening the drawer.

Inside was about £80 which I handed over. Sub Zero looked at the cash for a few seconds. Obviously, this was not the result he was expecting. We all waited. I watched him intently. I've got to get him out of here. But before I could think of anything, Sub Zero advanced towards me, blade held high.

'THIS CAN'T BE IT. YOU LISTEN TO ME, MOTHERFUCKER. YOU'VE GOT 10 FUKING SECONDS TO COME UP WITH THE REST OR THIS IS GOING ACROSS YOUR FUKIN HEAD.'

I backed up. 'Look, that's the lot. There isn't any more.'

This was too much for Sheona and she stood up to protect me. 'Leave him alone, leave him alone.'

'Sheona, it's okay, sit back down,' I told her, motioning with my hand. She sat back down. Thanks, Sheona, but this was my show. I looked closely at Sub Zero and could sense the doubt growing in his mind, time to go on the front foot.

'Don't you think we'd have given you the lot? You're the guy with the machete and the shotgun; you've already stabbed me.' I put my hand up to my head and pulled it away covered in blood. 'And you've hurt my mate bad, he needs a fucking doctor right now.'

Sub Zero looked down at Skater Boy and back at me, I could feel him waver.

'You've got what you came for... JUST GO!' I put every ounce of willpower into the last statement and stared straight at him.

He made up his mind and sprang back, sheathing the machete and whipping out the shotgun.

'RIGHT, LADIES, I'M GOING TO WALK OUT THAT DOOR NOW AND IF ANYONE FOLLOWS ME IN THE NEXT TEN MINUTES, THEN THEY GET THIS.' He brandished the shotgun and legged it out the door. Seconds later, we heard a car start up and screech off, tyres burning.

I jumped over to the window and thrust the curtain aside and looked out. Cool, they were gone. I turned to Smudge

'SMUDGE, WHERE'S THE FUKIN KEYS?'

But Smudge was just standing there in shock. I grabbed him by the collar and shook him.

'SMUDGE, SMUDGE, FUCKING KEYS.'

'They're... they're in the door,' he answered weakly.

I was off and running.

'But Keef,' he said, 'don't go out for...'

'SHUT THE FUCK UP, SMUDGE! AND GET THE FIRST AID KIT.'

Reaching the door, I grabbed the keys from the lock and legged it across the arch to the gates, taking a glance left and right to check all was clear as I battled to get the key in and turn the tumblers. Click, we were safe. The gate covered the whole arch and was made of thick solid iron bars. I legged it back inside, locking the office door behind me. By the time I got back into the office, someone had helped Skater Boy into a chair.

After swabbing off the blood, I got a good look at his cut and, as is often the case with head wounds, it looked a lot worse than it was but would still require stitches. I patched it up as best I could and got someone to look at my cut. Again, not too bad.

I sat down in my chair and let out the biggest sigh of relief in my life, reached for my cigarettes, lit one with a shaking hand, and took a long puff. Now I turned my attention to Smudge and said quietly,

'Smudge, you useless little arsehole, I told you to check the fucking spy hole.' My voice had a layer of ice to it and the menace wasn't lost on Smudge.

'But,' he started.

'But fuck all. So, you looked though and saw a big motherfucker dressed in black wearing a balaclava and clutching a machete and decided, "Oh, yeah, I'll just let him fucking in".'

'Keef, man, I'm so, so sorry, I just didn't think, I just...' his voice tailed off and he looked at the floor.

I looked at him, the thought of violence growing in my mind. I dismissed it with a shake of my head. What would I gain by battering Smudge anyway?

'Okay, what's done is done. Why don't you see if there are any beers in the fridge while I skin a joint?'

Smudge scuttled off, glad to have something useful to do. I went to the stash, came back with a 250g bar of hash, banged it down on the desk and started to make a joint. There was an intake of breath from the room as they stared in disbelief. I looked around at them. Sheona found her voice first.

'But, but, I can't believe you didn't... I mean, you could have been killed!'

'What? You think I was going to hand over all the drugs and money to that fucker? Fuck that!' I said and finished rolling the joint.

Lighting it up, I took a long drag and handed it to Skater Boy; he really looked like he needed some. Smudge came back with the cold tins. I drained mine in one, scrunched up the can, stood up, then grabbed the BMW keys and the baseball bat from behind the door.

'Right, Skater Boy, let's get you down to A&E.'

This event was what you might call a game changer. Something had to change at The Unit. Some of us were in favour of moving out but I was having none of it. First thing was a new rule; at all times the front gate had to be locked. Secondly, I fitted a secret bell behind the panel for the lock. There was already a normal bell so if a friend came round, they would reach behind and press the hidden bell and you would know all was good, but if the new bell went, well, it was red alert time. Next, I fitted two 500-watt halogen floodlights at eye level either side of the office door. They were operated by PIRs sensors so that if you approached the gates at night, you would get blasted by 1,000 watts right in the face. Meanwhile, we could open the office door and see who was out there without being seen ourselves. That just left the problem of getting in and out. My procedure on arrival was to drive right past The Unit, do a U-turn at the end of the road, and drive slowly back up checking if any parked cars were unoccupied. Then get out with my baseball bat in hand and quickly let myself through the gates. Once the gates were securely locked again, you could relax.

It seemed to work; there was no return Sub Zero the machete

maniac at any rate, but the happy-go-lucky days at The Unit were over. It was never the same again. Defence is much harder than offence. Attackers can sit in the house and choose their moment. Defenders must always be on guard, which is much more stressful. But bit by bit, things got better, parties continued, and life went on. I never did find out who was behind the robbery but I have my suspicions.

Then one night at a Unit party, I met a girl...

11

ELAINE

I met Elaine at the Unit when I was outside having a smoke. It was about two a.m. and I needed a break from the party and wanted to chill on my own. I was enjoying the solitude when Sheona came up to me and pulled me close. I could see someone else standing slightly behind her in the shadows, and Sheona leaned over and whispered in my ear, 'Keef, do u remember my friend Elaine I told you about?'

I didn't really but just kind of grunted, 'Err, yeah.'

'Well, she's here, do you want to talk to her?'

'Eh, yeah, okay.' It didn't look like I had much choice in the matter.

'Elaine, this is Keef.'

A tall, thin girl with blonde hair stepped forward into the light and offered her hand. 'Hi, I'm Elaine.'

The girl spoke in the sweetest angelic voice and added a little laugh at the end. I looked a little closer; Jesus, this girl was hot. My mind started accessing the part of my brain for chatting to leggy blondes with a view to scoring with them later on. It usually started with, '*Hi, I'm Keef, would you like a drink?*'

'Hi, I'm Keef, would you like a drink? Sheona's told me all about you.'

I lied – well, it might have been true, I just couldn't remember

Sheona ever mentioning her, and I took her hand. When I shook it, I felt a little spark and almost pulled back, static or something? I think she felt it too, and we looked at each other, puzzled.

My plan went to shit, and I stammered, 'Err, are you sure we haven't met before?'

There was definitely something about those eyes, something I couldn't quite put my finger on, something maybe familiar about her.

'No, no, I'm sure we haven't, but I've been watching you in there, waiting for a chance to talk,' she answered softly, and added in that cute little laugh again

Now I was thinking, that's a bit weird, watching, waiting and all that. Is this some crazy Desert Storm groupie stalker? I've met a few, and usually I find out too late; after the drink, the flirtatious conversation, bigging up the Storm, maybe a little line of coke and then an inevitable mad night in the sack. Then the next day, in the cold light, you realise they're totally loony tunes, and how the fuck are you going to get rid of them before your girlfriend gets back? Being the man behind Desert Storm (not to mention a handsome fucker) has certainly brought me more than my fair share of action. As Wu-Tang Clan sang, 'Spent a lot of dough, it's so hard to explain. And I fucked a lot of bitches, off the strength of the name.'

Maybe it was time to ditch this girl and boost back inside? But for some reason, I was entranced. Was it the voice? The eyes? The laugh? The legs? Or the whole package? Anyway, I didn't hit on her, I just got her a drink and we talked and talked, I don't know what about but we hit it off big time, and at the end of the night I drove her home in the crazy Storm machine. Okay, I snogged her a bit, but walked her to her door and asked her out for a date the next day, lunch at a nice restaurant, no less.

Next day, there I was in Cottiers Restaurant, a really nice, converted church in the West End, pawing through the menu, nursing my hangover and waiting nervously at the table. I kept looking at my watch, not even sure if she'd turn up. But bang on time, in she walked, looking just as fit as the night before and wandered over to the table, smiled and sat down.

'Eh, hi.' Shit, what was wrong with me, I'm never usually this nervous, even my palms were a little sweaty. Quick, get the drinks in as the waiter was hovering.

'Something to drink?' I offered, 'the wine here is pretty good.'

'I'll just have a pint of Stella, thanks,' she said, interrupting, and added that little laugh again.

Pint of Stella, eh? Unusual choice for a girl at noon, I thought, raising one eyebrow a fraction. Bit of a drinker then? I didn't know the half of it.

'I'll have the same, then. Two pints of Stella, please, waiter.'

With that we were off, straight back into the conversation of the night before, it was as if we had known each other for ages. Then suddenly, she stopped and looked into my eyes, all seriousness.

'Keef, I hear you have a girlfriend.' Not a question, and there was no follow-on little laugh. This was... unexpected, a little awkward and also very, very true. Usually I would have launched into my *'Oh well, the relationship's on the rocks, we hardly see each other anymore, you can't really call her my girlfriend, blah blah blah'*. Almost always a winner, but something stopped me, and looking at her for a few seconds, instead I said, 'Well, that's easily sorted.'

Eh, what? Did I just say that? What the fuck is going on here?

'Well, it needs to be,' she stated and followed it up with a bombshell, 'and you do know I'm still at school, your old school in fact.'

'Jordanhill College School?' I added pointlessly, spluttering on my beer.

'Of course,' she replied, with that little laugh returned.

WHAT? Now, this was something Sheona had omitted to mention, and had I heard her right? She had just ordered me to – and I had agreed – to ditch my long-term girlfriend. But... but... that meant she thinks that she is going to take her place, immediately, like right now! Was she mental? Still at school? I was confused, on the back foot completely and must have looked it. Jaw dropping, brow furrowed, staring blankly. She just started laughing. I had to say something.

'So, eh, school... what, er... year are you in?'

Now it was her turn to raise an eyebrow. Oh no, that had come out all wrong.

'If you're asking if I'm old enough to go to bed with, without going to jail, then yes, I am,' she replied matter-of-factly.

I stammered. 'Err, no, that's not what...'

She interrupted again, 'You haven't met anyone like me before, have you?'

Well, that was blindingly obvious. I just shook my head weakly and stayed silent.

'Well, then, that's that settled, shall we order?' She reached over and took my hand.

After the meal, Elaine went home and I split straight up to my mate Kris's. I had to talk to someone about this. Kris was one of my new mates, a rich kid, whose parents had bought him and his brother a really nice flat bang in the middle of the West End and a shiny new Range Rover to boot. But in spite of the silver spoon, he was a down-to-earth sort of guy, full of energy, and a hard worker. Not to mention, beer drinker, dope smoker, coke sniffer and serial womaniser, so as you can imagine, we got on famously.

'Yeah, Kris, you're not going to believe this...' and I relayed the story of Elaine, and how in the last twenty-four hours, I was ditching my girlfriend and was now going out with a schoolie.

Kris listened carefully and replied, 'I've just got one question, Keef, has she got any mates?'

Haha. That was Kris all right. I sat stroking my chin between finger and thumb thinking. 'Hmm, you know she was at the party with a girl, a little stunner too, must have gone home early.' We hatched a plan.

A couple of phone calls confirmed it, yes, she did have a mate, Jill, yes, very good-looking and yes, they would be interested in going away for the weekend camping, that's right, this weekend no less.

So, we planned a superdate. We would pick them up on the Saturday morning in the Range Rover (of course) and drive to Lochearnhead where we had booked a dinghy, then we would sail off out of the bay and go camping on a secluded beach I knew a few Ks up the loch, just the four of us. Throw in a ghetto blaster, cases of beer, wine, some dope, a bit of sniff, meat to cook on the fire – what could possibly go wrong, fantastic!

Saturday finally arrived and we picked them up. I don't know who was more excited – them or us? Kris and Jill were soon talking away and there seemed to be real chemistry between them, but Kris is a right smooth customer, rich and good-looking to boot. Elaine and I seemed to already be firm friends and it seemed hard to believe I had only met her a few days ago. We even managed a couple of small lines of coke off a CD; Jill held it for Kris and he sniffed it as he drove.

The weather had been sunny and mild when we left Glasgow but as we neared Lochearnhead, I noticed the wind was really picking up and wispy clouds started to whisk across the sky. I voiced my concerns but the rest just blew me out, such was the mood of optimism in the car. As the only sailor in the group, I wasn't so sure.

We arrived at the port and found what had to be our boat, a bright red Enterprise dinghy moored on its own with *Lochearnhead Boat*

Rental painted on the side. I noticed the wind had picked right up, and standing by the dock, I looked out and saw white tops on some of the waves rolling into the bay. The worrying way the little boat was being buffeted against the jetty was unsettling to say the least. I also couldn't help but notice that Jill was looking more than a little nervous. Then the boatman rocked up, an old geezer with a beard and a captain's cap, you know the ones with the anchor on. He looked like Captain fucking Bird's Eye.

'So, boys and girls, you'll be having second thoughts about the camping trip by now?' he stated, pointing out at the darkening water.

'Well, not really,' I replied, not much liking the way he was taking for granted that we would give up so easily.

He looked dubiously at us. 'Good sailors, then? I might even think twice about taking her out myself in this, must be force five already. But if you're decided, who am I to spoil the party?' With the last bit, he looked from me to Kris, then to the girls, looking them up and down lecherously, and added, 'Just make sure you sign the insurance sheet nicely, wouldn't want to lose my boat.'

Well, the old guy had our number, that was for sure, and he was right, if we didn't go now, this super date would be a total disaster. I looked out at the water once more, weighing up my sailing skills against the weather. I was a pretty good sailor, but most of my experience was in small, single-seat racing dinghies called Lasers. Oh, fuck it. I turned to the others.

'Well, I reckon if we can just force our way against the wind, get out of the bay and turn at the point, it should be all downwind from there and then it's only a few miles. I think we can make it.' I looked from face to face. Nobody said anything till Kris piped up.

'Well, if Keef thinks we can make it, I'm game, he's the sailor.' Nice move, that, put the blame on me, though I knew for sure why he was so keen to go.

The boatman looked incredulous, as he realised that I was the only sailor. Elaine still looked up for it and was already moving to get her bag from the car, but that's because she was mental though I just didn't know it yet. I turned to Jill, who looked properly scared, and asked her what she thought.

'Well, I don't know if it's such a...'

Elaine interrupted; she was good at that. 'Oh, come on, Jill, we've come this far, you can't chicken out now and ruin it for everybody.'

And that was that, Jill had been well and truly railroaded, we were going. Kris caught my eye and slipped me a wink. As we unloaded the kit, the boatman said he was off to get a deck chair and some binoculars, adding there was no way he was going to miss this.

After signing the paperwork, we loaded up, which was a task in itself as the boat lurched up and down, but finally, we were all in and settled, and I couldn't help noticing how low the boat was in the water. It was designed for four, but four and all the kit in this weather? I was checking and rechecking the fitting of everyone's life jackets when Captain Bird's Eye rocked back up with his chair and binoculars to cast us off.

'Yes, I'd tighten up them life vests if I were you, you might be needing them. Forecast says it's going to get worse, and you know there's no lifeboat on this side of the loch,' he said gleefully as he untied us and pushed us off.

I was starting to dislike this guy a lot.

'Oh, and another thing,' he added as we pulled away, 'watch out for the rip current at the edge of the bay, it tends to push you towards the rocks when the wind blows this way, hehe.'

Motherfucker! I turned round and gave him the finger, and then cast him from my mind, gripping the tiller hard in one hand and the main sheet for the sail in the other. This was going to be dicey. In my original plan, I had thought to mill about in the bay for an hour or so to show the others how to crew the boat before heading to open water. For instance, when the boat comes about, you have to change sides and release the jib sheet and move it across, and there was other stuff, but how was I going to do that now? It was crash course time.

'OKAY, LISTEN TO ME.' I raised my voice above the noise of wind and water to get their attention. 'In a few seconds, the boat will tilt to port, I mean to the left, I want you to carefully move to the starbo—right-hand side of the boat to even the weight, do you understand?'

They all nodded, although Jill looked like I had just asked her to jump into a pool of sharks clutching a bloody piece of meat. I suppressed a smile when I noticed she was clinging onto Kris's arm. With a deep breath, I pulled the tiller towards me, the mainsail filled with wind, and the boat tilted alarmingly to port.

'Okay, now,' I commanded.

They moved like their lives depended on it, which in some ways it did, and the boat righted itself and pulled off at fast lick. So far, so good, maybe this might work after all. The jib sail, the small triangular one at the front, was still flapping, so I got Elaine to tighten the sheet (rope) and it came under control. So, now to get out of the bay. The problem was the wind was blowing inshore hard, and as you can't sail into the wind, you have to cut backwards and forwards in a zig-zag fashion as close to the wind as you can, slowly making headway (this is called tacking). Sounds easy, but it's not, and with a strong wind pushing the water at you, you may think you're going fast but you may actually be going backwards! But at the present, all was going well. Now we were leaving the relative calm of the dock for the choppy bay and the boat was taking it in its stride, occasionally a bit of spray would come over the side, but we were cutting through the waves with ease. I looked at Elaine and smiled, she smiled back and leaned over and gave me a kiss. Well, she was fine anyway, damn fine. A glance at Kris showed him with his arm round Jill, looking out over the bow. But it was time to break up the happy party to explain to them the good news about going about.

'Listen up, people, in about thirty seconds I'm going to shout READY ABOUT and the boat's going to turn to the right and tilt hard the other way, then I'll shout LEE HO and you're going to cross over like you did last time.' They nodded that they understood. 'But this time, you've got to keep your head low because the boom,' I pointed up at the big bar above us with the sail on, 'is going to cross the boat quite fast and it could knock you into the water, so be careful.' (More like knock you into next week.) 'Okay?' They nodded more dubiously this time. Maybe I shouldn't have mentioned going in the water, because all the blood had drained from Jill's face. 'Okay, look, bad choice of words, nobody's going in the water.'

I hoped. God, please don't let me fuck this up.

Amazingly, it all went well considering the conditions. Okay, a little messy but we got round. I reckon any tack in a small sailboat in heavy weather where you don't go in is a good tack. We pulled off a few more and my confidence was rising but so was the wind, and now the boat was hurtling along, wind singing in the wires. What had I been worrying about? Old Bird's Eye can eat his hat. Now just one more tack round the point and we were free. I told them the plan.

'Okay, troops, you see the headland in front of us, we're going to come in fast and tight on it, go about, shoot past it, turn again and the hard part's over. Now, I won't kid you, the water there looks choppy so it might be a little rough but we can do it, right?'

A little choppy might have been a bit of an understatement, and as we got closer, I couldn't help noticing the water was dark and turbulent, and behind that were some nasty-looking jagged rocks. I hoped the others hadn't seen them, yeah fat chance, you could almost taste the fear onboard. The first I knew that something wasn't quite right was when the tiller went slack in my hand. Bit strange, that. I thought. Looking up at the sail, I saw it too had gone slack, but we were still speeding towards the rocks, now less than 200 metres away! But why would? 'Oh shit!' I must have said that last bit out loud because the others had all turned towards me, and if I looked as worried as they did, I must have looked REALLY FUCKING WORRIED.

'Err, I think we may be stuck in Bird's Eye's current.' For a few seconds, we all stared at the tips of the rocks breaking menacingly through the water. They would smash this boat into so much match-wood.

'STUCK IN THE FUCKING CURRENT?' Kris's normally cool and calm demeanour had temporarily deserted him. 'YOU MEAN THE FUCKING CURRENT DRIVING US TOWARDS THOSE FUCKING ROCKS? GREAT, THAT'S JUST FUCKIN' GREAT,' he screamed while wildly pointing.

I could feel my nervous laugh starting. Yup, that'll be dem rocks dere.

Jill was next, asking, 'But... but we're not going to go in the water, are we? Because... I... I... can't... I can't...' She sure had everybody's attention now.

I stared straight at her. 'You can't what, darling? I tell you what you can't, you can't be choosing this moment to tell us you can't fucking swim, that's what you can't!'

'Well, I'm not very good,' she admitted, looking at the bottom of the boat.

This sent Kris back off on one. 'YOU'VE GOT TO BE FUCKING SHITTING ME?' he ranted, moving away from her as if she had some disease.

'Look, I'm really sorry,' Jill replied pointlessly.

I looked at Elaine accusingly. 'And you knew about this?'

'Well, she swam a bit in the pool in Majorca, but she doesn't like the sea much, or waves.'

She doesn't like the sea or waves? Fucking hell, no wonder she'd been looking nervous.

'OH, MY GOD, LOOK!' Elaine pointed out over the front of the boat. 'THE ROCKS ARE GETTING CLOSER!'

She was right, much fucking closer! Something had to be done.

'Shit, we're wasting time with this bullshit. Kris, make sure her lifebelt is tight and maybe inflate it a bit. I've got a plan but it means we're going to have to turn back to shore, no camping.'

'WELL, FOR FUCK'S SAKE, DO IT, FUCK THE CAMPING.' Well, it looked like Kris hadn't calmed down much then.

I pulled the tiller right over and wrenched the main sheet fully in, and slowly, very slowly she started to turn. The rocks were only fifty metres away now.

'Come on, you bitch, turn. Please.' Elaine was clinging onto me and it looked like Jill had gone into shock. It was going to be close, but we should just about... oh, oh, now I could see waves breaking on previously unseen rocks lurking beneath the surface. I had time to shout, 'BRACE YOURSELVES!' and then...

BANG, CRUNCH.

We grounded out and everyone was thrown forward screaming and cursing. Panic time. The boat lurched sickeningly over, tottering on the brink of capsizing, and then incredibly... she jerked free, bounced and shot past the rocks and away.

Jill was still screaming as I got Kris to check if we were filling up with water. But no, we were sound, no holes. Elaine had a small cut on her leg but apart from that, we were all good. I let out the mainsheet, the sail filled with wind, and we set course for the pier.

The mood on board changed to euphoric; everybody was hugging, punching the air and congratulating me on my sailing skill. Even though I'd nearly killed us all, dry land was in sight.

Then it suddenly went dark. Eh? I was just wondering what the fuck was going on when Jill pointed back over the stern. 'What's that?' I had time to turn around just as it hit us. The squall from hell; cloud, wind and waves. It lifted the back of the boat right out of the water, ripped the sheet out of my hand and the sail blew clean out past ninety degrees, and then the starboard gunwale went under the water.

Jill had no chance; she gave a little squeal of help and was gone, tumbling backwards head first, disappearing into the dark water.

The boat righted itself, I regained control, and we were off, but Elaine was having none of it. 'JILL, I'M COMING.' She jumped up and prepared to dive in after her.

'KRIS... STOP HER,' I screamed. They struggled together, rolling about in the bottom of the boat. She was fighting like a banshee, screaming, 'Let me go, let me fucking go.' Then a bang. She'd punched Kris.

'ENOUGH! For fuck's sake, Elaine, stay in the fuckin' boat, we're going back, we can save her!' They stopped fighting and looked up, so I took my chance. 'GET TO YOUR FUKING PLACES NOW! READY A FUCKING BOUT... LEE-HO!'

I wrenched the tiller towards me, the bow slid round and through the wind, the boom snapped over, the main sail filled with wind and Elaine tightened the jib sheet. We had executed a perfect racing turn and were now heading back the way we came, scanning the water for Jill.

'There she is!' I cried, seeing a flash of an orange lifejacket and arms waving in the air. 'Okay, Kris, I'm going to close in on your side and go around her, stopping dead. You grab her in and we're off again, okay?' Kris nodded. 'And Elaine, for fuck's sake, stay on the other side of the boat to balance the weight or we'll all be going swimming.'

I came really close, almost too close, and for a second, I thought I'd run her over, but no, I brought the boat round, dead into the wind and Kris hauled her in coughing and spluttering and she lay gasping on the bottom of the boat, wet but alive. I tried to concentrate on the sailing, but in spite of the situation it was impossible not to notice how fit she was lying there in her soaking wet T-shirt and skimpy shorts.

We headed back, cold, bruised, and wet, nobody looking at each other, nobody saying anything. I was sure they were all thinking what an asshole I was for nearly getting us all killed and for coming up with this stupid idea in the first place.

Jill, still shivering, broke the ice. 'I swear that once I get back to dry land, I'm never ever getting in a fucking boat ever again.'

We had to laugh at that.

'When you went in,' said Kris turning to Jill, 'do you know what I was thinking?' She shook her head and we all waited for some soppy shit to dribble from his mouth. 'I was thinking, thank fuck I'd got the cocaine back off you in the car.'

Haha, nice one, I thought.

'You wanker!' she replied and gave him a playful slap, but knowing Kris, he probably wasn't joking.

As we neared the jetty, we could see old Bird's Eye standing there, looking smug with his binoculars in hand, waiting to tell us, 'I told you so.'

I groaned as Elaine threw him the rope, but he had hardly got past 'Well, well, I thought you were goners for sure after the young lady...' when Elaine let rip.

'Now, you listen to me, you asshole! Just one more word, I dare you, one more word...' she said, jabbing him in the chest. '...and I'll shove those binoculars—'

'Now, now, babes,' I said and managed to get an arm around her and lead her away, 'let's go and have a cigarette and unload the bags.'

Once we had loaded our wet kit into the Range Rover, we sat in silence shivering in our soaking clothes with the heating on, trying to warm up. Although I was happy to be alive, the weekend was now a failure. I stared gloomily out of the window, watching the worsening weather roll in off the water as the rain started to fall on the windscreen.

'I know what we can do,' said Kris excitedly, 'look over there.'

We looked and saw a sign that read *Lochearnhead Hotel and Bar, real log fire, home-cooked food daily*.

Yes, the answer to all our problems. Within minutes, we had two double rooms, had got changed (I tried not to watch her but failed) and were sitting supping beers in front of the fire, laughing about the terrible shit that had happened, which by now had turned into an incredible adventure. Wicked.

It's amazing how near-death experiences tire you out, and after dinner and a quick spliff out the back, even a line of coke couldn't wake us up and it was time for bed. Trying not to look like the cat that got the pigeons, Kris and I went off with a girl each to our separate rooms. Elaine and I threw ourselves on the bed exhausted, lay there for a few minutes, then I turned my head to her and said, 'Take off your clothes please.'

There was a slight pause. Then: 'All right then,' and that little laugh again.

Later, as I lay back having a cigarette with Elaine sprawled over me, with one arm across my chest, she gently poked me with her finger.

'Darling,' she whispered softly.

'Yes, babes?'

'If I ever catch you looking at Jill like that again, I'll...' I gasped as she grabbed my nuts and squeezed hard.

'Aaargh, fucking hell, okay, okay, never again.'

'You promise?' she continued, giving them another twist.

'Yes, yes, I promise. Fuck's sake.'

She relaxed her grip and draped herself back over me.

'Good night, darling.' And with that, she went off to sleep.

I looked down at her, stroking her neck and playing with her blonde hair while thinking, *Oh, my God, what have I let myself in for?*

12

MOUNTAINS OF THE WHITE STUFF

I love skiing, I've been doing it for a long time. It all began when I was fourteen and I went to Glencoe ski resort with the scouts. Typical me; get the chairlift straight to the top and learn on the way down. Since then, I've skied at all the resorts in Scotland numerous times, favouring Glenshee as it's by far the best. People scoff at Scottish skiing, but with the ice, horrendous weather, and rocks, I'd say that if you can ski in Scotland then you can ski anywhere, and I've given anywhere a good try. I've skied at Val d'Isère in France, Font-Romeu in the Pyrenees, the Dolomites in Italy, and Pranitha in Greece to name but a few! I like to ski fast, no poles, jumps, freestyle. I hate being passed over, and if I am, I want to see 'ski team' or 'ski instructor' on the back of their jackets or I'm really not happy.

I'm most proud of my skiing at Val d'Isère, on the Tignes glacier, now there's a fucking hill. I went there for the first time with my friend Rob as a guest of his rich dad and it didn't take long to get in with the chalet staff, courtesy of the large lump of hash I had smuggled there in the hollowed-out heel of my shoe. After they had finished their jobs in the chalets, we would meet up on the slopes and ascend to the top of Tignes. At 3,000 metres, your breath comes in gasps and the view is mind blowing. The piste down is one of the best in the world but that's not where we were headed. The chalet posse covered all the disciplines; snowboard (hard boot carve and soft boot), telemarking, and standard skis, and were never content with the easy way down. Our route would take us across a vast, off-piste snowfield and to the top of the dreaded couloirs (translating as passage between the rocks) above the ski village. This place is not for the faint hearted, you could only describe the route down as seriously dangerous; basically, it's a gully that cuts into a cliff and you must make about ten steep, tight turns on the icy snow (while managing to miss the rocks) and then turn at the bottom before you head off the cliff to certain death. Oh, and you'd better not get second thoughts because it's the only way down. They even had pay-as-you-view telescopes down in the ski village trained on the gullies to watch the action for Christ's sake.

Standing at the top of a couloirs gives me the same feeling as cliff diving. I lean out, looking down to assess the job for a few seconds, then straighten up shoulders back and GO. The push off is the moment of no return; you know you must make it or you will be fucked. This is the big one, the adrenaline rush of total madness and I love it. The knowledge that if you blow even one turn, then you're almost certainly going to punch out concentrates the mind no end, I can tell you! Now if you're a skier or boarder you may be thinking, ten turns on steep snow, no bother, but you're thinking of a piste or snowfield. This is different, you must turn when the gully dictates, not when you're ready. This changes everything and if you fuck up, well... Provided you make it, you emerge from the gully tunnel and speed along the top of the cliff stabbing the air with your hands shouting, 'YEAH, YEAH, I'M ALIVE,' and you know you really are.

If I hadn't been with the chalet staff, I would never have tried this shit and it gave me the confidence to do almost any hill, but that confidence was about to take a knock on something the chalet posse called 'Trip Tour Thursdays'. This involved taking fucking acid and doing the couloirs! Now remember, these people were a bit fucking mental so don't try this at home! I was a bit uncertain about it but they assured me I would ski better than I ever had in my life. I assured them I already was, but somehow, they persuaded me.

At first, it seemed they were right and I was off, all jumps and turns. By the time we reached the top of the couloirs, I was proper flying on the LSD, but so far, no problems, and I was just considering making my run when Rob went flying past, forgetting to slow down, before going over the edge. Oh shit. I could hardly watch as he made his descent. To his credit, he managed the first few turns but then the inevitable happened. He fell and just kept falling, rolling over and over, arse over tits and then plunged over the cliff! Oh, my God!

I made a panicky run down the gully, snatching at the turns, as the acid made the rocks seem to melt around me and the snow under my skis was covered in strange patterns. Reaching the edge, I gingerly looked over, shouting, 'ROB, ROB!' My voice echoed round the rocks and could have caused an avalanche, but there was no answer. Looking down, I expected to see his broken body on the rocks far below but there was nothing. Suddenly, one of the others called out, 'THERE HE IS!' Incredibly, his snowboard had caught on a boulder, nearly snapping it in half, but it had saved him, stopping his fall inches before the edge.

Rob had banged his head and had some cuts and bruises but was otherwise okay. Unfortunately, the fall had broken my mind instead. The acid had come right up and Rob's dice with death had brought on a bad trip. I quickly found out I had forgotten how to ski! Not the best place for it and the journey down was a nightmare. So, unless you're crazier than me (which I doubt), LSD and snow sports don't mix.

Anyway, I digress, this story was supposed to be about a ski trip Elaine and I took to Glencoe ski resort in Scotland so here it is...

Okay, we're driving to Glencoe to go skiing in midwinter. For some reason, I'd borrowed a car from a friend, guy called Normal. It was a battered old MG Mini Metro and we're late, so I've got the foot down overtaking cars all the way. We were making good time and were already on Rannoch Moor (a huge, barren glacial moorland strewn with massive boulders dumped there by the last ice age) with not far to go when the car started aquaplaning on the sleet. Immediately, I knew we were in deep shit; all four wheels had lost contact with the road and we were literally skating along at fifty miles per hour!

What to do in circumstances like this is to ease your foot off the gas, hold the steering straight, and pray the car slows quickly enough to cut through the water and regain traction. What you should never do is hit the brakes! I grimly gripped the wheel while screaming, 'COME ON, YOU BITCH, COME ON.' I was starting to get some feedback from the steering and turned to Elaine, saying, 'Yes, yes, baby, I think we're going to make it!' when we crested the hill and the wind took us.

It blew the car straight off the road and down the embankment. We went farming. At first, we stayed on the wheels as the car bounced off rocks and clumps of grass, but then the mother of all boulders appeared in front of us. We both screamed as the passenger side (Elaine's side) smashed into it with a grinding and tearing of metal on rock. The impact catapulted us into a vicious roll. CRUMP. We went in roof-first and the sunroof popped out. ROLL then CRUMP again. This time, the windscreen smashed and the roof crumpled in, ski boots and stuff started to bang about inside the car. Hitting another boulder, the car spun again and smashed to a halt upside down and nose first into another rock bigger than the car.

I must have been dazed for a bit because when I came to, I wasn't sure where I was. I hadn't been wearing a seatbelt and had been saved by the steering wheel which I still gripped for grim death in my hands. We were upside down as I stared out between my legs. I could hear a wheel still spinning in the silence but nothing else. Nothing else? Shit, Elaine! I looked over and saw her suspended by her seatbelt, long blonde hair hanging down to the floor, sorry I mean roof, silent and unmoving. I got a real fright then, I can tell you, but after shaking her, she came round and with difficulty, I got her seatbelt unbuckled and freed her. After a cuddle, we started checking ourselves for injuries. That is until Elaine said she could smell petrol! Panic ensued as we kicked out the remains of the windscreen and scrambled out into the driving wind.

One look at the car told its own story; it was proper fucked, every panel was smashed and buckled, windows smashed, roof caved in, it was hard to believe we were still alive! I looked back up to the road to see that a car had stopped and noticing that Elaine was shaking uncontrollably from a mixture of shock and cold, I led her up to the road and a kindly old couple gave her a blanket, put her in the back of their car, and offered to drive us to the nearest place. I thanked them and told them to wait just a minute and I would fetch our skis and the rest of our gear.

Back down at the wreck, I had managed to squeeze back in through what was left of the driver's window and was pulling on the skis trying to free them when I felt a sudden fear. What it was I don't know, sixth sense maybe, because I sure didn't hear or see anything. Anyway, next thing, I was wriggling back like a maniac to get the fuck out of there. I got clear of the car and glanced up to see a dark blue car in mid-fucking-air heading straight for me. I will never forget the look on the driver's face as he hurtled towards me. I threw myself backwards as the car crashed down, half on top of our car and half on the boulder. Recovering from the shock, I forced open the driver's door; he was still sitting there in shock, gripping the wheel and staring straight ahead.

'MATE, MATE, ARE YOU ALL RIGHT?' I shouted above the wind. It brought him back to his senses.

'Yes, yes, I think so, but was there anyone in that other car? The car underneath.'

'No, mate, we're all out of there.'

'Thank god for that!'

He nearly collapsed again with relief.

'Look, mate,' I said, 'maybe we should get out of here before another car makes the same mistake.'

Thirty minutes later, Elaine and I were sitting in the bar of the Glencoe hotel in front of the log fire sipping JD and coke and reliving the moment. I don't know if you've ever been in a proper car crash, but it's actually quite exciting. Especially if the only injury you've got to show for it is a few cuts and bruises!

I had called my mate Johnny Mac at his garage and he came up with another friend – Phil Hopper – to rescue us. Phil told me later that they were sure I was exaggerating. One car on top of another. Yeah, right. But of course, I wasn't. On the way home, we stopped off and John cast a professional eye over the wreck and told us that judging by the bends in the roof supports, he reckoned that one more roll and the roof would have caved right in crushing us both!!

Later that night I went round to Normal's with the bad news. I also brought along the still intact sunroof which I had rescued from the moor as a trophy. He wasn't well pleased and I think I eventually paid him £200 compensation. I didn't see him for years after that until I bumped into him in Goa of all places, where he had become a top trance DJ! He got me back for trashing his motor by dosing me up with shitloads of liquid acid, but that's another story.

After this, you might have thought that Elaine might be nervous about getting in a car with me. But not her, she didn't give a fuck and revelled in telling the story to her mates. Yet another reason I liked this girl so much... kindred spirits.

13

WHAT IS A RAVE?

What is a rave?

According to the Merriam-Webster dictionary, one definition is:

A large overnight dance party featuring techno music and usually involving the taking of mind-altering drugs.

If you look up the Criminal Justice and Public Order Act 1994, then it says this:

This section applies to a gathering on land in the open air of 20 or more persons (whether or not trespassers) at which amplified music is played during the night (with or without intermissions) and is such as, by reason of its loudness and duration and the time at which it is played, is likely to cause serious distress to the inhabitants of the locality; and for this purpose—

such a gathering continues during intermissions in the music and, where the gathering extends over several days, throughout the period during which amplified music is played at night (with or without intermissions); and

'music' includes sounds wholly or predominantly characterised by the emission of a succession of repetitive beats.

When you get right down to it, standing in a dark and dirty warehouse listening to banging beats at a ridiculously high volume while taking mind-bending substances for hours on end is quite a strange thing to do. Even I, as a 'professional' raver, have problems trying to find a rational explanation for it. However, the cosmic raver in me has no problem explaining it.

It goes something like this: raves have something to do with the distortion of reality. The trees, buildings, mountains and suchlike seem solid and real. But are they? Drugs like LSD and mushrooms give a hint that reality can be bent, and drugs like DMT show that reality can be blown away completely. Ah, I hear you say, the drugs have affected Keef's perception of reality (not to mention his grip on it!). But wait, what we call reality is in fact made up of subatomic particles and at this level, strange things are definitely going on. There is a test called Young's double-slit experiment, which deals with the duality of light: i.e. is light a wave or a particle (photon)? Many of you may remember an experiment in science at school where water waves were made to pass through two narrow slits. When they reconnected with each other they formed an interference pattern. Where the crests of the waves met, they would double in size and where the troughs met they would double in depth. This experiment can be done with light. Again, you find the same interference pattern. So what, you may ask? But here's where it gets interesting. Light behaves like a wave and a particle (hence the duality of light). For many years, scientists have wondered which one it is.

Anyway, this guy (Thomas Young) designed an experiment where you would shine the light at the slits, get the interference pattern, but you would also set a detector at one of the slits to see which one the light passes through. This gave an astonishing result; when you turn on the detector and observe the slits, light instantly becomes a particle and the interference pattern disappears, replaced by a dot.

Turn off the detector and it returns to being a wave! Now think about this for a minute, by merely observing an event you have changed the result. You have looked inside reality, forced its back to the wall and it has revealed a secret about itself. Reality is (at least in this case) created by the observer.

Now, Young's experiment was initially theoretical but has now been carried out in real life (see New Scientist, etc., blah, blah, blah). If you think that this is no big deal, then you need to think again. 'God does not play dice,' Albert Einstein once said, expressing his contempt for the notion that the universe is governed by probability when he didn't like the direction his theories were taking him. In fact, he spent the latter part of his life trying to disprove his own theories without success (see *A Brief History of Time* by Stephen Hawking). This opens a whole can of worms; if reality can be created by the observer, then how do we know it really exists at all? I think, therefore I am. Okay, I'm pretty sure I exist, but you? Or this world? I can't prove that. It could all be some mad dream that I have spun to pass the time in the nothingness of the cosmic void. Unlikely, I know, but if all I know for sure is what my senses tell me and now I know that my senses can affect the reality around me... Do you see where I'm coming from?

Anyway, what does all this have to do with the rave? Well, I think ravers are on a mission to investigate the meaning of reality, okay, maybe not at a conscious level. But I did a survey of the people that travelled with me as I was trying to find a common thread that connected us all. It wasn't easy; we were all from different countries, backgrounds, ages, etc. Then I hit upon this strange fact; almost all of us had taken magic mushrooms or LSD in our early teens. Could it be that this had opened our minds to something we wanted more of? Terence McKenna believed that man was raised to intelligence by ingesting magic mushrooms in the dawn of history (see his book *Food of the Gods*). The rave breaks you down through lack of food, lack of sleep, mind-bending drugs, flashing lights, pounding beats and the energy of the crowd. At such times, you start to feel reality bend and begin to fall apart. I think that this is meant to happen. The positive rave energy is needed on a cosmic level, it balances out things that are missing in the modern world, it harks back to a simpler time, a time of magic and the spirit world.

Or maybe this is all bullshit and people just like to get out of their heads and have a good time. One thing's for sure; it's addictive. When we did our first party in Barcelona, we had a maximum of nine ravers on the dance floor at any one time. Less than a year later, we had more than 5,000 in a warehouse on Barcelona beach!

Rave on.

14

JUSTICE FOR CRIMINALS? PROTEST TO SURVIVE!

It's November 1994, Park Lane, Hyde Park, London, and my friends and I in Desert Storm sound system have driven down to London to protest against the Tory government's plans to outlaw our life of hedonistic rave parties for good with a double-dipped hit of draconian legislation called... The Criminal Justice Bill.

The camouflaged Desert Storm sound system van, with its internal PA system, had been blaring out techno music at the head of 50,000 protesters all day, leading them pied piper-style through the streets of London. We had long ago lost sight of the rest of our posse in the matching convertible staff car. They were last seen at Trafalgar Square, heading the wrong way towards the Houses of Parliament right into the clutches of hundreds of tooled-up riot cops, a group of drunken drug-crazed anarchists hanging off the side. Oops! I hoped they were all right, but in the meantime I had my own problems.

In the front of the van was myself and Simmy, our heavily medicated and schizophrenic sound engineer. His dark, wide eyes and tangled mass of curly hair made him look even madder than usual.

On the roof was our look out, Sheona, my neighbour's kid, only sixteen and on her first trip out of Glasgow. The back of the van had nobody in it due to the lethal concentrations of deadly fumes from the on-board generator. We were all dressed as soldiers.

I was losing my voice as I had been MCing to the crowd all day through a microphone gaffer-taped to the sun visor, shouting, '*PROTEST TO SURVIVE*' and '*KILL, KILL, KILL THE BILL, KILL THE CRIMINAL JUSTICE BILL!*' and suchlike all day.

Things had been going quite calmly for the last ten minutes or so (well compared to the madness of before) and it looked like we might even make it to the end of the march, the final rally in Hyde Park. In fact, protesters had started to file past us, up Park Lane, hoping to get a seat on the grass. That's when it all went tits-up!

The first I knew that something was amiss was when Sheona's upside down head appeared at my side window. She was screaming above the music, 'Keef, Keef, they're coming. Oh, my God, they're coming!' and then her head disappeared back up to the top of the van.

I glanced over at Simmy, and the look of alarm on his face must have mirrored my own, as he demanded. 'What's happening? Who's coming?'

'Well, it's not the fucking Easter Bunny, that's for sure, Simmy,' I replied.

I was right. It wasn't the fucking Easter Bunny.

The people that had been calmly filing past a few seconds before, were now surging back towards us, a wave of panicking bodies trying to force their way back into the crowd. People were being trampled.

As the crowd cleared we could see now who was coming. Hundreds of riot cops, that's who, some mounted and some on foot, charging towards us. There was no chance of reversing back. We were fucked.

Looking over again at Simmy, I saw him frantically trying to wind up the window and lock the door. I let out a nervous laugh. He had no chance. The window winder was broken and the lock completely shafted. Mine however was working just fine. But as I reached towards it, I remembered poor Sheona on the roof!

Meanwhile, the police weren't taking any prisoners. After the chaos we had brought to the streets of London, they were finally being let off their leash and charged the crowd, beating all before them with wicked-looking long wooden batons. They were nearly upon us.

That was when the first bricks and bottles started flying over the van and into the advancing blue line. I saw a cop fall, helmetless, blood pouring from his face. A wounded horse reared up and turned back into its own lines. Protestors dressed in black, faces covered in bandanas poured past the van to take on the police.

They had also taken up my chant, but dropped the Criminal Justice bit, and now it was just...

'KILL, KILL, KILL THE BILL.'

'KILL, KILL, KILL THE BILL.'

It was at that moment someone appeared at my window with a pen and paper.

Leaning in, he introduced himself as Paddy and calmly asked, in a broad Scots accent, if there was any chance he could get my phone number as he had a gig for us.

A gig? He must be mad, I thought. 'You must be mad!' I shrieked. 'Can't you see there's a riot going on? Leg it, mate, before you get your head caved in.'

But he wasn't to be deterred, so I scribbled down my number and thought no more of it as he melted back into the chaos.

Strange how your life can change in such a small moment of time.

I didn't know it then, but I'd be seeing Paddy again. Paddy had a gig for us, all right. That was for sure, and it wasn't his mate's birthday bash down the local boozer. It was a trip to the front line in the former Yugoslavia. Bosnia, no less. Smack bang in the middle of a war zone for a New Year's rave. I could never have guessed that one.

To find out why we got involved in this crazy demo you have to go back about two months.

* * *

I was standing in my favourite record shop in Glasgow, 23rd Precinct, waiting my turn to buy the latest vinyl and looking at the posters covering the walls around me (I would always do this as I needed to keep tabs on the local events so I could be outside at the end with Desert Storm flyers). One poster suddenly grabbed my attention; *PROTEST TO SURVIVE*, it proclaimed, *BE A SPANNER IN THE WORKS NOT A COG IN THE MACHINE; MARCH AGAINST THE CRIMINAL JUSTICE BILL*. It continued and there was a contact number at the bottom. Record shopping forgotten, I pulled out my mobile phone and banged in the number. March against the Criminal Justice bill? Too fucking right! It rang for a few seconds and then someone answered.

'Campaign against the Criminal Justice Bill, how can I help you?'

Sounded on the ball. A good start, I thought.

'Hi, I represent the Desert Storm sound system from Glasgow and I'm interested in taking part in your demo. I have a sound system built into a van, do you think you could fit us in?'

There was a noise of scrabbling as the person on the other end gathered together a pen and paper. 'Just a second while I write this down. Desert Storm sound system, okay, van with built-in sound system. From Glasgow, you said?'

'Yes, Glasgow,' I replied, pride in my voice.

'Okay, we'd be more than happy to have you on the march. But first what you have to do is phone the number I'm going to give you and tell them the van registration and your name.'

'Whose number is that then?' I asked.

'It's the Metropolitan Police number.'

What? 'Sorry, can you repeat that? I thought you said the Metropolitan Police number.'

'Yes, that's right, I did. This is a legal demo; we do live in a democracy, you know.'

Fair enough. I copied down the number, but didn't phone right away as this required some thought... all of two seconds of thought. Us in a big demo in London blasting out the fucking tunes? I punched in the number.

The next day, all plans of demos came to a shattering stop, you could even say a bone-shattering crash if you wanted.

I was in the unit after another top night, in bed with Elaine (we had discovered that we both liked drink, drugs, parties and mad sex when we got home, or in Elaine's case even before we got home, like in the cupboard of the local nightclub Reds or even the toilets of posh restaurants like the Ubiquitous Chip off Byres Road), when a motorbike pulled up outside, revving its engine and beeping the horn. We got up to see what was happening. Even Smudge, who was crashed out in the rave arch next door, crawled out of his pit.

It was my mate Steve on his lovingly rebuilt air-cooled Yamaha RD250, a real classic. After a coffee and a spliff I dropped the question.

'So, eh, Steve, how about a spin round the block then?'

He was none too happy, but I can be very persuasive, and within a few minutes I was doing up the helmet strap and I was off. The last thing I heard him shouting was, 'For God's sake, be careful.'

I love motorbikes, and although the RD is only a 250cc it has a two-stroke engine which means it picks up much faster than its larger four-stroke cousins. Throttle back, balls over the tank, and I was away. Banking hard off York Street, I turned towards the West End going like the wind. Down Byres Road zooming in and out of the traffic, up past the university nearly going airborne at the top of the hill, wicked. After about ten minutes and a couple of loops of the area, I decided to turn back as Elaine would be getting worried. Coming past the park, I saw a silver van pull into the side off the road. Eh? What's he up to, I wondered. Next thing, he pulled a snap U-turn without indicating! Oh, my God, the van's going to hit me! I just had time to bank the bike and open the throttle in an attempt to get round him but there was no chance. BANG! The fucker turned right into me! The front corner of the van smashed into my left arm, shattering it in two places. The bike catapulted away and off down the road. I did a complete somersault and landed on my head. Crack, the helmet came off. I somersaulted again. Smash. I landed on my now unprotected head a second time. also shattering my shoulder. Then I lay there, staring up at the sky and wondering, *what the fuck!*

Next thing, some binmen that happened to be travelling along the road were peeling me off the tarmac. 'Are you all right?' Yeah, right, I thought, just fine.

'We saw it all, mate, we've got that bastard here and we're calling the cops.'

Hmm, the cops might not be such a good idea as I had no bike licence or insurance. I managed to mumble through the pain, 'No, don't.'

The binman picked right up on it. 'Okay, son, got no documents? Right, we'll hold him here and you get to fuck... If you can.' He looked dubiously at my smashed-up body.

Somehow, I got up off the road and staggered over to the bike. By now, the place was crowded with shocked onlookers. How I picked up the bike with my injuries and started wheeling it away into the park,

I'll never know, but I'll tell you one thing, the pain was intense. I'd got a few hundred metres and was out of sight of the road when a council parks van pulled up. The guy rolled down his window.

'Right, son, the game's up, I know it was you that crashed down there and you're going to wait here with me till the cops come.'

As if to emphasise the point, a cop siren started wailing in the background getting closer. But I wasn't having any of it, and leaned over towards him, blood dripping on the deck.

'Now you listen to me, you fucker, you have no idea who I am, and if you don't fuck off right now, you're a dead man.' And then I added in for good measure, 'and your family too, I'll even have your dog killed. You haven't seen anything. So, fuck off... NOW.'

In some places this wouldn't have worked but in Glasgow it's a different matter. The guy quickly weighed things up, very quickly, and next thing he was gone. I smiled grimly to myself and continued to push the bike away, but the pain was so great that my vision was swimming and I was sure I was going to pass out. Then a stroke of luck; a friend of mine appeared from nowhere. 'Keef, what the fuck? Oh, my God, what happened to you, are you, all right?' It was a stupid question, smashed bike, broken arm, busted-open head, blood everywhere, and he asked, 'Are you all right?'

'Of course I'm not all right!' I croaked between clenched teeth. 'Look, I need to ditch this fucking bike fast, can you help me, there's not much time.' I turned as I heard more cop sirens coming.

The guy —bless him – took the bike off me and hid it in an old railway tunnel nearby. Clever boy, these railway tunnels were always dropping in and out of my life. Anyway, without the bike, it was easier – I said easier, not easy – to continue my journey and sneak back to the unit undetected. I don't remember much of the trip back, but I do remember the look on Elaine's face when I fell into her arms and half-passed out. Her, Smudge, and Steve led me into the unit and cut the clothes off me and looking in the mirror, I could see the injuries were horrific; there was hardly a square inch of my body that wasn't cut or bruised and the broken arm and shoulder were swelling up to a frightening size. Hospital, immediately, was the only option. Even now, writing this nearly twenty years later, I'm cradling my left arm as the dull ache of half-remembered pain returns like the distant memory of a bad dream.

Now there was a hospital just up the road, the Western, but the cops would be bound to look there first (black guy with road traffic injuries, not hard to spot), so we all got in my car and Steve drove me to a hospital on the other side of town. Of course, the traffic was bad and as the shock and adrenalin had well-worn off by now, the pain was so bad I was passing in and out of consciousness. By the time we arrived, I was a mess and they had to lift me out of the car and into a wheel chair then straight into the emergency department. We had planned a cover story, I had fallen off a wall and down some stairs and I gave that and a false name and passed out.

'Craig? Craig?' I dimly heard this voice pulling me out of a dark dream. 'CRAIG? CRAIG!' Louder this time. 'Craig,' I thought, that's not me, just let me sleep and the darkness enveloped me again. 'CRAIG!!!!' Much louder this time accompanied by a sharp pain in my ear.

It all came flooding back; the crash, I was in hospital... and Craig, fuck's sake, that was the dummy name I'd given. I sat bolt upright and opened my eyes and shouted, 'CRAIG, yes, yes, that's me!' The doctors and nurses that had been bending over me trying to bring me round got the fright of their lives and jumped back scattering medical equipment to the floor. But the effort was too great and I collapsed in a heap.

Later that day, a doctor came to see me and explained how lucky

I was, yeah, right!

'You're a lucky boy,' he began, 'usually when the outer forearm is broken, the force of the tendons contracting shatters the inner forearm as well, resulting in a much more serious injury. But in your case, the elbow joint dislocated and we have had only to insert one metal plate instead of two.' *Lucky, eh?* 'All I can say is you have much tougher than average bones. In fact, your muscle structure is unlike anything I have seen. I had a really hard job to cut through you, and the operation took twice as long as I had expected as I just couldn't get through the tissue.' The image of him sawing into my left arm was not a helpful nor a pleasant one, so I changed the subject.

'Err,' I croaked, 'so what about the shoulder?'

'Ah yes, the shoulder, dislocated A/C joint, a tricky one. In the past, a screw would be inserted...' God, this guy had some bedside manner. '...but we found that they would come out inside the body and another operation would be needed to remove it.' I felt sick. 'So, we're just going to leave it as it is, and with care, it should be okay in about six weeks, but it will heal fully and will never be the same again.' I just had to get rid of this guy.

I leaned forward. 'Look, pal, why don't you just fuck off!'

'Well, I never, there's gratitude for you,' he said and scuttled off.

Drugged up on morphine, I slept for, well, I don't know how long, but when I eventually awoke, I wanted just one thing (apart from a piss of course) and that was to phone Elaine. At first, they wouldn't bring me a phone, but when I started to cause a scene in the ward they soon caved in and a phone was wheeled round to my bed.

Ring ring, please be in, *ring ring*... 'Hello, Docherty house.' It was her; I felt a massive sigh of relief.

'It's me, I'm in the hospital.'

'I know that, you eejit, I took you there, remember?'

Oh yeah, of course.

'How are you?' she asked.

'I'm... I'm not so good. Listen, Elaine...' I paused.

'Yes?' she replied softly.

'Look, err, you're not going to dump me or anything are you?'

'Keef, don't be silly, of course not! What on earth gave you that idea?'

'Well, it's just that I'm pretty fucked and I was worried that...'

'For God's sake, no way, leave you when you're down? Anyway, the bits that matter are still working, or at least I hope they are.'

Haha, nice one. I laughed weakly in spite of everything, but it hurt too much.

'Yes, that's still working.' But then I got a sudden weird feeling inside me, warm but cold, beautiful but somehow frightening.

'Elaine?'

'Yes, darling?'

'I love you, babes.'

That was it, it was out, love had never been mentioned in our relationship before. I had thought that, well, she was young and I didn't want to scare her off with commitment. As for what she thought, I could only guess.

There was a pause.

'I love you too, I have since the moment we met and I'm coming up to see you. John McCarthy is driving me up tonight, and I'm bringing a fat joint as well to cheer you up. So, for now, get back to sleep, that's an order.'

As I passed out again, I could hear the old biddy in the next bed talking to someone, 'Oh, that's so sweet. Oh, to be young again.' And I faded back to black.

Visiting time arrived and so did my visitors bearing the obligatory grapes, Lucozade. and hopefully stashed somewhere, the fat joint I had been promised. Since McCarthy was there, it was hard to continue our conversation from earlier, but something subtle had changed between Elaine and I, a closeness that hadn't been there before, and if it wasn't for the fact my shoulder was trussed up like a chicken, my left arm was swollen to twice its size, and my head bandaged like a mummy, I would have been very happy.

Late that night, I began the long, slow, and painful shuffle to the end of the corridor to an open window to spark up the fat one. Elaine's joints really do look like joints, wide at the business end and tapering down to a slim cardboard filter. After many long cool puffs, I retired to my bed fucked out my face.

Next day, I was getting restless, I became a terrible patient and by eleven a.m., I was already demanding to be released. A doctor was summoned and I pleaded my case.

'Look, doctor, I'm okay now—' yeah, right – 'I'll be fine back at my place, my girlfriend will look after me, and I've got my medication, what can possibly go wrong?'

It was the same doctor I had abused the day before.

'Well, Mr Robinson, I'm afraid that many things could go wrong. Have you heard of osteoporosis?' I shook my head. 'Well, in some patients the plate doesn't take and bone wasting occurs and this, if not checked in time, can lead to amputation or even death by septicaemia.' God, this guy really was a bundle of good news; I was starting to wonder if he enjoyed giving his victims the worst-case scenario. 'And just as serious...'

This was definitely not making me feel better so I interrupted him and cut straight to the chase.

'Look, let me put it like this, you can't keep me here. I'm not a fucking prisoner so I'm going to sign myself out no matter what you say, so be a good guy and give me some drugs and advice on how to look after myself and I'm out of here. Oh, and no more doom and gloom scenarios please.'

He looked long and hard at me, sighed, and caved in.

Later that day I was back at the unit realising I should be back at the hospital. I couldn't even dress myself or make a cup of tea, I could hardly even wipe my own arse. Elaine claims she even did this for me, but I have no memory of it so it didn't happen. Anyway, without her help I would have been shafted and that night I felt really, really sick; weak, sweating, shaking, and I nearly went back to hospital with my tail between my legs. But in the back of my mind was the nagging doubt that maybe the cops would have got round to widening their net and I would be nicked, so I held on.

The next day, I felt a little better and was ready to take the doctor's advice; no physical activity, no driving, and loads of sleep for at least six weeks. The last thing in the world I should be thinking about is driving to some crazy demo in London for maybe the maddest weekend on record.

Just then, the phone rang...

'Hello? Desert Storm International, which department please?'

'Err, hello, am I speaking with a Mr Keith Robinson?'

This sounded official so I was instantly suspicious.

'Eh, yes, who's calling please?'

'It's the Metropolitan Police. We're phoning concerning the information you gave us about the vehicles you want to include in the forthcoming demonstration.'

Shit, the demo. With everything that had happened, I had completely forgotten about it.

The voice continued. 'In respect to the Bedford van registration number, WIA 618 with an internal sound system, you gave the colour as camouflage, but the DVLA assure us it is registered as white. Also, you have given no named driver for your other vehicle, the camouflaged... it says here...Triumph Convertible staff car? Again, the DVLA say this is also registered as being white. Mr Robinson, can you please clear these matters up for us?'

I cleared them up, all right, and it was game on. London town, full steam ahead.

A meeting was called, phone calls were made, people were informed, and by eight p.m. that night we had gathered. There was John McCarthy (Johnny Mac), my old friend from school, for whom I now worked for at his car garage a couple of days a week, Sheona, who although only sixteen was now an indispensable part of the organisation doing phone calls, flyers, postering and security (she did the lot), John Owen, a bit of a peace-loving hippy but a good friend nonetheless (I don't generally like hippies), Smudge, another hardcore member, Mad Dog (need I say more), Brian Bowes, a couple of the DJs, Simmy (our half-crazed sound engineer, Elaine and, of course, myself.

The first order of business was the camouflaged car. Although I had already committed it to the demo, I hadn't actually cleared it with the car's owner, Johnny Mac. The car had been built and recently finished over the last three months in John's garage. It was an old Triumph 2000; the doors had been welded up, the roof cut off, the car MOT'd, Desert Storm's logo stencilled on the sides, and finished off with a wicked camouflage paint job. I can't remember if we built the car for any specific reason although the cosmic raver in me suggests it was for this event, which we hadn't even known about, of course.

He said yes surprisingly quickly and that was that, so now I knew how many seats we had for the long journey down to London, three in the van and four in the car. Now to find out who wanted to come.

I was surprised again that although right up for events in Glasgow, not so many were willing to risk their neck in what the media was already calling a guaranteed riot. This was a problem I came across more and more as time went on; as the missions got madder, only the maddest were up for the missions. Not for the last time, I wished my dear friend Bruce was still alive, he would have been there in a shot. I didn't know it then, but he would not be the last of my friends to go to the big rave in the sky.

Anyway, back to the mad and the living. The mad were me (of course), Sheona on her first trip out of Glasgow for fuck's sake, Simmy, who was mad anyway, John O, who although a hippy was an anarchist as well, and Brian Bowes. Elaine was desperate to come but her parents had already heard that this was no peace and love, stop the war event, but the demo of the decade, where an angry populace were to vent their spleen at a piece of legislation that many felt attacked the very core of our democracy, so she was grounded. Oh yeah, and a few crazy ravers who just wanted to party. I couldn't even get any of the DJs to come, even using all my, not inconsiderable, persuasive skills. Lucky I'm pretty good on the decks then!

I was driving the camouflaged car as it was an automatic and I wouldn't have to change gear (a good idea as I had broken my arm and shoulder), and John O drove the van. With our convoy, the staff car out front (Desert Storm pennants fluttering from poles on the wings) and the strange-looking Desert Storm van with what looked very like a large missile launcher bolted to the roof, we were certainly attracting a lot of attention on the trip down the M6 to London. Oh yeah, I forgot to tell you, the staff car was not really a convertible. As we'd just removed the roof, there was no roof to put up, so it was wind in the hair and jackets if it rained time! Cars passing had one of two reactions. Toot the horn and wave, or more often, slow down as they passed us, peering over with dark looks, at a black man with dreadlocks dressed as a soldier, driving a fake army car followed by more weirdos also dressed in army kit driving some other kind of freak machine. The looks of disgust on their faces cracked Sheona and I up every time it happened.

For these people we had one of two reactions; for the friendlies it was all smiles and waves back, happy nice strange people saying hello. For the disapproving people, it was a different matter; we would wait until they were right up beside us and then turn around pulling bizarre faces. I would make disgusting licking motions with my tongue leaving them to speed off gazing at my middle finger proudly sticking up over the windscreen. Once, before I could stop her, Sheona stood up in the passenger seat and pulled her top right up shouting, 'Get a load of these, you fuckers!' The look on the lady passenger's face was indescribable as she turned to her hubby screaming at him to put the foot down and stop gazing at Sheona's breasts. Amazing. The journey down was a total laugh and when we stopped at the services, it would bring the whole place to a grinding halt as people stared in disbelief

As we passed Manchester, we noticed a lot of other strange vehicles on the road also travelling south, old buses with smoke stacks sticking out of the side, battered vans filled with hippy freaks. We soon realised that these were others heading down for the riot... sorry, I mean peaceful demonstration, and our excitement levels raised another notch from very, very excited to unbelievably excited. The horn was on constantly but I had forbidden Sheona from exposing her breasts anymore. We pulled in around nightfall and spent an uncomfortable night sleeping in the vehicle, my injuries had been aggravated by the drive and I had to double-drop my medication. We were rudely awoken the next morning to find the cops banging on the door to check our documents; they were all in order and on we went.

Eventually, we arrived at the end of the M1 and outer London and onto the next problem; even though I had stolen a London A to Z map at the services, my knowledge of the city was limited and with Sheona navigating it was a nightmare. Also, my arms were hurting, it had been not so bad on the straight road down, but now with the twists and turns, the pain was really bad, and it was more by luck than anything else that we arrived at the meeting point around ten a.m., perfect timing.

Cops were everywhere and it wasn't long before we were flagged down.

'Stop there, sir, this is for authorised vehicles only.' He looked down at me with obvious distaste.

'Well, officer,' I replied from behind my mirrored sunglasses, 'I think you'll find we are authorised. Keith Robinson, Desert Storm sound system. We have two vehicles; this, and the van behind,' I said, pointing back at the Storm machine.

The officer looked doubtful, but began to consult a large list he had pinned to a clipboard and moved round to the front to look at the registration plate. Then he was straight on the radio. The tension in our car was incredible... please, please let us be on the fucking list.

After what seemed like an eternity, he walked back round. 'Well, sir, I've radioed in... and ...and...' I wanted to punch him. 'And yes, it would appear your details are down. If you'd just like to continue up this road and pull in when you see our command vehicle, someone will check your documents.'

'The command vehicle?' I queried.

'You'll know it when you see it, sir. Now move along.' He waved and a barrier was pulled aside and we rolled in. YES!!!

He was right about the command vehicle, you couldn't miss it; it was an elderly Transit van, Mark 1, I think, with a large glass turret sticking out of the roof, looking a bit like the Popemobile.

Our documents were checked and there was a problem. I was named as the driver of the van and John O as the driver of the car, and they weren't budging. It would be insane for me to try to drive the manual van with my broken arm, changing gear, stopping and starting all the time, for hours in this march, but fuck it, I got straight out and we swapped places.

The march didn't leave till noon so we had a bit of time to take in our surroundings and we all sat in the car chatting. The place was pretty chaotic, the cops had cordoned off the area but were having problems keeping back the streams of protesters that desperately wanted to be at the front of the march. I stood up on my seat and as far as I could see masses of people were converging on this very spot. Cool, I got a rush of excitement knowing that we were in and as far as I could make out, we were right at the front!

Sitting back down, I scanned around and right away my eyes fell on a flatbed truck covered in the largest speakers I'd ever seen. 'Simmy,' I said to our sound engineer, 'check those fucking bins out man!'

We all turned to look and were suitably impressed.

'But Keef,' said Sheona, 'if those speakers are on, will people still be able to hear the Desert Storm van?'

I looked over, rubbing my chin with my forefinger and thumb. 'Shit,' I replied, 'Sheona, you're bang on. If that thing is playing within a block of us, people won't hear shit.'

'More like people won't hear anything ever again,' said Simmy.

This was the first downer of the trip and we all sat in silence for a bit staring over at the massive speakers. Then a group of people in front of the truck caught my eye. They were all dressed in black and silver, with skip caps and sunglasses and although we couldn't quite hear, they appeared to be in the middle of an animated discussion.

Next thing one of them broke away from the group, a girl, and started walking towards us. As she got closer, I noticed she was well fit; short dark hair, tight black leather trousers, and a tight black T-shirt with a strange silver motif on the front that looked like a kind of face with mushrooms on, and she topped her outfit off with an expensive pair of wraparound shades. She must have felt my gaze because she smiled and gave me a little wave. I managed to smile back and was just thinking of something to say when she cruised past us heading for the popemobile. She arrived at the back door and started banging on it hard.

'Hey, open this door, I want to speak to the boss.' She kept on banging. The door opened and out stepped a cop with more gold braid on his hat than I'd ever seen before, he looked like he'd been dipping the peak in scrambled eggs. This guy had to be the chief, and Scrambled Eggs did not look happy.

'You again, Miss Griffith. I've told you already that your truck is definitely not getting into this march while I'm in charge,' he said firmly, pointing over at the massive sound system.

'But...' the girl tried to continue.

'No means no, young lady. You should have got your registration and other details into us last week at the very latest, as you know very well. Now, you're wasting my time. If you don't get that vehicle and that bunch of degenerates out of my sight in the next ten minutes, I'll have it impounded and the lot of you arrested for obstruction. NOW GO!' With that, Scrambled Eggs got back in the popemobile, slamming the door behind him.

The girl stood there for a few seconds then turned and started back. 'FASCIST FUCK!' she shouted over her shoulder, not smiling now. As she passed us again, I looked more closely at her tee shirt.

The design was somehow familiar, and underneath I read two words. SPIRAL TRIBE.

'Fucking hell,' I muttered to the others under my breath, 'that's fucking Spiral Tribe over there.' We all turned to stare. Even Sheona had heard of Spiral Tribe, they were superstars of the techno underground, they'd even made the six o'clock news with the now infamous Castlemorton event. In some ways, and I don't mean this in a bad way, it was their fault that the Criminal Justice Bill included powers against raves in the first place. Jesus, they were banned from the march while we...

My thoughts were broken off. Scrambled Eggs had got out of the popemobile again and was purposefully striding towards our car.

'Who's Mr Robinson?' he demanded and I answered that it was me. 'Well, I'm the assistant met commissioner and I'm here to inform you that we're moving the start point as there's too many people gathering here, so I want you to get these things fired up and follow my command vehicle. We move in five minutes. Oh, and one more thing; when we arrive at Trafalgar Square I want you to pull into the left and park. Under no circumstance are you to enter the square, got it?'

'Eh, yes, but what order do you want us in, the van first or the car?' I asked.

'Listen, son, I don't give a damn which vehicle is first, just get them moving!' And with that, he stormed off and got back into the popemobile.

We didn't need to be told twice and we got sorted, Simmy and I in the van with Sheona on the roof and John O and Brian in the car.

'Shall I start the generator?' asked Simmy.

I looked at him and raised an eyebrow. 'Well, Simmy, we didn't drive all this way just to watch the fucking march!'

'Okay, okay.' And off he went into the back to pull the starting cord on the generator and turn on the amps. I heard the familiar whoosh and pop as the amps powered up. I tapped the head of the microphone which was gaffer-taped to the sun visor, with my fingers and heard a dull thump come from the sound system. Everything seemed in order, so I leaned forward and cleared my throat.

'One, two... one, two.' The words echoed off the buildings and everyone in the area, from cops to Spiral Tribe, everyone turned round to look at us. I just waved back with a big stupid grin on my face.

Then we were off. My last view of Spiral Tribe, as we disappeared, was of a large scary-looking dude, who appeared to be missing some fingers, violently kicking the front of their truck.

We pulled away at a slow speed keeping about twenty feet from the back of the popemobile and the crowd surged after. We took the next right onto a large road. I couldn't tell you which one as I had never even been to Trafalgar Square before much less Hyde Park and then the madness began.

Basically, the march had started, no matter what Scrambled Eggs thought, so it was time to fire up the tunes. This was the moment we had been waiting for! Our hearts were going like sledgehammers.

I turned to Simmy. 'Okay, Simmy, fucking hit it!'

He started fumbling with the cassette deck. 'Which fucking tape, man, which tape? He was flapping big time. His eyes, which normally protruded out, were now bulging as if they would break free of their sockets. Looking at him, I hoped he had remembered to take his medication. In fact, maybe I should ask him for some of it too!

'Well, definitely not your goddamn Dire Straits tape! Find any fucking tape that says Desert Storm on it and... GET IT ON!'

'Okay, okay, no need to shout.' I saw him select a Desert Storm tape and slot it into the deck, pushing the door closed. As he reached forwards for the play button his hand was shaking. Click.

BOOM, BOOM, TSSST. BOOM, BOOM, TSSST. Like a bomb going off, Desert Storm techno sounds blasted out from the van shattering the peace of central London as it bounced off and around the buildings. Behind us, a huge cheer went up, temporarily downing out the tunes. I leaned out the window and shouted out to Sheona on the roof.

'SHEONA, SHEONA, what's happening?'

She leaned over. 'Oh, my God, Keef, you won't believe it; the people are going crazy!'

'How many people are there?' I asked as I couldn't see shit in the mirrors.

She briefly disappeared to look back down the road. 'I don't know, thousands and thousands, as far as the eye can see!'

WOW. We'd done it. Desert Storm, the provincial sound system from darkest Glasgow, had pulled it off. It was more by luck than anything else that we had given our details to the cops, only because we were coming from so far away, but none of that mattered now... this was definitely going to put Desert Storm on the map.

Broken arms forgotten I got on with the driving and started MCing to the crowd.

'DESERT STORM IN THE FUCKING AREA. DANCE, DANCE, MOTH-ERFUCKERS. KILL, KILL, KILL THE BILL, KILL THE CRIMINAL JUSTICE BILL! PROTEST TO SURVIVE.'

The crowd loved it, and all around us were people dancing in the streets like maniacs. On the roof, Sheona was dancing so hard it was starting to dent the fucking roof!

Suddenly, Simmy and I could hear a new chant.

'GET YOUR TITS OUT, GET YOUR TITS OUT, GET YOUR TITS OUT, GET YOUR TITS OUT FOR THE LADS.'

We looked at each other, no way!

Sheona's head appeared again at the window. 'Keef, they want me to... what should I do?'

'Sheona, I don't know what you should do. They're your tits.'

'Okay then.' And she went back up. Moments later, there was a deafening cheer accompanied by whistles and clapping.

I turned to Simmy, shaking my head. 'Oh, my God, looks like she got them out then. If her mother finds out about this...'

'Keef, it's not her mother you should be worrying about.'

Fair point; her dad was a detective inspector with Glasgow's finest, and could defo make life difficult for me. Oops.

Looking back, it could be partially the fault of Sheona's breasts that the riot started in the first place, because at the same moment as she was displaying her breasts to the world, we came up to a McDonalds restaurant and the crowd, worked up into a frenzy, swarmed towards it, smashing the windows with litter bins, bits of concrete, and anything they could get their hands on. To them, it was a symbol of capitalism at its worst and it had to go.

'Oh, my God!' was all I could say as I watched the devastation take place.

After a short while, or maybe a long time (I have no idea), we arrived at Trafalgar Square.

'Keef, remember what the cop said, pull in on the left,' Simmy reminded me.

So, I tried to pull over but the crowd just followed me. There was no way I could stop; the march would have bottlenecked and people would have been crushed. I drove a bit further round and tried again, same shit. The next turn was larger but when we looked down it, it led to the Houses of Parliament and a little way down the street at least 500 mounted riot cops were lying in wait, blocking the way, defo off the menu! As we drove past, Sheona was at the window again, obviously in a state.

'Keef, Keef, Johns O's not behind us anymore! He's turned off towards the fucking cops!'

No fucking way! But it was true, out of the side window I could see the Storm car peeling off and heading towards Parliament and an almost certain bad end. At least ten full-on old-school punks with Doc Marten boots and spiked hair were sitting on the bonnet and boot drinking from bottles of Buckfast! Had he lost his fucking mind? I screamed to him over the PA system.

'JOHN O, HAVE YOU LOST YOUR FUCKING MIND? FOLLOW THE STORM VAN!!'

But he just carried on, taking an element of the crowd with him. We couldn't stop and he was soon lost in the chaos.

Now we were in the shit too. We had almost come full circle and in a minute were going to crash back into the march again! In the front, Simmy and I were starting to panic. For some reason, turning off the music (the thing that was drawing them on) never occurred to us. Just as it was all about to go tits up, I saw Scrambled Eggs running across the road towards us, ripping out his radio headset and flinging it to the winds.

'GET INTO THE SQUARE, GET INTO THE FUCKING SQUARE,' he screamed, realising what was about to happen.

Not a fucking problem and I did as the man said, bumping up the kerb, horn on, and shouting through the PA system for people to get out of the way, and we slipped in, now safely surrounded by thousands of demonstrators.

There was no time to waste so I jumped out, ran to the back of the van, and threw open the doors to reveal the Technics turntables and mixer all ready to go. Reaching into my record box, I pulled out a pre-selected tune, Desert Storm's first vinyl release, the eponymous 'Desert Storm' track (the other side was Scoraig 93). I kissed the centre label, placed it on the turntable, picked up the headphones, and began to cue it up. For effect, I flicked the switch on the mixer from line to phono, thus killing the music. The entire square turned round to face us, the dancers in front of the sound system froze mid-step. Where had the music gone? Trafalgar Square had gone almost dead quiet. I definitely had their attention now. Raising my left hand, fist clenched in the air I screamed at the top of my voice, 'DESERT STORM IN THE FUCKING AREA!' and reached forward with my right hand and pressed the start button. The haunting melody of Desert Storm (the track), with its newsreel intro, permeated the square... 'The skies over Baghdad glowed'. Then the kick drum came in and the crowd went wild, thousands of people dancing and screaming, an unrepeatable moment in my life.

I played on for about forty-five minutes but knew if I didn't stop soon, I was going to piss myself, so I handed over the headphones and did a quick body swerve out of the square. Soon, I saw a likely spot and ran round the corner, only to stop dead with my hand frozen on my zip. In front of me were about a hundred cops with their backs to me, but not your normal run of the mill Met cops, not even your riot cops. These guys were dressed in light blue army-style jumpers with no shoulder numbers and blue balaclavas, like the ones armed robbers use so they can't be recognised! And most worrying of all, another cop had a tray with strange little silver vials on it which he was handing out and the cops were snapping off the tops and necking the contents. That's when they noticed me. I got an overpowering feeling that I had just witnessed something I shouldn't have and turned tail and fled.

I found another spot to piss and thought over what I had seen. Those cops didn't look very friendly. I mean, I couldn't imagine one of them helping an old granny across the street, the one that had been nearest to me even had a wicked-looking scar just visible under his balaclava. Who the fuck were they? And what was in those silver vials, hippy bashing juice maybe? (I didn't know at the time, but they were the Met's infamous TSG tactical support group, a clandestine force of basically boot boys unaccountable to anyone.) And, more importantly, what were their plans? Also, just up the road I noticed loads of mounted cops saddling up and checking equipment. The conclusion was inescapable. They were going to clear the square the hard way.

Something had to be done, but thinking about it, who was there to talk to? I hadn't seen sight nor sound of the organisers all day, not even stewards. This was a mess. I looked over to the popemobile parked nearby and decided to grasp the nettle. Taking a deep breath, I strode over, only to be stopped by a cop guarding the door.

'Fuck off,' he said pushing a hand into my chest.

'Well, actually,' I replied, 'I'm here to see the assistant commissioner, I'm from the van playing music in the square.'

The cop stiffened up. 'Are you Mr Robinson?'

'Eh, yes,' I reluctantly admitted.

The cop grabbed my arm. 'Right, Mr Robinson, I'm arresting you under section—' blah blah – 'of the Public Order Act 19 blah blah on suspicion of causing a public nuisance.' He grinned from ear to ear as he reached round for his cuffs. 'Sir, sir,' he called, kicking the door of the popemobile with his heel. 'I've got Mr Robinson right here.'

The door opened and Scrambled Eggs stepped out onto the road.

'Ah, Mr Robinson.' He motioned to the cop to move off and the cop backed off a few paces but kept the cuffs in his hands. Was I under arrest or not?

Scrambled eggs looked me straight in the eyes. 'So, Mr Robinson, what's your next move?'

'Well, I was just wondering what time we would be moving off for Hyde Park?' Now this was the million-dollar question.

'So...' he replied slowly, 'you're planning on moving this circus on, then?'

I didn't really like this. By answering, I would be accepting some of the blame for the demo. Images of McDonalds being smashed up came to mind.

'Whenever you're ready. For my part, I could get moving in about fifteen minutes.'

He looked at me again. 'I'm not sure if I trust you, Mr Robinson. Maybe it would be more prudent just to arrest you right now and clear the square by force.' The other cop moved a little closer to me. I knew it! So that was the plan.

'You could do that and have a full-scale battle on your hands. I mean, surely you don't think these people are just going to leave? Why not use my van to lure them away and on to Hyde Park as planned?'

Scrambled eggs looked thoughtful as he considered this... and then decided.

'Okay, in fifteen minutes your van is ready to go or we will move in. Got it?'

I sighed with relief. 'No problem. Just one thing, which way is Hyde Park?'

Scrambled Eggs looked at me in disbelief. 'Just follow me.'

Saying I'd be ready to leave in fifteen minutes was a lot easier than doing it. First, I had to explain to my posse – speaking of which where the hell was John O, not to mention Johnny Mac's camouflaged car? No one had seen him and my lot were reluctant to leave the safety of the square, even after I had explained the situation. This was wasting precious time. I looked at my watch, only eight minutes left! There was nothing else to do, so I pressed stop on the turntables and moved to the front and grabbed the mic as people booed and jeered.

'Please, your attention for a minute, ladies and gentlemen. I have a very important announcement to make.' That got them listening and the noise died down a little.

'Everyone, we must move from the square immediately. You see those 500-plus riot cops down there?' I pointed to the blue mass down the road. Everyone looked. 'They are going to clear the square by force. I REPEAT, BY FORCE! We must continue the march to Hyde Park as planned. The Desert Storm van will be moving off in a few minutes so please move out of the way and follow it. Thank you for listening.'

There were many calls of 'fuck off', 'suck my dick' and suchlike, but it had to be done. I jumped in and started her up while Sheona and the others tried to clear a path behind. It was a total nightmare, most of the protesters were totally fucked out of their tiny minds and how no one was crushed, I'll never know, but finally we were on the road behind the popemobile and ready to roll.

We kicked up the sounds again and off we went. Sheona reported that the march was following, we had done it. As we pulled off, a girl came to the window. I was just about to tell her I was a little busy when I realised it was the Spiral Tribe girl from earlier. I asked what had happened to their truck.

'Well,' she explained in a London accent with exaggerated hand gestures, 'Well, it's like this, the pigs have taken the truck and the rig and nicked a few of my posse *(I thought back to the fingerless dude kicking the truck grill)*. I told them to put in the details but they wouldn't listen, boys eh? It's quite embarrassing really. I mean, this is our town and we can't get it together to get our system on the march. And you guys, Desert Storm? Is that right?'

'Yeah, Desert Storm from Glasgow,' I replied.

'And you guys come all the way from Glasgow, oh pukka van by the way, with your details all sorted. Oh well. Anyway, I've got a favour to ask. *(just name it, I thought, anything)* Can you put on a Spiral Tape for me, it would mean loads to my lot.' And she produced a black tape with SP23 written on it. 'Oh, and I'm Debbie by the way,' she said, offering her hand.

'I'm Keef, but I can't really shake your hand.' I showed her my damaged arms.

Debbie's eyes opened wide. 'Oh, my God, how the fuck do u drive this thing?'

'With difficulty,' I replied, and gingerly took the tape.

'Wicked, thanks a lot. Oh, and we're having an afterparty and we want you and your posse to come along. Here's the flyer, just phone the number this evening and we'll sort you out, cheers geezer.' And she was off.

Simmy put the tape straight on. It was much harder and faster than the Desert Storm sound, but still minimal, and the crowd seemed to like it. I could see what had to be the rest of Spiral Tribe, dancing with the crowd beside the van. Our van! Wicked!

Throughout the day, people had been putting flyers in through the windows; flyers for clubs, raves, and after-demo parties (obviously those got kept to the side) but one flyer stuck in my mind. It was from the Lesbian Mothers Non-aggression Society – LeMoNS, or some shit like that – and its headline was '*Keep it fluffy*' and then it went on to explain how not to antagonise the police, pick up your litter, and how to take witness statements in case you saw the cops beating people, good stuff really. We had only got maybe another mile down the road when the anti-flyer to 'Keep it fluffy' was thrust into my hand by a hooded and masked anarchist, dressed in black. It was titled '*Fluff off*', and went on to explain the best way to throw a brick without hitting your own guys, how to break off bits of metal from bus shelters to use as weapons, and more mad shit like that! It finished with the line, '*Hoods up, heads down, let's cause some trouble.*' I thought to myself, maybe there will be a spot of bother soon, I wasn't to be disappointed.

Groups of similarly hooded trouble makers started ranging off to the sides of the march, bricking the cops and smashing windows and then slipping back into the crowd before the cops could react. Very clever, I thought, but as time went on, they got braver and braver and started to stand and fight, some even had goddamn baseball bats for fuck's sake. Things were rapidly getting out of control and I had no idea what would happen next.

What did happen next was that the cops tried to force a wedge between us at the front and the crowd, trying to divert the van off into a side street. Cops were running at the doors. Oh shit, they were going to drag us out the fucking van! They nearly made it too; just as a burly riot cop was about to smash my window with his baton, the crowd reacted violently and forced them back (I last saw him go down under a sea of fists and feet). A titanic struggle ensued that made all that had gone before seem like a tea party! Sheona called down that she was scared, I told her she wasn't the only one and to lie flat on the roof. The cops were beaten back by sheer numbers and the popemobile was gone, replaced by low flying police helicopters. But now I could see Hyde Park approaching. Another ten minutes and we'd be safe.

We nearly made it, but the cops had regrouped and were back with a vengeance. This time there was no stopping them, people were being hospitalised, but they didn't care, they were beating men, women, and children. It was shocking. As the blue wave descended on us I just covered my face with my hands and ducked down. I heard one of the wing mirrors smashing off and looked up again. Unbelievable, the battle had swept by us and we were on the other side of the police lines.

'SHEONA, GET THE FUCK IN THE VAN,' I screamed up at her. In seconds flat, she jumped off the roof and into the van, looking like she'd just seen a ghost. I wasted no time and put the foot down and accelerated down Park Lane, engine screaming. It's quite hard to get off Park Lane because of the barriers and bollards but fuck that, I turned past a no entry sign, going the wrong way up the one-way street, and screeched off, scattering road cones to the wind and away.

Five minutes later, and we were still at large, the expected pursuit had not materialised.

'FUCK'S SAKE, KEEF!' shouted Simmy, 'slow down, we've made it, we're clear.'

I slowed down and checked the mirrors, correction, mirror, and he was right. There was nobody behind us so, seeing a parking space ahead, I pulled in, we collected some belongings, abandoned ship sharpish, legged it up the road to a bar, and sat outside at a table, hoods up and sunglasses on (looking dodgy as fuck) and watched the van.

'I'm going in to get the fucking drinks in, keep an eye on the van.' And I got up and walked into the bar. Somehow, we had escaped, and that called for a beer.

Back outside sipping on my drink, the adrenaline that had been coursing through my veins all day started to fade and the pain of my injuries came back with a vengeance, no doubt aggravated by the madness of before. Again, I pulled out the pill bottle marked '*do not drive or operate machinery and never exceed the stated dose*' and double-dropped them, washing them down with a generous slug of lager.

We sat there talking about the day and comparing stories from our different perspectives but kept coming back to the whereabouts of John O and the Storm car. Every few minutes, cop vehicles would come screaming past, sirens on, heading in the direction of the park, and we would turn away hiding our faces, but they weren't interested in us at all. I was checking my phone for a signal when it rang.

It had to be John O, so I eagerly answered, but it was Elaine, and she was excited, very excited.

'Keef, Keef, what's happening down there? I just watched the news. It's amazing; I saw the Desert Storm van with Sheona on the roof. You're all on the fucking TV, man. The news estimates 50,000 protesters. No way, it's on again now. Jesus, it's a full-on riot! Where are you, are you okay?'

I turned to the others and said quickly, 'Elaine says we're all on the news...' Sheona looked a little worried so I couldn't resist adding, 'She says Sheona had her tits out on top of the van.' Sheona's mouth just formed one big O. Hahaha.

Switching back to Elaine, I quickly explained the main events and told her I'd phone back because we were waiting on John O to call. We weren't disappointed, he soon rang, but it wasn't great news. The car had been impounded by the cops and he and Brian had been arrested but let go and he wanted to come and meet us. I gave him the name of the pub and the road and we waited. After about forty minutes, they trooped up and John O handed me a bit of paper; DB9 certificate, statutory off-the-road certificate from the Metropolitan Police, great!

'But I thought you said they impounded it?' I asked.

'Well, they might as well have,' he replied. 'This certificate says it can't be moved except by tow truck. It's still round the corner from Trafalgar Square... as far as I know.'

To tell you the truth, although glad they were out of jail, I was none too pleased and I told him straight.

'And anyway, John O, why the fuck did you turn down towards

parliament in the first fucking place? Didn't you notice that every cop in London was standing there tooled-up to the max? Why didn't you just follow me, for fuck's sake?'

He mumbled some shit about the cops telling him to pull in but it didn't wash with me. Well, there was nothing we could do at the moment, there was no way I was going within two miles of Trafalgar Square anytime soon!

After a few more beers, we were all exhausted and so we decided to crash in the van for a bit and then find out about this afterparty later. After a couple of hours kip, I phoned the number and asked for Debbie. She sounded well pleased to hear from me and gave me the address of the event. It turned out to be on the other side of London in some place called Epping Forest, great, so I got directions and we set off. After a nightmare journey of wrong turns and getting lost, we finally arrived at the meeting point, completely shattered.

It turned out it was lucky we had come as they still hadn't got their rig back and basically, we were the only sound system. So, we drove onto the field and in minutes the tunes were pumping. I was totally shafted so we just let them play and as it got dark, stragglers from the march started to arrive and soon there were loads of ravers and it was kicking off.

Debbie took me aside to meet Spiral Tribe. It turned out she and her boyfriend Mark were the main organisers and I was introduced to so many others that it was hard to remember their names but Mark was not an easy person to forget. He spoke calmly and quietly, but for some reason it was difficult not to listen to him. His voice was hypnotic, and within a few minutes, I was totally absorbed in his spiel as he told me his anti-establishment philosophy and the history of Spiral Tribe. It seemed that for him, at any rate, it wasn't just about parties, it was about effecting a change in society, starting an unstoppable movement through the vehicle of rave that would transform things. It was a bit deep for my tired mind, but he was a persuasive guy and I could see why his posse followed him. Left alone with him for much longer, I would have fucked off out of Desert Storm myself and joined SP23 right there and then, that's how magnetic his personality was. Totally disarmed, I found myself telling him things about the problems I was having in Glasgow with the gangsters, hopes and fears that I hadn't even shared with my friends yet.

I told him the sorry tale of how we had been having problems on the door, guys with knives, and stuff like that, so we had hired these heavies to do security and now it had all backfired and they had taken over and wanted control, so much so that I had stopped doing large events completely and only did small afterparties in the unit. His reply was to set in motion a change that meant that things for Desert Storm would never be the same again.

'Look, Keef,' Mark began, 'the way I see it, the solution is simple. Stop charging money and the gangsters will soon go away.'

I thought about this for a minute, but right away I could see a problem. 'But how will I pay everyone? DJs, doormen, etc?'

'That's the beauty of it; at a free party, everyone works for nothing, they work for the rave. Ok, you take donations at the door and you get the bar money to cover costs, but you don't charge an entrance fee. That way, the authorities can't get you on not having a public entertainment licence and the gangsters will fuck off. Rave on, simple.'

He made it sound easy but I was still doubtful. I mean, I really couldn't see DJs like Michael Kilkie from 23rd Precinct working for a couple of Jack Daniel's! And I told Mark this.

'Well, fuck him off then. There are plenty more DJs that will be dying to take his place. It sounds to me that you're in a tight spot anyway, so you've got nothing to lose.'

Now that was a home truth, make no mistake, we were in a tight spot all right. As I mulled it over, the sense of what he was saying hit me and I had an epiphany. I was convinced and at that moment, Desert Storm as a free party organisation was born.

Most of the rest of the event, I spent talking to Debbie and soon we were firm friends, so firm in fact that Simmy, a friend of Elaine and always the gentleman, came over and took me aside. 'Now, Keef, remember the saying, it's okay to look at the menu so long as you dine at home!'

Yeah, thanks for that, but nothing was going on. Not that I didn't find Debbie attractive, her slight build and almost elfin face in contrast with her strong character and steely gaze were very appealing, and I could certainly see what Mark saw in her.

The party went on till around dawn and then petered out. I reckon most people (myself included) were totally fucked from the day before anyway, and it was with much relief that I stopped the music and killed the geny. The silence after so much noise was almost deafening and the gentle tweeting of the birds and other countryside sounds were a pleasure to hear.

It was agreed that we would all head back to the Spiral's squat in North London for a bit of R&R. This was totally cool with my lot and off we went, but then I remembered about the Storm car, still stranded near Trafalgar square; we had to do something about that first. Well, it was John O's fault that the thing got DB9ed in the first place, so he should drive it to North London, but he refused point-blank, and short of pulling out his fingernails with rusty pliers, I couldn't force him to. So, guess what, he would drive the van and muggins here would drive the car.

We arrived at Trafalgar Square early doors and sure enough, there was the car with a huge *Police Aware* sticker plastered on the windscreen. I don't know if you've ever had to try to remove one of these fucking things, but let me tell you, they don't just peel off. Ten nervous minutes later, and I was inside firing her up and off. Well, there was no point in messing about, it was all or nothing. Sometimes you just gotta do what you gotta do! Surprisingly, we made it, no problems, and in less than an hour we had pulled up outside the Spiral's squat. We knew we had arrived by the pounding techno blasting from inside. Sheona was not impressed.

'For god's sake, don't these people ever stop?' she said, 'I was looking forward to some sleep!'

But it seemed that sleep was the last thing on the Spirals' agenda and on entering the house, the volume increased to concert volume. I couldn't help thinking I wouldn't want to be their neighbour! Right enough, I wouldn't want to be my neighbours either, or then again maybe I would. Anyway, we were welcomed in, and by the state of them, it looked like they had started without us. Debbie spotted me and came dancing up.

'Keef, excellent, so you made it. Here, have one of these.' And before I could protest, she had shoved an acid tab in my mouth.

Forty-five minutes later, I was dancing like a maniac in the living room with the rest of them when I noticed the guy with no fingers from earlier come up to me and pull me aside away from the speakers. They must have let him out of jail then.

'Are you Desert Storm Keef?' he asked.

'Yes,' I replied, looking up at him. He looked even bigger and madder on acid, I thought.

'Hi, man, I'm Terminator Cris.'

Of course you are, I thought. He offered his fingered hand and I shook it. (I later found out that his loss of fingers was no accident but the result of some dealers tying him down and chopping them off for a drug debt!)

'Well,' he continued, 'is that your friends out dancing in the road?' I nodded and he continued.

'Well, you'd better tell them to get the fuck inside because there's going to be a drive-by in a minute.'

What? 'A drive-by?' I repeated dumbly.

'Yes, geezer, a drive-by. You know, people are going to drive by the house and fire guns. A drive-by, I just got a call to warn me.'

Oh shit. I ran out of the front door and sure enough, there was Sheona and the others dancing in the road. By their faces, it looked like Debbie had got to them as well. I had to basically drag them inside and, as everyone hid behind the walls for cover, music off, Terminator peeked over the windowsill with a shotgun in his hand. This was scary stuff, let me tell you. After about thirty minutes, the alert was called off and the music went back on. I wasn't so sure and firmly told our lot to stay well away from the windows.

Things got a bit vague after that. I think I went out and bought some bottles of wine and maybe took some more acid, but the last thing I remember is lying on the floor in a corner as Debbie tucked me up in a grubby sleeping bag... and zonk!

Next day, I was up early, and after a search of the house drew a blank, I finally found the others curled up outside in the van. I made tea and we discussed our next move. It was now Monday and some of us had to get back up the road. Sheona for one now looked like one of the undead, her face was chalk-white and her hair splattered all over the place, sticking up in big lumps. The problem was the car. We talked about it round and round and decided on a plan. We had an RAC recovery card so we would vandalise the car a little and take off the distributor cap, thus immobilising it. We would then phone the RAC saying that we had come out this morning and found it like that, and they would then tow us back to Glasgow. We could even blame the damage on anarchists from the demo. Perfect, what could possibly go wrong?

Terminator Cris, that's what. It turned out he had a big problem with anybody in uniform, and not just the police, anyone! When the RAC man arrived, he swallowed the story hook line and sinker and was just about to winch the car onto his low loader when the Terminator came flying out of the house face twisted in fury. He attacked the RAC man, I just couldn't believe it. By the time we had calmed him down, the RAC man had done a runner leaving the storm car, now vandalised as well, still sitting in the road. Fuck! Terminator Cris was one crazy dude... and we were back to square one.

So, the only plan left was not a good one. I would drive the car up to Glasgow. We said our goodbyes, I got a hug and kiss from Debbie, and off we went. Soon, we were on the M1 heading north. So far, so good, and I was just starting to relax a little as we came up to Watford gap services when I saw a traffic cop car passing me very slowly staring in. I just ignored them and hoped that maybe they would just go away. Alas not, they pulled in front of us and a rolling red led sign in their back window scrolled the words:

POLICE>>>PULL IN >>>AT THE NEXT EXIT

Well, that was it, the game was up. I didn't know how much shit I was in for driving a car with a DB9 certificate in place but for sure it was deep. I pulled in at the services and sat in the car as the cops walked over. The van pulled in too, but sat back one hundred metres away not getting involved. Chickens.

'Right, Mr' Robinson, out of the car.'

I wondered briefly how they knew my name as the car wasn't registered to me. But soon, all was revealed.

'Yes, Mr Robinson, heading home from the demo, are we?' The cop continued, 'Desert Storm sound system. These registrations come up with red flags all over them. It says you're a bit of a rave-organising anarchist.' The cop smiled as he he seemed to enjoying it

Well they were right there, there was no point in even denying it. Next was the bit I had been dreading.

'Oh, and I take it you're aware that this vehicle had a DB9 certificate served upon it on Saturday afternoon?'

Okay, time for some grade-A bullshit.

'DB9 certificate?' I played dumb. 'What's one of them, then? I have all the documents just here.' And I reached into the glove compartment and pulled them out, noticing that you could still see the bottom of the orange *police-aware* sticker stuck to the window.

'No, no, Mr Robinson,' said the cop shaking his finger, 'these documents are of no use to you now. This car has been deemed unfit to drive on a public road by our esteemed colleagues in the Met. You're in a lot of trouble!'

My face was a picture of disbelief.

'But, officer, I'm only driving this vehicle because the driver disappeared at the demo and I had no choice. Maybe he knows something about the... DB9, did you say?'

I felt like telling him that the halfwit driver was sitting in the fucking van just there. But that wouldn't have helped anyone. It was a good try but the cop wasn't wearing any of it.

'Ah, well, you know best, Mr Robinson. How about you just step out of the car and hand me the keys.'

I did as I was told. It looked like this was it. The cop jangled the keys in front of me and glanced over at his partner then back at me.

'Well, then, Mr Robinson, what do you think we should do with these?'

I just shook my head with my palms up, not sure where this was going.

'Well,' the cop continued slowly, 'we're not the Glasgow cops, or we'd just beat you up. We're not the Met cops, or we'd just jail you. We're the Watford cops, and this is what we're going to do. If you can recover these keys from the fast lane of the motorway, you can have the car and off you go.' And before I could do anything, he made to throw the keys high and long into the road! I let out a gasp, and was just about to start running out into the traffic when he held me back.

'No, son, only joking.' He laughed and opened his hand to reveal the keys. 'It's your lucky day.' And he handed them back to me. 'Okay, off you go.'

I was stunned, but thanking him, I wasted no time in getting back in and moving off before he could change his mind. Looking in the mirrors, I could see the Storm van pulling out of the services behind me and behind them. Nothing. Incredible but true. We were on our way again. Now, I'm not too keen on cops as a rule, but even to this day, when I think of the Watford cops I get a warm fuzzy feeling inside.

Luck was still on our side and many hours later, we pulled up outside the unit utterly exhausted. I crawled in to find Smudge asleep on the couch and Elaine sitting up in bed wiping the sleep from her eyes.

'Hi, darling,' she said, 'do you want a hand unloading the van?'

But it was too late. I had already collapsed on the bed and fallen fast asleep.

15

BOSNIA OR BUST

It was Tuesday morning and the fallout from the criminal justice demo was still front-page news and it was no surprise when the phone went and it was some journo from the Daily Mail, his name something like Dave Conchetti, asking for Desert Storm sound system. I asked him where he had got my number.

'Oh, I got your number from the march organisers,' he replied.

Well, that was good enough for me and I answered all his questions as honestly as I could as he seemed like a nice guy. So, the next morning we were first in the queue at the newsagent to buy our copy, then straight back up to the unit for coffee, cigarettes, and a quick ego massage. I was making the brews and called through to Elaine – who was reading the article – and asked how it was.

'Err, I think you'd better come and have a look for yourself.'

Now that didn't sound good. I quickly walked through for a look and read it.

'Desert Storm sound system was one of the main agitators in the riot that followed... blah, blah, blah... systems like Desert Storm have been linked to a string of drug deaths around the country, some involving school children as young as fifteen. These dangerous and unsanctioned events are putting thousands of youngsters' lives at risk every week... blah, blah, blah... Desert Storm's mouthpiece, Keith Robinson, freely admitted to his part in the demo that led to the rioting and... blah, blah, blah... and they showed their true colours by the mindless violence meted out on unsuspecting Londoners last weekend. Police sources said... blah, blah, blah.'

And on and on and so forth.

I looked at Elaine, shock written on my face. 'But, but...' I stammered, 'I told my mother to get a copy of this... this...'

Words failed me as I scrunched it up into a ball and snatched up my phone.

'Hello, directory inquiries? Can I have the number for the Daily Mail head offices in London please?' I scribbled it down.

'Now, Keef, chill,' Elaine warned.

'Yeah, right,' I replied, and punched in the number. Within a minute or so, I was through to the rat Conchetti's desk and it was ringing. I raised an eyebrow at Elaine and smiled grimly. She just shook her head.

'Hi, Dave Conchetti, Daily Mail, can I help you?'

'Hey scumbag, it's Desert Storm sound system's mouthpiece here, remember me? Today, you accused us of killing schoolchildren, who the fuck do you think you are? I'm going to sue your ass until you're standing in the street in only your boxer shorts, you motherfucker.'

'Now, wait here, Mr Robinson, I can understand you're annoyed but...'

'Annoyed? You piece of...'

'Yes, I can understand you're annoyed, but if you read the article carefully then you will see that we never directly say that Desert Storm are responsible for any deaths...'

'Bullshit, I just read that crap and...'

'...or directly link you with any crime. Our lawyers have cleared the article, so see you in court.'

I had already uncrumpled the paper and was speed-reading. It was true; it said, 'systems like Desert Storm admitted...', 'events leading to...', etc, etc. We'd been had.

'B-But, I trusted you,' I said pathetically.

'Well, Mr Robinson, I think you just learned a valuable lesson in dealing with the media and...'

I hung up. The bastard.

There were quite a few of us there; Smudge, Elaine, Rob, Simmy and me, and we sat and discussed our dealings with the media. I mean, I thought we'd always used them to our advantage, Mixmag, DJ Mag, even the local papers. Like when we planted the story about the first Desert Storm rave in the tunnel to use on the next flyer. But it looked like this time we were out of our league. The phone rang, maybe it was Conchetti again. I had already thought of some new insults for that bastard, so I snatched up the phone.

'Hello, can I speak to someone from Desert Storm sound system please?'

It wasn't Conchetti, this person had a Scottish accent, but I was still suspicious...

'Who's this?'

'Hi, I'm Paddy, I got your number at the demo in London, remember?'

I didn't really, but just said yes anyway.

'Err, I think so.'

'I came up to the van, Scottish guy, curly black hair.'

'Oh yeah,' I remembered now. 'The crazy guy who wanted my details as the cops were attacking, I remember you!'

'That's me. Well, I said I had a gig for you.'

'Yes, that's right.' I was imagining some rave maybe up north or something.

'Well, I was just wondering if you would like to take your system to Bosnia?'

I paused. Had I heard him right? 'Sorry, did you say Bosnia?'

'Yes, Bosnia, this New Year for a rave.'

I didn't know what to say, I mean what do you say to that. Remember, this is 1994, right at the height of the conflict.

'Eh, just a minute, I'll ask the others.' I put my hand over the phone.

'Guys, some dude wants to know if we'll take the rig to Bosnia?'

Their faces were a picture.

'Bosnia? Isn't there a war on there?' Smudge asked.

'Yes, Smudge, there's a war on there,' I replied sarcastically. 'Well, do we or don't we?' I pressed. 'The dude's on the phone right now.' I was surprised to see heads nodding.

'Hi, Paddy, are you still there?'

'Aye, I'm here.'

'The answer's yes. We'll do it.'

The die was cast. Bosnia or bust.

The conversation turned to the logistics. I mean, how would we get there? Surely he didn't think we would be going in the van? How would we pay for it all? Where in Bosnia were we going? Who was coming with us? I had a hundred questions, but Paddy was a sharp operator and he had all the answers.

The plan was to go with some outfit called Workers' Aid for Bosnia, which mainly consisted of students from various universities around the country and we would tag along behind them (they were taking food aid). We would be going to a place called Tuzla, a city in the north of Bosnia (Paddy omitted to tell us it was basically under siege by the Serbian forces and had to be reached via a pass called Snipers Alley, but never mind). As for paying for it all, as WAB was a registered charity, collecting tins and stickers would be sent up and we were to collect the money ourselves, supposedly enough to buy a truck and pay all the fuel, food, etc, for there and back. Oh yeah, and we would leave in about eight weeks. Writing this now and reading back the last paragraph, I find it amazing that I accepted all this at face value.

Maybe I am crazy after all.

True to his word, the tins arrived two days later with a note that said 'good luck'. The first thing I noticed was that although it said W.A.B on the tins, the charity number was something totally different. Paddy assured me that apparently this is legal, but I'm not sure how. Anyway, Sheona, Rob, and I headed out with the tins and started the ball rolling. I must say we were nervous as fuck going into the first bar on Byres Road to shake the tins and ask for money. But Glasgow people are a generous lot; many had heard of Desert Storm already, and if we were crazy enough to go to Bosnia to hold a rave, then fair play to us, they knew that the people there needed a good party and the tins soon filled up... and up and up. Soon, we were going round collecting while dressed as soldiers, getting articles in the papers (not the fucking Daily Mail, of course) but The Scotsman, Glasgow Herald, etc, and this helped loads.

In five weeks, the floor of the unit was awash with coins. A count was organised and we had over £5,000 already, unbelievable. It was at this point I started to realise that maybe we were going to pull this off and the reality of going to a war zone began to sink in, and not just with me. Of the Desert Stormers that had been so keen to go a few weeks ago, the list was narrowing rapidly. Very rapidly. Sheona – of course – wanted to come, she would have jumped down a dragon's throat for Desert Storm (if she didn't fall over her own feet first), but this time her parents put their feet firmly down (who can blame them) and said no. I wanted Elaine to go, but she was in her last year at school and had exams, etc., and this was no weekend away! Smudge said he was going but then got cold feet after there was some massacre in Bosnia on the news. Etc, etc, etc.

As it drew into the last few weeks, only myself and Rob were definite. Two people. Oops. This was bad news, and as for Rob, well, he was my mate and a good guy, but a little scatter-brained and prone to taking strops if things didn't go his own way. I wasn't sure I could handle being cooped up with him in the cab of a truck for so long, but he was keen and he was definitely mad enough, so that was that. He had proved that on a skiing trip to Val d'Isère in the French Alps, as he led the way off-piste down the side of Grande Motte glacier and the legendary deadly couloirs, which we were both lucky to survive. A crazy guy for sure. As I've said before, as the missions get madder, only the mad go on the missions. And this was by far the craziest yet!

Sheona and I sat going through lists of prospective candidates. The problem was, we needed someone who was mad enough to go but not mad enough to put the mission in danger. One by one, for one reason or another, we crossed out the names until there was none left and then we sat there wondering what to do.

'Wait a minute,' I said, 'why don't we try widening the net?'

Sheona grabbed my address book and started turning the pages. After some time, we had settled on three names. Two from Manchester; Danny Baxter and Joe Marshall, and one from Nottingham, James Hoo Smiles. Sheona was a bit doubtful about Danny Baxter and said so.

'Keef, you know what he's like, if he goes with you, in nine months' time, there will be a little Danny in every fucking town from here to Bosnia!'

She was right. He was a serial shagger and had even hit on Elaine last time he was up. But he was a top DJ and defo mad enough to go.

His mate Joe was an inspired choice; a good friend, cool-headed and sensible but still hardcore. If he could be persuaded to come, the mission would be looking a whole lot better and I'd be a whole lot happier. Finally, James Hoo Smiles the Nottingham DJ. Him and his girlfriend Kerry were good people, keen and efficient, and again James was a top DJ. What did I have to lose? So, I got on the blower.

As I waited for an answer, it occurred to me that now I was in Paddy's place, phoning people out of the blue to ask them if they wanted to come to a war zone to do raves. Oh yeah, and at short notice! The boot was well and truly on the other foot now.

'Hello, James, it's Keef from Desert Storm. How's it hanging?'

'Hey, Keef,' replied the ever-bubbly James. 'What's happening, fella? You got another gig for me?'

'Err, yeah, you could say that.' I paused. 'Err, how do you fancy coming with us to Bosnia to do a rave this New Year?' The million-dollar question.

'Sorry, did you say Bosnia?'

'Yes, Bosnia, in the former Yugoslavia.'

'The war zone?'

There was no way out of that one. 'Eh, yes.'

Long pause.

'Yeah, okay.'

Wicked! He had agreed. As I filled him in on the details, I noticed I was downplaying the risk and overplaying how much I really knew about the whole deal. I wondered if Paddy had done the same with me? Anyway, James was in. One down, two to go.

Incredibly, Danny and Joe were totally up for it as well so now we had five definite, which in my mind, with a little help from WAB, was enough to hold a half-decent rave, cool!

There were only a few minor details to sort out now. Like a truck for a start! Unfortunately, none of us had ever driven a truck before and knew nothing about them. After looking in Auto Trader, we found a 7.5-tonne Leyland Daf Roadrunner for sale for £2,500; it had a large box and an electric tail lift. Seemed ideal, so we went to look at it. They say you should never buy the first thing you see, but it's always worked for me (but then I've got the devil's luck) and after a few minutes, the money changed hands and we were driving off in our new Storm mobile.

Greg (the dope-smoking joiner), who had kitted out the Desert Storm van, was called in, handed a big bag of weed and asked to crack on with the conversion. I wanted the back split into two parts; one a living area with three bunks, window, door, cupboards, sink and cooker, and then a dividing wall with a door leading to the storage area for the rig, etc. in the back. I helped Greg with the work while Sheona and Rob started making lists of things to do. The lists were long, the time was short, and it was just one week before the off.

We cut it right to the wire; the truck was still in a DAF garage getting serviced overnight on the day before we were due to leave. Finally, all was ready and Desert Storm gathered at the unit to say goodbye. The worried faces told their own stories, but I didn't give a shit, I was totally excited and raring to go. After a long parting with Elaine, I fired up the truck and without looking back, we were off.

We were to meet WAB, Danny and Joe in Manchester and then pick up James in Nottingham, so we took the M6 and were soon in the bleak windswept border hills heading for England. As for driving the truck, it was learned on the job and I couldn't help noticing how slow it was on the hills and how much the wind buffeted the huge box on the back; this was going to be a slow trip. But we arrived in Manchester with no dramas and soon were at the meeting point, a community hall in Hulme. Danny and Joe were already there waiting with bags and record boxes.

The other travellers were gathered too and we got our first look at them. There were eight trucks going together with a motley collection of well-spoken student types, a Geordie guy called Brian (I couldn't understand a word he said), an older guy who seemed to be in a bad mood and was already complaining about something (I had him figured as the morale hoover), the vegan chef (we had no idea how much trouble this would cause), Paddy and his girlfriend Lisa (an attractive blonde with a nice smile) and then there were us.

We all trooped into the hall for a meeting. It seemed so far that Paddy and Lisa had everything under control. They did a passport check, document check and then we sat and discussed the journey. Looking over, I was not surprised to see Danny was already in the corner deep in conversation with one of the student chicks, and by the way she kept shifting in her seat and looking into his eyes, I could tell it wouldn't be long before he had charmed the pants off her and she was on her back in the Storm truck being pumped silly on top of the bass bins. Meanwhile, I asked a few questions about the road, what countries we would be passing through, where we were getting the ferry from, things like that, and I had to admit it all looked sorted. Right away the morale hoover was trying to find problems, questioning Paddy's leadership, the guy was a nightmare and we hadn't even set off yet, for fuck's sake! Then I figured it out; he thought he should be in charge and was going to fight Paddy all the way, this guy was trouble. Anyway, the meeting finished and as we were going to Nottingham first, we set off and arranged to meet them in Dover.

James Hoo Smiles's friends were all at his house to see him off, and by the looks on their faces they thought it was for the last time. His girlfriend Kerry (another fit blonde), whom I'd met before in Glasgow, was there fussing over him, checking he had everything. James, however, seemed totally relaxed, if anything excited, but no sign of fear. James and his friends had collected aid to take, which seemed to consist mainly of hundreds of tins of baked beans and pork sausages, which I looked over doubtfully (was Bosnia not a Muslim country? If so, they don't eat pork!) but I said nothing and loaded them on the truck to be polite. Well, at least we wouldn't starve. He had also been given collecting tins so he could raise some money, but it seemed he had lunched it and had little cash. Luckily, we had shit loads, about £3,500.

On the road again, we rolled some fat spliffs. I had brought a good supply of hash (but probably not enough) and James had a bag of grass so it was a very stoned Desert Storm truck that arrived at Dover where the rest were waiting at the port.

Paddy looked at us knowingly as we opened the door and a cloud of ganja smoke poured out of the cab and into the night. I just smiled at him and we checked in. Joe and Danny had been in the back on the way here but as they climbed out, even I stared in disbelief when the student chick from Manchester also jumped down with her face flushed and her clothes a mess! I mean, how the fuck did he manage it? She must have been stashed up in there all the fucking way to Dover.

These days, and a hundred crossings later, it would be just be another ferry trip for me, but then it was fresh. I hadn't even driven on the right-hand side of the road before, so pulling off the ferry at Calais and into the dawn light was the beginning of an adventure and we were all hyped up to the max.

We stopped in at the next services, to cook a meal in the car park, take on fuel, and sort the route out. Right away, the morale hoover was challenging the direction, the timings, the lot. The rest were being very diplomatic with the guy, trying to talk it all through, but I'd had enough of this dickhead already and decided to act.

'Listen, pal, why don't you just shut the fuck up. Paddy's in charge and if he says we do this or we go that way then that's what's going to fucking happen, okay?'

The morale hoover opened his mouth to say something, but catching sight of my angry black man stare, thought twice about it, and with the dirtiest look he could muster, fucked off back to his truck.

Some of the others looked shocked. Such language! This wasn't the way WAB committees conducted their affairs, but Paddy looked at me with a half-smile and a nod. I could tell that we were going to be friends. As for the rest, only Geordie Brian seemed to openly support me, but as I couldn't understand a word he said, I wasn't sure. Well, they had invited Desert Storm along for the ride, so it was like it or lump it time. The cook prepared a vegan meal. We were starving, and although I knew in theory what a vegan was (no meat, dairy products, eggs, etc.) the reality of eating it was a different matter. It tasted like fucking cardboard. James, a fellow carnivore like me, just tipped it in the bucket, while some of the others complimented the chef as they desperately tried to swallow the inedible goo. Luckily, we had a year's supply of baked beans and sausages in the back of the truck!

The journey after that consisted of long periods at the wheel with shorts stops and even shorter sleeps. It got to the stage where we were changing drivers while moving! Don't try this at home folks; the driver would lean forward over the steering wheel while the next one would slip in behind. Well it was better than falling asleep at the wheel, just.

France, Belgium, Germany all rolled past, and by the time we had reached Bavaria in south, the novelty of driving a truck had totally worn off, so when we started to climb into the snowclad mountains of Austria, it was a welcome change, except for the freezing cold that is; temperatures at night in the back of the truck dropped to -17 degrees and it was common to wake up with your sleeping bag frozen to the side of the wall, but at least during the day we had the heater in the cab, unlike the Leeds University truck which had no heating at all!

Finally, the border with Slovenia was reached and we crossed over. This was our first taste of things to come; stuck at the border waiting for our papers to be cleared, nightmare. Twenty-four hours later, we got through and soon were on the coast road and into Croatia. The Dalmatian coast is a place of extreme natural beauty and as the sun rose over the Mediterranean and onto the white faces of the surrounding mountains, they glowed red in the dawn. It took our breath away. Mind you, so did the road which winds along the side of the cliff with only the occasional concrete block between you and a deadly one-hundred-metre drop onto the jagged rocks below. That focused the mind and we were no longer messing about in the cab but staring ahead and judging every turn.

There are two winds in that area, and they have names. The first is the Yugo, the wind that comes in from the sea, cool as it blows against the mountains and the other is the Mistral, a different beast, chill and strong, it gusts down the gullies and blasts out into the Med. It was full on Mistral as we began our journey down the coast and every so often, the truck would be buffeted towards the edge of the cliff and we would have to brake hard to regain control and continue on. After many hours of this, nerves were frayed and as the wind worsened, we were starting to think it would be safer to pull in before disaster struck. After an extra strong gust, I was just telling the others that we should stop.

'Look, guys, I don't like this. That last gust nearly had us over.'

Looking down at the dizzying drop, I could see a smashed truck far below on the rocks. 'Shit, look down there.' Rob and James leaned over to look. Well, there was no way you were walking away from that one.

'We'll be okay,' said James, who had just rolled a spliff, 'fate wouldn't put us over while we're smoking this.' And he held up the joint.

At that instant, a gust many times stronger than any that had come before grabbed the side of the truck. I looked over at James and he was right up in the air, and out of his side window all I could see was sky. We were up on two fucking wheels only metres from the edge.

'Oh shit, we're going to die,' I said, stating the obvious as James and Rob slid towards me. In the back, the rig and the cargo banged over to my side with a horrific crash making the situation even worse. A corner going the wrong way was coming up and it looked like the end. The only thing I could think of was to force the steering wheel hard to the left. This caused the truck to dip forward onto my front wheel. The suspension and running gear groaned in protest as the whole weight of the vehicle shifted forward, passing the design tolerances by a factor of umpteen as the suspension springs bottomed out. We hung there almost on one wheel for an instant as the truck decided whether to flip completely and plunge over the edge or right itself. Well, if it hadn't righted itself you wouldn't be reading this as the writer would have been dashed to bits on the rocks, but how it did so, I'll never know. A hundred to one chance, I reckon, but it did and the wheels scuffed the edge of the cliff as I hauled her back to safety. We pulled in on the wrong side of the road, as close to the wall as possible, and just sat there in shock with the engine off.

I grabbed the spliff off James and started toking for Scotland.

'James, don't you ever, ever say anything like that again!'

James just nodded weakly. Then there was a faint knocking noise coming from the back. Shit, we had totally forgotten about Danny and Joe sleeping in the bunks! Leaning out of my window, I saw Danny's head appear out of the side window of the box, hair all over the place and sunglasses totally squinted to one side with the lenses smashed. All he said was, 'What the fuck?' I burst out laughing.

After a long discussion, it was decided that we would continue. The rig and aid cargo were loaded onto the coastal side of the truck and it was agreed that as the wind got up or we approached a gully, the Desert Storm truck would pull onto the wrong side of the road and a cover truck would move in beside us in case it happened again. So, we slowly and carefully continued on our way like this with our next target, the coastal town of Split, still many hours' drive to the south.

As we neared Split, the road wound its way down to sea level and the wind dropped, much to our relief. Split itself was a disappointment; I had seen photos of Dubrovnik, the picturesque walled medieval coastal town that was further south and I was expecting much the same, but Split was a nasty modern industrial port and at first sight, the locals looked none too friendly, not a smile in sight.

We were to park up at the UN base outside of town and we arrived to find a vast area of white military vehicles and a warehouse and camp surrounded by razor wire. Although it was only early evening, WAB all went straight to sleep, (except for Geordie Brian, who had wasted no time in attaching himself to Desert Storm) but we wanted some beers and headed into the town. Parking up the truck, we soon found a booze shop and I was leafing through my Serbo-Croatian phrasebook as we waited at the counter. But the assistant must have heard us talking, smiled, and broke into pretty good English.

'Hello, my friend, what would you like?'

'Ah, yes.' I put away my phrase book. 'I want beer, one case, cold beer, please,' I replied, keeping my English simple.

Soon we had an ice-cold case of finest Croat Pivo but the guy wasn't letting us away so easily. He wanted to know if it was our first time in Croatia, wasn't the coast road beautiful, etc, etc. I was pretty certain this was leading somewhere and sure enough next thing, he was trying to flog us some of the local fire water called Slivovitz, a plum brandy. Anything for an easy life, so we took a bottle. His last question was where we were headed to. Without thinking, I said we were part of an aid convoy to Bosnia. His face went hard and cold as he stared at me, friendly no longer. Oops, I suddenly remembered, these guys are at war. Talk about putting your foot in it! He basically threw the change at me and as we beat a hasty retreat, we could hear him shouting to others in the back shop. We legged it.

We were nearly back at the truck, crossing the final road, when James roughly pulled me back, nearly throwing me to the ground, as a small white car screamed past at an insane speed. I could just make out two soldiers in it. The car had no chance of making the corner and crashed though some road works, jumping fully a metre in the air and landing on the front end on top of a huge concrete block, a pool of fuel and oil forming quickly underneath it. We just stood mouths open as the driver tried to start her up! The concrete must have punctured the engine casing because as it turned over, sparks were flying from the damaged flywheel onto the road and into the fuel, but even if it had started, the front wheels weren't even touching the ground. It got worse as the passenger got out with a cigarette dangling out of his mouth, a rifle slung over his shoulder and started shouting encouragement to the driver. It was then I noticed a bottle very similar to the one we had just bought dangling from his hand. It was too much for me and I ran over; had they not seen the petrol on the deck? I pulled up short as he swung the rifle round in my direction while swaying unsteadily on his feet. I backed up slowly, keeping both my hands in view. Fuck them if they wanted to die in a burning fireball, good luck to them, so we headed off. Just as we pulled away in the truck, an explosion rocked the area. James looked down at the plum brandy bottle in his hand. 'Slivovitz, eh, must be pretty strong shit,' he observed. We shouldn't have laughed but couldn't help it.

Back at the UN base, we sat smoking the last of the dope and drinking. The slivovitz tasted like shit, I mean really bad, but chased down with cold beer it certainly worked, and by midnight we were all totally panelled and had the stereo in the cab blasting out the tunes as we danced about drunkenly in the car park. It wasn't long before the morale hoover was up complaining about the noise. We told him to fuck off and get a life. He fucked off all right, but I doubt if he ever got a life.

Next morning, as we sat nursing our hangovers, there was stony silence and withering looks cast by some tired-looking faces in our direction. The morale hoover looked pleased as for once, some people were on his side.

I couldn't be arsed with the petty politics and headed over to talk to some British squaddies that were standing at the gate to the base.

'All right, guys?' I ventured. 'What's happening then?' They looked cold and despondent.

'Oh, not much, we've been staging on this gate for the last twelve hours. We're fucking snapped.'

'Oh,' I replied.

The other one spoke up.

'Hey, was that you guys playing the tunes in the car park last night? They were pumping. I don't suppose you got a cassette? I've not had any new music for months.'

I explained that for sure I could sort him a cassette and that we were Desert Storm sound system headed to Bosnia for a rave.

'Bosnia for a rave?'

They looked at me as if I was crazy but I was used to this by now.

'Whereabouts in Bosnia, then?' they continued.

'Eh, Tuzla, as far as I know.'

'TUZLA? Fucking hell, that's way up north.' They exchanged stunned looks. 'Even we wouldn't dare go up there, that's bandit country!'

'Hmm,' I replied. Not really what I wanted to hear, so I changed the subject.

'So, it's Christmas Eve tomorrow. What's your plans?'

They looked dejected again.

'Nothing, we're just stuck here. There was some trouble in town last week so we're confined to base.'

That gave me an idea.

'Confined to base? Does that include the loading bays over there?' I asked, pointing over to the nearby abandoned warehouse.

They looked over.

'No, we can go there, it's just the town that's out of bounds. Why do you ask?'

A couple of hours later, we parked the trucks against the raised roofed loading bay to make a wall, set up the rig and backdrops and were planning a trip into town to get the bar. Rumour of the party spread like wildfire and squaddies were coming over constantly to check it out. This was just what they, and us, needed and even the morale hoover got stuck in and helped look for tables for the decks and bar.

It kicked off at ten p.m. (or 2200 hours in military speak) and it was heaving! The place was crammed out and the drink was flowing like water. It didn't matter what records we played, the soldiers had been cooped up for so long they didn't give a shit. There were no women there apart from the WAB ones, and it was a little worrying to see grown men in blonde wigs, bras, and suspenders dancing on the bar. But I suppose that's just what squaddies do. More worrying was the obvious bullying that was going on; some of the meaner-looking ones basically had the weaker ones as slaves, fetching them drinks, etc, and they referred to them as their 'bitches', but apart from that, it was all pretty friendly and we all danced in a group, arms around shoulders at midnight and sang 'Rudolph, the Red-Nosed Reindeer' at the top of our voices while pouring drinks over our heads.

By about three in the morning, the CO obviously had had enough and sent the MPs over to clear the place out and that was that, but a good night was had by all.

Next day, Christmas Eve was a late rise. I staggered out of the truck, mouth tasting like an ashtray, to see the guard on the gate throwing up in the bushes. Paddy got everyone up and told them we had to get moving as we were cutting it fine for getting to Tuzla for the New Year. There were some complaints about it being Christmas, but Paddy would not be moved, so soon it was time for the off and waving goodbye to the base we drove away. As we left, I couldn't help noticing how well-armoured the UN vehicles were and remembered the conversation with the squaddies about how even they wouldn't dare go as far as Tuzla. I kept these thoughts to myself.

The road to Bosnia wound its way up high into the hills and bit by bit degenerated into little more than a wide farm track. Going was slow and tempers were fraying when we finally reached the border and stopped in the inevitable massive queue at the customs. Great, looked like we would be spending Christmas stuck here!

We had hardly stepped out of the cab and the morale hoover was already kicking off. We should have gone a different way, we should have done this, it was all Paddy's fault we were stuck here. I was wishing he would go a different way. If he just took a few more steps back he would, right over the fucking edge and a good one-hundred-feet drop into the forest below. Finally, he shut up, stormed off, and we all sat in silence smoking cigarettes waiting for the daily vegan gruel to be cooked. Today's variation of lentil death finally appeared and even the normally polite Leeds students couldn't bring themselves to look pleased at the green slop. As I lifted the spoon for my first mouthful, I sniffed the air, was that meat I could smell? I looked over at the source to see the morale hoover greedily tucking into a plate of sausages.

'What?' he asked, looking back at me, 'I couldn't handle another day of that puke he calls food. Thinks he's a chef? My dog eats better than that, so I knocked these up, and they are very nice too!'

For once, I had to agree with him, but he wasn't offering any out. The chef looked over at him as realisation slowly dawned on him.

'Meat? Where the fuck did you prepare that?'

The moral hoover replied, 'In the kitchen area, of course, where do you think?' and continued eating.

'You... you... cooked MEAT in my kitchen?' The chef was shaking with anger. 'Which fucking pan did you use?'

By now, we had all stopped eating and were looking at the two of them. Realising maybe something was wrong, the morale hoover stopped eating and looked up.

'Well, err, I cooked them in the frying pan of course. What else should I use?' he replied defensively.

The chef stood up, throwing the lentil death on the ground, he looked like he was about to cry.

'You used my good pans to cook meat? That's them ruined; I can never cook in them again. You selfish bastard, you... you... Neanderthal!'

'Now steady on, chef,' replied the morale hoover, 'I'll wash them up, okay?'

But chef was having none of it and stormed over to the cooking area and started throwing the pots over the fucking cliff edge, and not just the frying pan! The morale hoover got up to try and stop him and soon they were pushing each other in the chest getting ready to fight.

I couldn't help laughing. This was top entertainment and I shouted out, '20 Deutschmarks on the hoover!' But it didn't come to blows and

I left the rest and headed back to the Storm truck with Danny's girl shouting after me that I should grow up and a guy like me should be trying to calm the situation instead of always inflaming it. I shouted back that I hoped Danny shagged her to death and slammed the door. Well, well, tensions in the group were certainly growing, that was for sure.

Christmas Day was spent as expected, stuck in the line at the customs. To relieve the boredom, our crew got out our passports and walked through the border to a shack that passed for the local bar and drank the day away then staggered back to the trucks and crashed out. Next morning, the papers were finally cleared and we trundled away very hungover and in need of a shower, well glad to leave the border and head down onto the plain.

Time was short now, so we drove hell for leather north for Tuzla passing through such delights as Mostar. The main delay was the interminable check points; sometimes these were just a few barrels and some hillbillies with AK-47s. They just wanted money, so Paddy would grease some palms and off we would go. After forty-eight hours, we were making good progress. It was 27 December and it looked like we might make it in time for the New Year!

Publisher's Note

The Dayton Peace Accord was signed in December 1995, which prompted Desert Storm's trip to Bosnia one last time. Sarajevo, the capital which had been under constant siege for the previous three years, would be their final stop, and this time they would ditch the university students and aid convoys who they'd accompanied the previous two times to carry out one more ultimate, if risky, party. After all, they'd organised parties across Europe during the trip there to raise money for those affected by the war, so it was only fair that the people of the capital got to have the Desert Storm-standard rave experience too, right?

But it wasn't smooth sailing. First, they were confronted with a £2,150 charge to cross the Austria-Slovenia border due to the documents they needed to sign to declare the statistical value of their equipment (totalled at £4,300). They didn't have the savings and opted to falsify the documents instead.

James: So, what we're now doing is falsifying the documents to try and get across, so we're gonna change it to something we can afford, like 20p and throw it at them.

Keith: Unbelievably, the forged documents got us through the border and into Slovenia. Desert Storm are used to overcoming obstacles, there's always a way of sorting it. However, our next problem was much more serious.

Next, the truck's gearbox broke and they were stuck in the middle of a field in Slovenia. They found a nearby pub and, after a few pints for their sorrows, phoned DAF in Scotland to supply a new one, paid for on James's dad's credit card. With nothing to do other than wait and drink, and with Desert Storm soon becoming the talk of the town, they decided to put on a rave in a local venue. A good time had by all, the next day they fit in the newly arrived gearbox in sub-zero temperatures and drove two days through Croatia, non-stop, to make up for lost time. After hearing that a Christmas party for 1,500 squaddies in a UN transit van was cancelled, they decided to stop in Split and throw a free party to raise the mood. They invited the squaddies and made preparations (Danny: 'I am actually sorting the aid out as well at this stage, I'm not just looking for the [magic] mushrooms.' James: 'Apparently they've got the sniffer dogs out as well, [they can] sniff out the magic mushrooms for us.'), it was time to get on the decks.

Keith: It was a bit of a disaster, really. Only about ten people turned up. The rest were all too scared of getting caught by the military cops.

Joe: The military police turned up, like nineteen-year-old lads – one of them looked like he was on fucking speed. Shone their little touches [and yelled], 'Seen any squaddies round 'ere? Seen any squaddies round 'ere?' I said, 'No, mate, no'.

Keith: I mean, it worked okay as far as I'm concerned. It was fine.

As they drove towards Bosnia, they encountered more signs of the war: overgrown weeds, crumbled buildings and an air of trepidation. Keith's determination and the importance of Desert Storm reaching Sarajevo amidst the reality of the war-torn landscape only intensified.

Keith: People may ask, 'Why take a sound system to a warzone?' Well, we don't think music's a luxury. We think it's an essential. Yet it's always one of the first casualties of war. As the conflict drags on, the stress of living with the constant risk of death increases daily, building up like a pressure cooker. People need to forget the war and feel like normal human beings again, even if it's just for one night. How can anybody put a price on that?

Closer now to Sarajevo, and with a truck full of hitchhiking soldiers, they passed through another border check and arrived at the capital the following morning. Radio Wor, a local young person's radio station, invited Keith to play some music as a sample of what to expect the following day in person, and he encouraged everyone who was listening to spread the word and come. Everything was looking up.

They stopped at the local orphanage and delivered aid and toys to the children who had been orphaned or separated from their family during the war. Although there was a language barrier between the kids and Keith, they seemed to get on just fine, and Keith had them in fits of laughter with his expressions and gestures.

Soon enough it was time for what they'd travelled across Europe for. Driving through the streets of Sarajevo all afternoon, they blasted their tunes to publicise the free party they were to throw that evening.

Passersby, with encouragement from Keith, James and Joe, danced in the street as the truck drove past – kids even held onto the doors and ran in tandem with the moving vehicle! With spirits up, it was time for the much-anticipated event…

Keith: Klub Obala was packed, and the people were desperate to dance. Obala was the only club to stay open during the three-year siege. It was the climax to our trip. We had brought what we did best in recognition of what they had been through, and the need to forget about the war just for one night.

If you would like to watch the documentary footage of Desert Storm's trip to Sarajevo, narrated by Keith Robinson, you can find it on YouTube under the title 'Storming Sarajevo (Desert Storm.flv)'. All dialogue featured in this extract is from the aforementioned video.

16

SPIRALLED ON A DMT TRIP

I was sitting in my Kersland Street flat in Glasgow on a slow Friday night with Sheona and Smudge when the phone rang. It was Debbie from Spiral Tribe. I answered with my usual bullshit.

'Hi, Desert Storm International, which department please?'

'Yeah, right, Keef, it's Debbie SP23 here, are you busy?'

'Busy?' I replied, a little puzzled, 'What right now? No, not really, why?'

'Well, do you think you could come down to London?'

'Can't see why not. When?'

'Now.'

That got my attention. This sounded interesting. I sat forward in my chair. 'Right now?'

She got straight to the point.

'Yes, right now. I've been saving one hit of a special drug from South America here just for you.'

At last it had happened, it could only be dimethyltryptamine – or DMT for short. DMT was more myth and rumour than reality, at least for me and my mates. It was supposed to be the ultimate hallucinogenic, lets you talk to the gods and shit like that. Danny and I had first heard of it, a couple of years ago, from this old hippy weirdo at some party. He was banging on about it, how incredible it was. He said DMT is stored in a gland in the back of your neck, and when you die, it's released into your brain to move your soul into the after world, or hippy heaven in this guy's case, (unbelievably this bit is really true) so by smoking it when you're still alive, you're fooling your brain into thinking it has died! Serious shit. The strange thing is it only lasts around fifteen minutes to an hour. This is because your body recognises it and quickly breaks it down. Now, most normal people wouldn't try this shit if it was the last drug on earth, but for me and Danny, it was top of the must-do list. When asked where we could get some, the hippy replied it was only made in South America, from some weird plant though I later learned there were also trees and even a toad that produced it, or something very chemically close to it.

It was a yellow/orange powder or a white powder or white/yellow crystals. There seemed to be various versions depending on how it had been extracted. To ingest it, you smoked it. But as to where we could get it, fuck knew, as it was very difficult to find. But if we cultivated an air of expectancy, it would come to us. Now that's a weird thing to say; 'cultivate an air of expectancy and it will come to you'. But we did exactly that and low and behold, seemingly it had come.

'Debbie, are you talking about DMT?'

'Eh, yes, how did you know that?'

'Let's just say I've been expecting it.'

'So, you're coming down then?'

'On the next train,' I said, bade Debbie goodbye and hung up.

Jumping up, I grabbed my towel and headed to the shower, shouting behind me, 'Sheona, can you phone me a taxi to Central Station, please. I'm off to London.'

For some reason, or for no reason at all, my anticipation reminded me of the time I'd opened a coffee shop on Kersland Street, called The Cosmic Café. But this wasn't any old coffee shop; we wanted to bring the weed-selling cafés in Amsterdam to the streets of Glasgow's West End. The printed menus displayed the names of the products including Power Plant, Purple Haze and Hindu Kush, as well as ready-rolled joints, cold beer, coffee and space cake.

Now the problem with space cake is it tastes so good (ours was just a chocolate brownie mix with hash butter melted in). You just want to eat more and more and it takes ages to come up on it, so you think that it's not working and you munch more (also, due to inexperience, we had maybe put a tad too much hash in it). Soon the punters were totally fucked, high as motherfuckers and rolling about in fits of laughter and spilling beer.

My mate Dougie Kennedy's girlfriend had eaten too much especially. She was convinced that we were all out to get her and had to be persuaded not to jump from the window. The last thing I remember was locking the door behind the last customer as he staggered out and then I crashed out in a corner, only to wake up much later wondering where the hell I was. But all in all, it was fucking wicked. A total success. We repeated it once a month for about four months until we got bored of it.

I arrived the next morning and jumped the number 20 bus for Tulse Hill and the Spiral house. After the hellos and a little small talk, we got straight down to business.

'We only had twelve hits of this stuff and there's only one left. I decided it should be you who gets it.'

As Debbie talked, I looked out of the window and beyond her to the bus depot across the road. There was a line of number 23 buses parked facing me, and the image of her short dark hair and piercing, keen, gaze surrounded by 23s gave me a weird feeling in my stomach.

'So, Debbie, you've taken this stuff?'

'For fuck's sake, of course!' she replied

Then I asked the burning question. 'So, what's it like?'

She paused. 'Well, it's hard to describe, I think it's different for different people, but it's not like other drugs. This is the real deal. It's like what I thought drugs were like before I had taken any. It's not like acid, where you come up gradually and reality distorts at the edges, you take this shit and you're gone instantly. The only way to find out what it's like is, to, well, take it.'

With that, she put her hand out, palm up, and opened it slowly, to reveal a small bag with orangey-looking crystals in it.

I could feel my heart rate increasing and, looking her in the eye, said, 'Well, there's no time like the present, let's do it.'

'That's what I like about you, Keef, no bullshit,' she replied laughing, and stood up to close the curtains.

She sat me on the floor on some cushions in the darkened room and explained what was to happen next.

'Okay, you need to be on the floor when it hits you, because basically, you'll pass out and I wouldn't want to bang your head. I will hold the pipe for you and you suck for Scotland and hold it in as long as you can, you've got to get as much as you can in you because it's not like a spliff; you can't smoke half and get half the hit. It's more like...' she paused, trying to find the words. '...more like a horse jumping a fence, it either makes it or it doesn't.'

She started loading a small glass pipe with the crystals. My heart was pounding now.

Debbie pulled out a lighter, knelt beside me and got ready to light the pipe. My palms were sweating and I had to wipe them on my trousers a few times and take some deep breaths.

'Are you scared?' she asked softly.

'Yes,' I replied.

'Well, you should be, this shit is mental. Oh, and another thing, I stopped breathing when I took it, so remember to breathe.'

Fuck's sake, I thought, nice time to tell me.

She lifted the pipe to my mouth and lit the lighter. 'Ready?' she asked.

'Ready as I'll ever be,' I replied, trying to remember what she'd told me. Breathe deep, hold in, jump the fence, fucking mental, remember to breathe.

'Now,' she said, and the lighter flame danced on the DMT. I sucked for fucking Scotland and noticed a sharp, not unpleasant tang as the smoke went down my throat. I was just thinking... well, nothing so far, when it started.

First there was a ringing noise in my ears, then patterns of colours like Paisley pattern fractals covered over the shapes in the room, and Debbie stooping over the burning pipe looked like some elfin sorceress from Lord of the Rings. Then I was gone.

It was like, what I imagine, taking off in the space shuttle is like, incredible acceleration, a weight pushing down on you, and then weightlessness. I remember thinking, oh shit you've really fucked it this time, then I passed out. When I came to, I was somewhere totally different. It felt like outer space or a void or something, and there I was curled up in the foetal position, naked, just floating there, scared shitless, convinced I was dead.

It was then I heard the laughter. It seemed to come from thousands of voices, and to be all around me, maybe coming from the little white lights buzzing about my body. Then they spoke to me.

'We have been waiting for you, don't be afraid, we have things to show you.'

It sounded like hundreds of people talking at once, but clear as a bell.

And before I had time to even think about it, we were off, high above the earth, zooming down to the surface at an impossible speed. The only thing I can compare it to is the way Google Earth zooms in to show you where stuff is on the news. Anyway, we arrived at a hotel room in Moscow, where two people were making out on the bed. I understood that this was my mother and father, my beginning. Then away and off to Scotland, the images of my life flashed like a camera shutter in front of me, many years in a few seconds. Sometimes it paused for an instant as if some crossing point was reached, I think they were trying to tell me that that's where the timelines crossed and things could have been changed (I know that doesn't make much sense), then quickly off to South America and a strange-looking man, a shaman maybe, picking and preparing the plant, then it crossed the Atlantic. Next was my journey to London and there I was in the Spirals' house talking to Debbie.

They spoke again.

'Don't you see that all the things in your life have led to this moment...' More laughter... *'but your life is not real, this is what things really are.'*

We were still in Debbie's front room but now everything was transparent, and you could see millions of flashes of energy connected by a spider's web of filaments covering everything.

The image of London faded and we were back in the void. Something was forming in front of me, a face, but not a human one. It was vaguely human-like, a little lion-like too, and golden, with a swirling mass of kind of gold dreadlocks with sparks coming out of them, and the eyes were just glowing orbs. What is was I couldn't tell you, a god an alien, fuck knows, but it looked like a cross between the Predator alien and the Sphinx. Then, he, she, or it spoke, without moving the lips. The words echoing in my mind.

'LISTEN CAREFULLY.' Yeah, right, what else was I going to do. *'WE HAVE A JOB FOR YOU. YOUR JOB IN THIS REALITY IS TO PUT THE MUSIC ON.'* Okay, fair enough, I can do that. *'DON'T WORRY ABOUT WHAT HAPPENS TO YOU WHEN YOU GET OLDER. WE WILL LOOK AFTER YOU. NOW GO!'* Cue more laughter.

With that, I was gone. I slowly opened my eyes and realised I was on my back on the floor with Debbie over the top of me, shaking my shoulders.

'Keef, Keef, wake up. Oh, thank fuck for that. You had stopped breathing. I thought you were... were... gone.'

'So did I...' I replied, croaking as my mouth was so dry.

'Here, sit up and drink this.' She put a glass of water to my lips and I eagerly gulped it down.

'So how was it?' she asked, looking into my eyes.

I felt this all-encompassing smile spread across my face. 'It was... it was...' Words failed me. '...unbelievable!'

Debbie nodded. 'It was the same for me.' And she gave me a big hug. Time passed.

'Debbie?' I said finally.

'Yes?'

'I've got a job to do.'

Okay, now you're probably thinking this guy is truly loony tunes, or he's making it all up, that is if you haven't taken DMT of course, then you'd know exactly what I'm talking about. But as you may have noticed already, in some ways I'm not quite playing with a full deck, and in another way, I am making it up. Let me explain...

I have given quite a few people DMT and I, like Debbie, have guided them through the process. And when they first come round, they all have that strange smile and a faraway, dreamy look. When you ask them what it was like, they can't describe it. They know what happened, but they just can't seem to express it in words. I believe this is because there are no words to describe it, the place you go is so different from this reality that there literally are no words for it. Picture this, imagine trying to explain to a caveman what a motor car was. He might get the '*you sit in it bit*', maybe even '*it runs faster than a deer in full flight,* but the gearbox, wheels, bonnet, exhaust pipe... starting to get the picture? Of course, it would be impossible. Now although the drug only lasts 15–45 minutes, the aftereffects go on for weeks, even years, maybe you're never the same again. Anyway, over the next few days, you will find yourself suddenly remembering the trip. Things that were unclear before will start to form into solid ideas. This is you putting an interpretation on things you don't understand. Back to the caveman. Let's say you take him for a quick spin in the motor car. It's going to be a bit of a shock for him. After you drop him off and you're gone and he's trying to explain to his woman what happened, well he's got a problem there, hasn't he?

'*Darling, roaring animal, breathing fire from the back, climbing inside the belly of the beast, running fast, faster than antelope, now I'm back.*'

'*Dear, have you been on those mushrooms again?*'

So, two options. You tricked your brain into thinking it's dead and your soul goes to another reality where you talk to aliens?

Or...

Your brain shuts down in some way and invents all these things to pass the time, and subconscious fears surface, like my fear of what I'm going to do when I get older, for instance?

Who knows? But one thing for sure, when you think you're on a mission from aliens, you sure get on with the job!

17

NAPLES, ROBBERY, MAFIA AND DRUGS EVERY DAY

The walls of Fintek were closing in; the rats, the rubbish and the 'lost its' were getting on our nerves so we decided to head south, leave Rome for a bit and rave it up in Naples (or Napoli as it is correctly known). One of the girls in Hekate was from there so we already had our local contact.

First, we needed fuel, so a midnight mission was organised, robbery by night. Myself and a few others headed out in Alex's van to look for a target, but the problem was we had skanked that much diesel around Rome already that it was hard to find a new place. Eventually, we decided to revisit an old skank, never a good idea, but we had no choice, the idea of paying for fuel wasn't even mentioned. Hoods up, hoses out, we scaled the fence and found what we needed. It seemed the yard didn't give a fuck anyway and hadn't upped security since our last visit. It went like clockwork and soon we were headed back to Fintek, stinking of diesel, with all the fuel we could need, nae bother!

Next morning, we were ready to roll, the three sound systems (Desert Storm, Tomahawk and Hekate) in at least eight trucks, a van, and a car, lined up at the gates, revving their engines, and then we were off! I led in the military truck, soft top rolled back, side windows folded away, and Kerry and the dogs in the front, stereo pumping, big smiles all round and enjoying the sunshine.

It's always great to hit the road again after being stopped for a while, especially in a squat as nasty as Fintek, and to be going to a new town to do some parties was a good feeling. The atmosphere in the convoy as we rolled out the gates sounding the horns was ecstatic! It's why we were on the road in the first place. What could possibly go wrong?

Naples is about 150 kilometres south of Rome and we planned to travel along the coast, and with Kerry navigating, there should be no problems. As soon as you go south of Rome, you can't help but notice a change; the people are much poorer, out is the Dolmio advert of plush olive groves and smiling grannies of the north and in are the potholed roads, dusty rundown towns and the litter-strewn beaches. This was unexpected and took a bit of the gloss off the trip, for me at any rate, and when we stopped for lunch, the beach was covered in cotton buds, tampons and syringes, a sure sign that raw sewage is being pumped into the sea nearby. No swimming for us then.

On we went and pulled up for the night, not far north of Naples, on another nasty beach, outside a little town, Shitsville South Italy. Immediately we were being dicked around by guys on Vespas, circling the trucks and then zooming off. Normally, people were curious about us and they would stop in to see what was happening, maybe even join us for a beer. Italians are sociable people, and there were Italians with us, even some of the English, like Charlie, spoke the lingo pretty decently, so right away it was strange and unwelcoming, and usually you could bet your bottom dollar that within the hour the local cops would pay a visit to make sure we weren't stealing anything or planning to stay permanently, but they didn't show either. Myself and a few other of the older heads had a bad feeling about this place and with much moaning from the rest of the posse got the trucks moved into more of a circle for defence rather than strung out all over the place. We lit a fire and settled in for the night.

I was tucked up in bed with Kerry just going off to sleep when I heard the noise of a speedboat in the bay. Now that's strange, I thought, speedboats at night? Next, I heard motorbikes and a vehicle approaching and our dogs started barking. Tahi the pitbull was up, face pressed to the window, letting out her fearsome *I'm going to eat you motherfucker* growl. Kerry nudged me with her elbow and ordered me to get up and see what was going on. Reluctantly, I did as I was told, got my boots on and pulled the curtain to the side, peering out into the night. Well, something was happening anyway. Vehicles were parked, engines still running, about twenty metres away from the trucks with their lights off. Could it be the cops, I wondered. But lights off? And what about the boat? Slipping a metal bar from under the bed, I slid it up my sleeve, grabbed my torch, and headed out with the dog.

By now, a few others were up and we headed to the edge of the circle and looked out. Immediately. three men moved towards us and started shouting in Italian. One had a pickaxe shaft in his hand, so I got ready to lose the pole. Tahi jumped forward barking but I called her back.

Unable to understand what they were saying, I turned to my Italian mate Marco.

'They say,' he translated, 'who gave you permission to stay on this beach? This is our beach, you have no business here, I give you five minutes to leave, or we're going to fuck you up.'

Obviously not the cops then.

'Their beach, yeah, right. Tell them to suck my dick and taste the difference, Marco.'

I was just about to add go fuck your own asses in my best Italian when Marco grabbed my arm.

'No, no, Keef,' he said urgently, 'these people are mafia, very dangerous. We must go, go now... via, via.'

Well, Marcos isn't what I would call a shrinking violet, and if he reckoned we were out of our league, then we should split. Luckily, the French Tomahawk posse hadn't bothered their arses to get up, as they wouldn't back down to anyone and things would have, for sure, got nasty. A quick chat with the rest and it was agreed. In double time, we packed the trucks and got moving. The last image I had as we pulled away from the beach was of something being loaded out of the speedboat and onto the shore! We rejoined the road and pulled in at the next services and parked up there. Before I turned in Marco came over to my truck.

'Well, Keef, welcome to Napoli,' he said, smiling grimly.

I didn't say anything. I was mulling over a conversation back in Rome when the idea of going to Naples had first been mentioned. As I recalled, Marco had been dead against it, warning that it was a heavy town, controlled by something called the Camorra, a faction of mafia by all accounts. Well, it was too late now. We had set a date, the flyers were already out in Rome, and the rave was two-weeks tonight. That was that.

In the morning, we went our merry way, the plan being to park up on the outskirts of Napoli and get the train in for a look around and some flyering. We parked up on a quiet street across from a police station and jumped the train into town. Arriving at the station, I was hit right away by the hustle and bustle of the place, there were hawkers everywhere selling stuff, everything from dodgy DVDs to aftershave. Settling down at a bar in the square, we had a beer and an ice cream then split into groups – some to flyer likely punters and others to find the local record shop etc, and meet back at the station in two hours. Flyering is easy once you get the hang of it; you don't give them to everyone, no way, that would be completely pointless. It takes a certain type of person to want to go to an illegal rave, and probably no one on the planet was better at spotting them than us.

Everything went well and we met back up to return to the trucks. On the train back sitting with the dogs, looking out of the window at Mount Vesuvius above, and the bright blue Mediterranean below, and with my arm round Kerry, I was content, life was good.

As we walked to the trucks in the sunshine, we discussed our next move, and it wasn't till I got close to the door, I realised something was wrong, very wrong.

'Oh shit. Kerry, did you leave the window open?'

'No,' she replied, and I got that fear feeling in the pit of my stomach.

Rushing to the door, I could hardly get the key in the lock as my hands were shaking so much. I opened it and looked in. 'Oh no, no, no,' I muttered. Right away, my worst fears were realised. The live setup was gone and all the lights. Not the live setup! I had worked like a slave on that, countless hours sitting in front of the machines, until a cramp had set in and I could hardly even stand back up. And not just my music was on there but B, Alex and Charlie's too. Desert Storm's ability to play music had just taken a severe nose dive.

Okay, we still had the disks to play on the decks, but the live setup? We had worked so hard to earn the money to buy it; three months of parties in dingy warehouses saving every Lira. I took it badly. Why the fuck hadn't I left the fucking dogs in the truck? Because there had been no shade to park in and since we were stopped outside the cop shop, I thought it would be safe for just a few hours. If only... what if... I just sat with my head in my hands on the pavement, nearly crying. The dogs nuzzled up to me. Kerry tried to give me a cuddle but I was having none of it, I could feel the red mist lowering over me and anger took me. I got a pole out of the cab of the lorry and started smashing it against the lampposts and litterbins, anything I could find, everybody kept the fuck out of my way, and the dogs hid under the truck. Kerry – the voice of reason – snapped me out of it.

'Darling, for fuck's sake, the police station is just there so calm the fuck down. Do you want to get thrown in jail as well?'

She was right and I lowered the pole.

'And another thing, look what I just found,' she said, showing me what was in her hands. The box of disks from the live sets! This was good news. In their hurry, the thieves had dropped these crucial items. With these disks, I could buy the same equipment again, simply insert the floppies and load up the live sets. There was hope, though of course, where the fuck I was going to get the £5000 to do it with? Well, that was another matter. I gave her a big kiss and hug.

Just then Kamikaze sound system rocked up. Steve, the head honcho, was quick to tell me it straight.

'Keef, you're a fucking idiot, why the fuck didn't you leave your dogs in the truck? I mean, buy a pitbull and bark yourself? It's a joke.' Now Steve is a straight talker, and he was right, but there is a time for home truths, and this wasn't it. Next thing, we were squared up on the road, head to head. The abuse started to flow, Kamikaze had a sticker they put on all their kit; *'Kamikaze, we live in hell, but we live well.'* but Steve's posse had changed it to, *'we live in hell, but Steve lives well.'* I hit him with this and it didn't go down well. Now it was pushy-pushy time on the road. Just when the first punch was about to be thrown, Charlie came running over.

'Guys, there's a bar up here and I think they're going to try to get our stuff back.'

Conflict forgotten, I headed up to the bar. It seemed there was a chance as the bar owner was a nice guy and when he heard we were in Napoli to do a party for the locals, he sent his son out to find out info. First, he asked if we had gone to the cops. Yeah, right, the cops in Italy don't really solve crimes, in fact most of them are the criminals. Then he said maybe he could help us but we would have to pay something to get the kit back, and since luckily the robbers hadn't found the stash of cash, hidden under the filing cabinet in the truck, we had about a grand in English pounds in there. I sat there in the bar downing beers and chain-smoking cigarettes waiting. Finally, the son came back. Yes, he had found the guys that had ripped off our stuff... my heart jumped and I leapt up... but unfortunately, they had already sold it on. Fuck!

So that was that. I went back to the truck and apologised to Steve, we hugged and made up, and I sat and thought about a solution. I find that, almost no matter how bad a situation is, if you calm down and think things through, there are usually still options. So, I came up with Operation Rabbit Run (more later...).

Well, what doesn't kill you only makes you stronger... and all that bullshit. With less than two weeks to the rave, we still had to find a park-up, much less a venue, there was postering to be done, etc, etc. So, putting the disaster to the back of my mind, I got on with the job.

First thing was a park-up. Looking at the map, it seemed that there was a large industrial area down by La Porta Vecchia (old port in Italian) pretty close to the centre, and that an overpass led straight to it. This looked like a good place to start, so taking Alex's van, a few of us hit the auto-route and headed in. As we approached the auto-route gate to collect our ticket, I noticed that as well as the obligatory hawkers selling cigarettes, they were selling white t-shirts with a thick black band running diagonally from the shoulder to belly. What the fuck?

But then I remembered that the Italians had recently passed a law that required seat belts to be worn and Italians hate new laws and this was their response: a T-shirt with a seatbelt printed on it. Wicked! We thought it was cool as fuck and bought one each.

The sign for the flyover was just ahead and we turned off, drove about 200 metres up the ramp and I suddenly slammed on the brakes, throwing everyone against the windscreen with a bang. The road ended in mid-air, and all that stopped you falling fifty metres to your death were a few boulders placed on the road! What the fuck? Thank god it hadn't been dark! We checked and rechecked the map, and sure enough, it clearly showed a flyover running over the city. This was another introduction to life in Napoli. It turned out that the road may have been on the map, but the corrupt city officials (with the mafia) had simply stolen all the cash and built fuck all!

Nonplussed, we reversed back to work our way through the city streets, which was a nightmare in itself. The locals don't stop for the red lights and if you do, they go crazy on their horns screaming at you out the window. It took hours to get through the gridlock. Finally, hot, sweaty and totally pissed off, we reached the old port. To say it was a bit run down would be the understatement of the decade! The place was fucked. The slums surrounding it were falling down. Rubbish filled the streets, (apparently there is always a rubbish collectors' strike in Napoli) and burned-out cars half-blocked the roads. I turned to the others, 'Maybe better lock the doors, eh?'

Then we found La Porta Vecchia. This looked a bit better, for parking up at any rate. A large waste ground surrounded by falling down warehouses and a dock, totally abandoned. We went back to get the trucks.

After we were all installed, I took a good look round. Well, there was a usable warehouse at any rate. Ok, it had a few large cracks running up the walls and a couple of holes in the roof but we had a venue. Marco had gone back to Rome for a few days but I knew in my heart of hearts that his idea of a venue would not be within five kilometres of La Porta Vecchia! Okay, maybe not the perfect place, but at least we had a backup venue, which is always a good idea. There's no denying there's a risk involved in promoting a gig when you don't have a venue, some might even say a foolhardy one, but nothing gets the workers moving more than knowing that there's only a couple of weeks to go till the gig! This also might be why my hair started greying in my twenties.

It seemed La Porta Vecchia was a good choice for a base. Close to the centre, it was perfect for flyering and postering and teams were sent out daily with buckets, paste, and stacks of flyers. To help with this, we sent along our special forces PR team: three Roman girls, all gorgeous, who we had nicknamed the Spice Girls. The boys would slap up the posters, while beside them, the girls would flyer the likely punters, a perfect combo.

Meanwhile, the van was covering the entire Naples area, desperately looking for another venue. I went on these trips with Alex driving and maybe B in there as well. Usually, it's pretty easy to find an empty warehouse; you drive round industrial areas in the day, marking on a map the empty places to come back at night to check out. Ideally, you're looking for a place that's been empty for a while. You can tell this by a lot of means; for a start, there's nobody about, the gate looks unused, rusted padlock, weeds growing around the place, smashed windows are a dead giveaway too, and maybe a for sale or to let sign outside. But try as we might, it seemed every fucking warehouse within ten kilometres of our park up site was either in use, squatted by gypsies (you don't fuck with them), or unsuitable for one reason or another. More and more areas on our map were being scored through with thick red markers and time was getting short. Three days of fruitless searching later, we'd used up nearly all the diesel and definitely all the willpower, and the backup venue was looking more and more appealing.

The next day Marco reappeared back from Rome.

'Well, Marco, what do you think of the venue?' I asked, pointing around at the abandoned warehouse.

'Porco dio, Keef, you know I think whole plan is bad.'

'Yes, yes, but what about the venue?' I pressed.

'Keef, the venue is a good, nice warehouse, but the place? Porta Vecchia? The old port, it is the worst area in the whole city, the centre of Camorra territory, it is madness to hold a rave here!'

'Okay, I admit that it's a bit run down, but the gig is in four days, and as you know, we've searched high and low for another place. It's this or nothing.'

'Well, nothing then. People from Rome won't come anyway when they find out it's in La Porta Vecchia.'

Cancel the rave? I couldn't believe he was saying this. No way, Desert Storm had never cancelled a gig in our lives!

'Look, Marco,' I said sternly, 'we've done raves in dodgy places before, Glasgow for a start, Marseille, the suburbs of Paris, how bad can it be?'

I was starting to suspect that Marco's fears were based on a kind of snobbery that Roman people have against other Italians; they think they're superior and look down on them, especially people from south of Rome. To Romans, they were basically just peasants.

'But Keef, you forget the Camorra?'

'Fuck the Camorra, Marco, we've dealt with mafia before. Remember in the hills above Rome? They even gave their blessing for the party as long as we tidied up the rubbish for fuck's sake.'

'Porco dio, you're not listening. The Camorra are different, more like a gang. With the mafia, you talk to the boss and sort things out. Here there is no boss of bosses, it's like a jungle. They will come here and then you will see.'

'Well, what more can they do, they've already nicked all our kit, and we've got nothing left to be robbed!'

'You still have your lives.'

This was serious. I'd never seen Marco like this before, there was no budging him, he was dead set against the rave and that was that. I sighed and looked around at the others checking out the warehouse, chatting happily, wondering where was best to hang the backdrops.

'Okay, Marco, I'll think this over, but I beg you, don't say anything to the others, at least not yet. Wait until I see if there's another option.'

Marco looked doubtful.

'Okay, I will keep quiet, but If nothing has changed by tomorrow, I must phone my friends and warn them. Maybe it would be best to get them to bring down some guns, a shotgun at least.'

I smiled grimly to myself. This rave was getting a little interesting. The dark side of me was waking up. Bring on the fucking chaos!

* * *

Another day passed and with no new venue, we had a meeting and decided it had to be at La Porta Vecchia. I noticed Marco slide off afterwards to phone his mates. Well, at least we had a plan, and with Alex off to try to rent some lights, we took B's truck to go and get the bar. B, Amy and I pulled onto the auto-route all proudly wearing our fake seat belt T-shirts and headed out of town, but had only got a few kilometres when B realised we were low on fuel and as we had used all the diesel venue hunting, we were going to have to buy some! There was no choice. We pulled into the next service station with B puffing on a huge joint. I told him to put in 20,000 lira (about £8), gave him the cash, and he made to get out, dreadlocks stuck to his face and still puffing on the joint.

'Hey, B, don't you think you should lose the reefer?' I advised him.

'Oh yeah,' he replied, stung out of his face, and left it in the ashtray. I promptly grabbed it and had a puff.

'Watch this,' said Amy, nudging me with her elbow and pointing to the door mirror. 'I bet he forgets to put the fuel in.'

Sure enough, B, the stone head, started walking into the garage.

'B, you waster,' we shouted out the window, 'the fucking fuel.'

'What?' he replied.

'PUT THE FUEL IN, DIMWIT,' screamed a laughing Amy.

'Oh yeah,' he said, and he moved over to the pump.

A few minutes later we were ready to roll, and with a crunch of gears we pulled off fast and... BANG, there was an almighty crash and the truck stopped dead, stalling. We all looked at each other half-laughing.

'Shit, what the fuck was that?' I asked.

'I think we hit something,' said B nervously.

'No shit, Sherlock,' I replied and leaned out the window to take a look.

I could hardly believe my eyes. B, the idiot, had put the fuel in all right but had forgotten to take the nozzle back out from the tank, and it wasn't one of the spindly little car filler hoses either but a big fuck off fat bastard truck one! The damage was immense. The pump had been pulled right out of the ground (bringing the half the roof with it) and lay mangled on the deck, diesel pissing out onto the forecourt. I leant back into the truck.

'Is it bad?' B asked. I replied, 'JUST GO, FOR FUCK'S SAKE, GO, GO!'

B needed no more encouragement and started her up and gunned out of the services, onto the auto-route, and away.

'Are we being chased?' asked Amy and I leaned out of the window again peering back.

'Can't see anybody, but one thing is following us, the fucking nozzle and hose is still sticking out of the tank, trailing along the road!'

For some reason, this was very funny and it was some time before we could stop laughing and pull in to get rid of it. It was at this point B made a fatal error, one that would cost us hundreds of man hours and stressed out times to follow. Obviously, the fuel cap had gone, and the tube to the tank had stretched to almost twice its size. In fact, it was amazing we still had a tank at all, so bent were the brackets. Anyway, B hunted around in the cab and came up with one of those plastic emergency caps, you know the ones, they sell them at every garage, black plastic things that fit any tank and he placed it in.

'Lovely,' he said and we went on our way, but it wasn't lovely, because every time you pull the bitch in and out of the tank, tiny slivers of plastic come off and over time these get sucked into the fuel system causing the truck to randomly stop running, usually at the worst possible fucking moments. It took us more than a year to solve this problem, so if you're ever tempted to use one of these, then don't, take it from me.

We got the bar stock with no problems and headed back to base, taking a different route to avoid passing the services, wondering if they had captured the reg plate on video! Back at Porta Vecchia, all was running smoothly and the info lines were starting to ring (a good sign), with eager punters trying to get directions to the rave. Of course, they were only told *'Napoli area, phone back in the night.'*

By now, I was into a routine, up in the morning while the site was quiet and off to the local café, just down the road, with my A5 diary to sit with a cappuccino plus cigarette and plan the day. They were starting to get to know me in there (black sunglasses-wearing rave promoters with dyed blond hair aren't very common in Napoli). When the old guy saw me enter, he nodded knowingly and pulled down the bottle of brandy, to mix me a cappuccino Vecchia. Now, drinking in the morning is usually not a good idea, but on the continent it's surprisingly common, and by ordering a capo Vecchia, you were fitting in with the crowd and the locals liked it.

After that, I would head back to the site, list in hand, and wait for the rest of them to claw themselves out of their pits! Except Kerry of course, who was always up and about early doors. That morning I was surprised to find a photographer taking shots of one of the Spice Girls posing in front of a truck. There was no denying she looked well hot in her cropped top and tight-fitting jeans and when I asked what was going on, was told it was just some guy writing a book on raves and thought no more of it. The build up to the event was proving surprisingly trouble free, and since the phrase live set had been banned from conversation, I felt pretty good about it all and when rave night came, we were ready, come what may.

BOOM, BOOM, TSSST... BOOM, BOOM, TSSST. I loved that sound! The walls of the warehouse were vibrating to the techno beats. In fact, the bass was so strong that I was getting worried that the huge cracks in the building would rupture, bringing the building crashing down and killing us all.

It was eleven p.m. and the place was filling up, maybe not the 1,000 we had hoped for but there was a good few hundred inside already and there was still plenty of time. The lights Alex had hired were pretty naff, more suited to a school disco than a pukka techno rave, but better than nothing. I got a small twinge of anger as I remembered the theft for the umpteenth time. No live set for me tonight unfortunately, but maybe this was for the best as I had other priorities, security for one.

Marco's mate with the shooter had arrived and we had it stashed in his boot in the car park, loaded and ready to fetch at a moment's notice (this fact was only known to the three of us). Tahi the pitbull was tied up under the bar and I had my trusty metal bar in the long back pocket of my baggy jeans and my large black Maglite torch in my hand. We took it in turns to cruise the dance floor, car park, and around the trucks, but so far no more than the usual amount of dodgies and 'lost its' were about and all seemed normal. Well, as normal as an illegal rave can be; it seemed there was a lot of LSD about that night. Thinking back, I had watched people dripping acid onto blotting paper back at Fintek, so no doubt it was that. Risky affair as you might get a tab with hardly any on it or one with far too much. No way was I going to trip tonight and I tried my best to dissuade the others too with mixed results. Marco, however, had his usual king-sized bag of cocaine which we hoovered up in my truck at regular intervals.

The night went on and the atmosphere was building. By now, there were a good 700 ravers in there and the combination of LSD, alcohol, flashing lights, and wicked beats was working them into a frenzy. The bar was doing brisk business and it was looking like another successful night when one of the French posse came running up to the bar obviously distressed.

'Putain, un voller, prendre ma drug et ma lira, et cassie ma tete, aide moi!'

Translated, *'Fuck, a thief has taken my drugs and money and smashed my head, help me.'*

Well, smashed was a bit of an exaggeration, but he did have a small cut above his eye. I gripped him by the shoulders and shouted above the music

'CALME TOI... DIE MOI... CEST QUES PASS?'

Calm down...speak to me...what has happened?

As best as I could make out with my imperfect French, he had been serving up some speed to a raver in the corner of the warehouse (bad lad), and three guys had come out of the shadows. One had smacked him on the head with a bit of wood, one held him while he was stunned, and most worryingly of all, the other had cut his pockets open with a knife and stolen his drugs and money.

Marco and I exchanged glances. Random bad guys or something more serious?

'Marco, let's split up, you find your friend and I'll do a quick cruise. Meet back here in five minutes.'

As I was about to move off, Marco put his hand on my shoulder. 'Keef, look, there,' he said in my ear, pointing into the shadows in the corner of the warehouse.

Looking over, I could see three guys who were definitely not ravers. They looked like extras from a gangster movie, long coats, the lot... shit. And they weren't alone as another larger group were now half-blocking the front door and punters were having problems getting in and out. These guys were definitely casing the place. Marcos's mate must have sniffed out the trouble because he suddenly appeared at our side. We didn't need to say anything to each other, it was defo time to go to his car and fetch the shotgun. The Camorra had arrived.

'Right, you two go to the car and get the gun, but be careful, go out the back exit then come back here and slide it in there.' I cautioned pointing to one of the open belly boxes in the army truck which was parked behind the bar where we were standing. 'I'll go warn everyone.' I repeated it twice to make sure I was understood because it's very difficult to communicate properly in a rave, you have to lean right into someone's ear and half-shout. By the end of most events, I'd lost my voice.

As they left, I had a quick look up the stairs and into my truck. Good. B, Alex, Kerry and Amy were in there shooting the shit. I jumped in.

'Sorry to interrupt you guys, but we may have a bit of a problem.' I quickly explained what was happening, leaving out the shotgun bit. 'Now, I want you to go and pass the word. Anyone that's fucking serving up needs to pack up and stash up their gear and the cash right now, and then get our lot gathered up around the bar and the system. Kerry, get the bar money and put it in the stash.'

All of them were up and on it. B even left his spliff burning in the ashtray. I'll be having that. I thought, and grabbing it, I went back outside.

By the time I got out, Marco and his friend were almost back and I could see they had a large black holdall with them. By the time we'd stashed it up, people were starting to gather at the bar as word was spreading. Tahi, always a barometer for trouble, was alert too, so I untied her and lifted her onto the large bar table where she sat bolt upright ears pinned back, her studded collar flashing silver in the lights. Good girl, not good for business maybe, but good girl for this situation. Now for the next move.

Our plan, such as it was, was not to start blowing people away with a shotgun in the middle of a crowded rave, that would be insane, the shooter was a last resort to blast at the ceiling and point at people, but hopefully it wouldn't come to that. First, we would try flattery. It wasn't hard to spot the leader, he just had to be the slightly older guy with the slicked-back greying hair and long cashmere coat standing by the door. If he was a raver, then I would be a bank clerk. Around him were some nasty-looking characters looking fucking hard and dressed in cheap-copy sports gear, a strange combo. Again, there's no way these people were ravers.

Taking a deep breath, I took Marco with me and marched up to Don Cashmere. As we closed in, two of his minders stepped forwards, but the Don waved them off. Through Marco, I introduced myself as the boss of the rave (complete shit of course) and welcomed him and his friends to the party (omitting the fact that they were already inside, of course). That seemed to go down okay so then I asked him if he wanted to come to the bar and I would get him a drink. This went down really well, and the Don, Marco and a couple of his boys walked over to the bar. I signalled our lot to back off a bit and ordered us all beers, which were passed over by a nervous-looking Kerry. It was reassuring to see my insurance policy standing by in the shadows close to the belly box, but all seemed to be going great and soon, through Marco, we struck up a conversation and yes, this guy really was from the Camorra. His family, at least according to him, ruled the whole Porta Vecchia, and if we wanted to do anything around here we needed his permission. He was actually an interesting guy and told me a few stories of shit that had happened in the old port and what it was like when it was a bustling dock.

I turned the conversation to matters of tonight and asked very nicely if he could call his boys off as one of our lads had been robbed. He had a word in someone's ear and off he went to presumably sort it out. I was just starting to relax when he started to turn the screw. Did I want to do other events with him? We could make good money as he could guarantee security... and we could sell drugs for him? The idea had about as much appeal as chopping off my own nuts with a rusty penknife but it was best just to play along for now. Yes, I replied, sounding very interesting, but maybe it would be best to talk about it another time? Soon after that, he said he was off home. I tried to look disappointed, and with the proverbial crushing handshake, he was off though he left a few of his lads, probably to keep an eye on us.

Fucking hell, it had worked. They say flattery will get you nowhere, well not in this case! I was really pleased with myself, and Marco massaged my ego even more by saying I'd make a good politician. With that, we stashed up the shooter again and disappeared into my truck for Jack Daniel's and lines of coke.

Now, this wasn't the first time I'd fronted out the bad guys and it wouldn't be the last. Always play to your strengths and their weaknesses, to them you're an unknown quantity and there's a lot of you, and their weakness is their egos. This might not have been the best gig we'd ever done but yet again, our 'never say die' attitude had won the day.

It was late morning and the rave was starting to thin out so I decided to body swerve to the café for my morning capo Vecchia. It's always nice to get a bit of you time after a long hard night, but as soon as I entered the bar something was different. The whole place turned round, looked at me, and started talking and laughing. Weird. Maybe they had heard about the rave or something, then the old bar guy started cutting out imaginary lines on the bar top, pretending to sniff them and shouting 'cocaine, cocaine' at the top of his voice much to the amusement of the punters. I was nonplussed. Had this dude lost his mind? I laughed along a bit, had my Capo, and split. Back on site, I was just trying to explain to Marco what had happened when shit loads of cops turned up, with what looked like journalists taking photos. This didn't look good. The head cop was out in front looking really angry. He was waving what looked like a copy of a newspaper and shouting. He walked right up to me and thrust the paper under my nose.

Looking at it, I could hardly believe what I saw. There was a picture of one of the Spice Girls on the front page, posing beside one of our trucks. I asked Marco what the headline said.

'It says,' he peered at the paper and paused, 'Porco dio, it says we take drugs every day, we live to rave.'

The cop was shouting in my face again.

'He says,' Marco translated, 'where is this girl?'

Of course, the guy that was supposed to be writing a book! He'd been a fucking journo for the local paper! So that explained the shit in the café, we were headline news. It didn't take long for the cops to locate the Spice Girl and she was led away in tears. She had proper spilled the beans too, the article went on to tell the whole tale, stealing diesel, venue hunting, drug taking, oh my god, but you had to see the funny side, or I did anyway. We take drugs every day, we live to rave, beautiful. Now, that's what I call a fuck up!

Amazingly, the cops seemed satisfied with the arrest of the Spice Girl and off they went. We sent a car after them to get her a lawyer and continued on with the party. By the next morning, the rave was over, we stopped the music and the generator, and peace and quiet once more fell upon La Porta Vecchia. I was just relaxing with a cold beer and a spliff after packing away the rig, when I spotted Don Cashmere and his cronies arriving. For fuck's sake, this is all we need. It seemed he was ready to talk more about doing some raves. Great. I was tempted to tell him the truth that we were fucking off and never coming back, when someone whispered in my ear that a dog had just been grabbed into a car and stolen, then Marco came over and urgently dragged me away.

'Keef, I just overheard one of them on the phone. He said we'll keep them talking and to get here in twenty minutes! I think they're going to rob us!'

Fuck, we had to split. I've never seen a site cleared so fast, we were out of there in record time. It was every system for itself and we split up, agreeing to meet back at Fintek.

Desert Storm headed straight for the auto-route. I had a quick glance in as we passed the services and saw the pump B had wrecked was still totally fucked with loads of red and white warning tape around it. If possible, it was even worse than I remembered. Oops. The plan was to get out of dodge as fast as possible, but the girls wanted to see Vesuvius before we left. I wasn't keen, having had enough of the delights of Naples, but was overruled and we turned off at the sign for Vesuvius and headed up the winding road to the top. When we had reached as far as we could drive, we stopped and got out. I looked suspiciously for thieves or dodgies, but as far as the eye could see was just heaps of ash, totally deserted. Satisfied, I agreed that a quick look over the edge couldn't hurt so off we went. We couldn't have been more than ten minutes but on our return, I discovered that the fucking stereo had been stolen from the front of the lorry! It nearly broke me, I looked desperately around. I mean where had these bastards been hiding? Did they drop out of the sky and then disappear into thin air? You could see right down the road almost to the auto-route, but there was no car speeding away. I demanded we leave immediately and this time, there were no dissenters. I have never been happier to see any town receding in the rear-view mirror. Even Kerry, usually calm and reserved, was screaming, 'Fuck you, Napoli,' out the windows and giving the whole city the finger.

Well, that was Naples and I'll tell you one thing, I'll not be going back. If we'd spent much longer there and I'd have been lucky to still have boxer shorts to cover my skinny black ass. We drove for a long time before finally stopping for the night. Rave off.

18

A TOUCH TOO MUCH

After splitting up with Kerry, I tried to get away from it all by playing live sets around the world, and soon landed a plum job in Venezuela's capital, Caracas, with my friend Darren. Darren was a man who can possibly take more drugs than anyone else I know; smack, crack, ketamine, LSD, cocaine, you name it and he can sniff it, smoke it, pop it and wash it all down with a flood of vodka, wine, beer, and still DJ a top set, even though he can barely stand. As I headed towards Heathrow airport, with my live set equipment, I knew this was going to be an interesting two weeks.

'Meet me at the bar,' Darren had said, and he wasn't hard to spot. Let me describe him. Darren wears expensive hoodies and jeans, but he likes them ripped and dirty. He has wild unkempt sandy-coloured dreadlocks which he matches with black wraparound sunglasses to hide his eyes. One look at him and you think 'DRUGGIE'!

Anyway, a quick glance around the bar and I had found him, half-cut, and slumping at the table surrounded by empty glasses. I tried to approach quietly but he had me spotted.

'KEEF, MA MAN, WHERE THE FUCK YOU BEEN?' he shouted across the bar, half getting to his feet, sending a few glasses smashing to the floor. 'I'VE BEEN HERE FOR FUCKING HOURS,' he continued, slurring loudly and gesturing with his hands at the empty glasses as he wound up for his finale. 'OH YEAH, YOU GOT ANY DRUGS TO SNIFF? I FINISHED ALL MINE.' The swish of heads turning from the surrounding tables was almost audible as Darren slumped back down.

'Shut the fuck up, Darren!' I murmured angrily from behind my hand as I sat down. 'You'll get us nicked.' And countering the disapproving looks from around us with my best big angry black guy stare, I manoeuvred Darren out of the bar and into the toilets, pulled out a wrap and cut out two lines of ketamine, hoping this might calm him a little, and offered over a rolled up £10 note. Taking the note, he glanced down disapprovingly at what I thought were reasonable lines and shook his head.

'NO, NO, NO! GIVE IT HERE!' he shouted, and before I could react, he grabbed the wrap from me and plunged note and nose deep in, sniffing hard.

I grabbed it back and we both looked down into it. It was nearly all gone. He'd just sniffed two-thirds of a gram of horse tranquiliser thirty minutes before check in.

'Oh, my God, Darren, what have you done?'

'What, man?' he replied innocently, palms upward, face covered in white powder, and cackling insanely.

'Well, thanks Darren, how not to attract attention. And I've got another ten grams in my bag!'

Darren cackled insanely again. I thought... fuck it, and sniffed the rest of the wrap as well as the two lines off the toilet seat.

I don't remember much after that, but somehow, we must have made the flight, because I definitely remember arriving.

Cruising through customs in Caracas, we collected our equipment and headed for the arrivals hall. I couldn't help but notice the three men standing by the gate looking like something out of the film Scarface. Tight coloured trousers, with loud flowery Hawaiian shirts unbuttoned to reveal outrageously large gold chains, all topped off with slicked-back Brylcreemed hair and matching extra-large mirrored sunglasses. I nudged Darren hard.

'Darren, check those three geezers out on the left, man!'

He looked over. 'Keef, that's our boys.'

'No shit!' I replied. I should have known.

As we got nearer, the hierarchy in the group was instantly recognisable. The fat one in the middle was obviously the boss, his whole upright manner oozed power and control. The skinny one on the left had to be the bodyguard, as his head kept scanning the crowd looking for threats. The other one, who was for sure lower down the pecking order, was smaller, with a pockmarked face and stood slightly behind the others, shoulders down, eyes down, head down, occasionally glancing up at the fat one like a dog seeking approval from its master.

For Darren, there was much backslapping, hugging, and hand shaking from the boss, while I stood somewhat awkwardly to the side, getting the up and down from the bodyguard.

Finally, the boss turned to me and said in perfect English, 'So, you must be Keef? Hi, I'm Carlos, welcome to my country.' He then gave me a crushing handshake, and turning to the bodyguard, added, 'and this is my friend Antonio.' I endured another crushing handshake and turned to the third one, waiting for an introduction. There was an awkward silence.

'Oh yeah,' Carlos added eventually, 'this is Jose, he works for me.' Jose didn't offer his hand.

To break the ice, I rubbed my hands together and said, 'Right, where's the car then?' and made to head off with my trolley, but Antonio placed a hand on it, stopping it dead. 'Jose, carry bags.' This was not a question, then he added, 'Cars, car park.' Cars, I thought.

Now usually I don't like other people touching my live set equipment. I mean, what if they drop it? I looked to Darren for help, but he just shrugged his shoulders. So off we all went, leaving poor Jose to carry thirty-five kilograms of equipment, two big record boxes, and the rucksacks.

As we entered the car park, I scanned it to see if I could spot our vehicles. We were headed straight towards the disabled bay. Parked across it was a brand new, silver Mercedes coupe, with blacked out windows and the biggest fattest alloy wheels ever. Behind that, also brand new, was a shiny black Toyota Land Cruiser jeep, even the windscreen was tinted.

'It can't be,' I thought, not for the last time on this trip. But of course, it was.

Darren went with the boss and Jose in the Merc, and I went with Antonio in the jeep. During the long drive into Caracas, I got my first chance to see the two levels of Caracas society. The haves and the have fuck alls. There were only two kinds of cars on the road, shiny new ones like the ones we were in with the obligatory tinted windows and the slow-moving smoking wrecks. There's no middle class.

As this was my first time in South America, I eagerly looked around, taking in the scenery, the bright red soil, and the jungle encroaching close to the road, well what little I could see through the outrageously tinted windows!

Antonio kept the jeep a constant ten metres behind the Merc, regularly checking the mirrors and not saying anything.

'So,' I ventured hopefully, 'are we going to the hotel?'

'No,' he replied, turning towards me, 'we go for a touch,' (pronounced tooouch) and laughed.

'Tooouch?' I replied, parrot-fashion. Antonio said nothing, and followed the Merc off at the next exit.

Caracas was still a distant haze of smoke and mist over the hills as we pulled off the highway, and soon the main road degenerated into little more than a farm track. Bumping along it, I looked up and saw the hillside covered in tin shacks and half-built houses. There appeared to be no plan or conscious design.

'What's that?' I ventured again, pointing up.

'That barrio,' Antonio replied and then added, 'very dangerous!'

Great, I thought as we headed towards it. For Antonio, as I was to learn, everything revolved around danger. It went on a scale of 'safe here' to 'very dangerous'.

As we entered the outskirts of the barrio, it reminded me of Bosnia during the war. Wrecked burned out buildings and bullet holes. Soon, we pulled up by what must have passed for the local bar, where a group of men sat sitting on crates, sipping beer in the shade of a burned out building.

'Yeah, man, I could murder a beer,' I exclaimed, and eagerly rubbed my hands.

Antonio looked around at me frowning. 'Hopefully no murder today,' he said and began to get out. I too reached for the door handle. 'No, you stay in car.' This wasn't a question. 'Very dangerous,' he repeated, and reached under the seat, pulled out a small black rucksack, and exited the Toyota. There was a long drawn out whirring noise followed by a clunk, as the special deadlocking mechanism engaged, and I was locked in, alone in the jeep.

Very dangerous, I thought, chewing a nail. Well, what the fuck are we doing here then? Tooouch? What the fuck is this tooouch? A horrible image filled my mind, of being dragged out of the Toyota screaming and into a burned out building to be tooouched up by crazed gay South American gangsters. I managed a nervous laugh.

Peering out of the windscreen, I could see Darren chatting in the Merc. God, I hope he knows what he's doing. Darren's idea of danger is running out of drugs...

Curiosity overcame my fears and I intently watched Antonio to see what he was up to. First, I noticed that the beggar-looking kids, who had approached when we pulled up, took one look at Antonio and quickly legged it. He swaggered over to the Merc, and the driver's window came down about three centimetres. After a few words with Carlos, he headed towards the bar. As he passed the table nearest the door, he flicked his fingers, pointing inside, and without a pause entered. After a few seconds and a few furtive looks around, a man got up and followed him in.

Within a few minutes Antonio was back in the jeep, handing me a cold beer. I looked at it doubtfully. 'This is a tooouch?'

'No,' he replied, and in one swift movement, out flashed a wicked-looking flick knife. Involuntarily, I shrunk against the door. Antonio just laughed and reaching into the rucksack produced a small white cylinder about ten centimetres long wrapped in plastic, and proceeded to pick at the top of it with the blade. That's when I began to realise that Antonio's idea of fun was to scare the shit out of you!

After a few seconds of picking and scraping, the tip of the blade reappeared with a pile of white powder on it. *Twice as sweet as sugar, twice as bitter as salt. And if you get hooked, baby, it's nobody else's fault, so don't do it.* Cocaine, it had to be.

Gently taking my hand, Antonio tipped the sparkling powder between the base of my thumb and wrist. 'Keef, a tooouch?'

We both laughed and I sniffed the lot in one greedy go.

There was just time for Antonio to have a tooouch before our convoy headed back to the highway to continue our journey. By now I was completely relaxed, jabbering on about raves, techno, Scotland, blah, blah, blah, you get the picture. Oh yeah, and hitting the coke like it was going out of fashion. That's the problem with cocaine, the hit doesn't last long, and you quickly want another. In Europe, it was about £50 a gram for shit that was about only sixty per cent purity if you were lucky. Here, it was only $5 dollars US a gram for ninety per cent purity! So back home, you chip in with your mates for a few grams for a night out, sniff it and it's gone, no problem, but what happens if cocaine is close to free and virtually unlimited, as in this case? Is it possible to sniff a line every fifteen minutes for two weeks? Well, Darren and I were about to find out.

Summiting the last hill, it was instantly obvious that Caracas is a city pushed for space. It's completely surrounded by steep hills and the only way to build is up; offices, apartments, and hotels, high-rise style, and the view from these could only remind you how lucky you were. Because on every steep hill surrounding the city are the barrios. No electricity, no running water, no roads, no plan and no hope!

Lucky for us, we were staying with the upwardly mobile members of society, the tinted window class. The kind of people who would never dream of pounding the pavement and don't have to. That's because a system similar to apartheid exists in Caracas, but instead of being judged by your colour (lucky for me), you're judged by your wallet. Whether you're going to the supermarket, the bank (especially the bank), your home, or in this case the hotel, there is absolutely no free way of walking in as there is no public entrance. You start your journey in a secure car park, guarded by machine gun-toting armed guards, and you finish in a secure car park guarded by machine gun-toting armed guards.

So, with our wallets well and truly on show (courtesy of our friends Mercedes and Toyota), the automatic gates of the Hotel Paradise, three stars, rolled back, the guards stood to attention, and we cruised in, with me still babbling bullshit.

Cross parking in the disabled bay, Antonio interrupted my frenzied drivelling, and said curtly, 'Keef, nose.'

'Nose?' I replied dumbly, and pulled down the sun visor to look in the vanity mirror, revealing nostrils and upper lip plastered in cocaine. I gave it a thorough wiping with the back of my sweaty hand, which I then licked clean. Disgusting I know, but a must with cocaine. 'Waste not, want not,' as my Scottish granny was fond of saying, although I reckon she was referring to my uneaten Brussels sprouts, not coke debris.

This time, I insisted on helping Jose with the bags, much to the amusement of Carlos and Antonio (you love everyone on cocaine, well, unless they cross you then you want to rip their heads off and piss down their necks). So, we loaded up, ascended in the elevator to the top floor, and entered the room, or in this case rooms. It was not what I expected. I had expected the usual we had on trips like this; a nice little private bolthole for Darren and I, somewhere to hole up and recuperate if things became too much, or to slink off to with some hot rave babe for a session, but Carlos had other plans.

'I'm sorry, but it's not the Hilton,' said Carlos as he showed us around the huge living room, kitchen, three bedrooms and expansive bathroom. 'But it's the only place I could find where we could rent the floor below as well, I'm worried about the noise.'

'You will be safe here,' Antonio added.

Fuck me! I thought, looking over at Carlos with new admiration. He's rented the whole top of the fucking building. Wow. This is a man after my own heart, and the twenty-four-hour party animal inside me started to run though the possibilities

'Right,' said Carlos, 'Antonio and I got to go to work.'

Work? What work, I wondered, images of unloading dismembered bodies into the river from the boot of the Merc, or of torturing the latest kidnap victim for his credit card pin numbers, flashed to mind.

'And we leave Jose here so you don't need to go out,' Carlos continued, 'anything you want, drugs, women, food, Jose will get for you.' To this, Jose nodded affirmatively.

As they reached the door, Carlos turned and added, 'Oh, and don't let anybody in except the boys with the sound system.'

'And don't go out,' reaffirmed Antonio, 'very dangerous.'

The boys with the sound system? Usually first with a witty response, Darren and I just stood there, jaws gaping and nodding dumbly.

'Whatever you say, my man,' was the best I could come up with.

As soon as we heard the lift machinery kick in we could contain it no longer, and started to run around the rooms screaming 'yeah, yeah!', high fiving and hugging each other. After a few minutes, we calmed down and I issued my first order to Jose.

'Jose, gimme the goddamn cocaine!'

After a couple of hours, sitting about, unpacking the bags, arguing over who got the best room, fiddling with the satellite TV, sniffing more coke, and sitting about some more, I started to get a little restless.

'Right,' I said, standing up and rubbing my hands, 'I'm going out for a beer.'

You see, I'm not used to being indoors. I live in a truck, okay a nice 4x4 army truck with double bed, kitchen, sitting area etc, but a truck nonetheless. I'm used to fresh air, being outside, and when I go to a new place, I like to go out to meet the people, and the best place to do that is in the local bar.

Darren glanced up from the TV. with a look that just said, you know they said not to go out.

Jose was also negative on the idea.

'No, no,' he replied and gently put a hand on my shoulder to sit me back down. 'I get beers, don't worry.'

But I wasn't to be deterred, and twitching my shoulder to shrug off his hand, I started to head towards the door. Too much coke brings paranoia, and even the walls of this massive penthouse suite were starting to close in.

'Look, man, I'm going out for a goddamn beer! You coming, Darren?'

At this, Jose started to flap big time. 'No, bad, bad idea, man. It's dangerous out there!'

I moved to the window and looked out and pointed down. 'Look, man,' I explained, 'I've been in war zones and survived. I can see people moving around down there, it can't be that bad!' I looked to Darren for support.

Now Jose looked really scared. 'Please don't go. If something happen you, boss kill me!' Jose pleaded, dragging his index finger across his throat and making a slitting noise with his eyes wide in fear. 'I get beers. Please sit, have another tooouch,' he added and frantically started chopping out lines onto a CD.

Darren just looked up again and pointed at the CD. 'Chop me out a fat one too, eh, Jose?' and then flicked the channel onto some blonde with impossibly big boobs romping on a bed with two blokes.

With a sigh I sat down, and looking over at Jose, I realised he was sweating as he chopped. Fuck me, I thought, he really is scared! But not scared for me. Scared of what Carlos would do to him if something went wrong. So, every silver cloud has a dark lining. I was almost a prisoner here! Nice prison though.

My thoughts were interrupted by a banging on the door. Darren, who can be a bit bossy, turned and said, 'That'll be the sound system. Get the door, eh, Keef?' He leaned down to sniff his line.

'Listen to Lord Muck, barking out the orders from his royal armchair!' I replied only half-jokingly.

'Oh, whatever,' he replied, 'Jose, get the door.'

This confused Jose as he couldn't both hold up the CD for Darren to take his line and answer the door.

'Fuck's sake, all right, I'll get the door.' I stood up, crossed the room, opened up the flap for the spy hole and peered out into the corridor, and then just stood there.

BANG! BANG! BANG! went the door again.

Darren looked up from his line. 'Fuck's sake, Keef, let them in,' he said irritably, before catching sight of the fear written on my face as I turned around. 'What is it? Who's at the door?' he said quietly.

BANG! BANG! BANG!

I said nothing.

'Keef, you're scaring me. Who the fuck is it?' he pressed.

Still saying nothing, I tiptoed across the room towards him, looked him in the eye and whispered in his ear. 'Shh, it's the fucking cops, man. No joke, it's the fucking cops!' Looking down at the CD that he had in one hand and the rolled-up note in the other, I added, ' and you'd better dash that stuff quick!'

Darren looked down as if seeing the drugs for the first time. You could have heard a pin drop.

BANG, BANG, BANG went the door again, this time louder.

Darren looked like a rabbit in the headlights. 'Oh, my God! You're fucking joking?' was the best he could manage, as images of years in a South American jail, cooking up cockroaches and being buggered nightly flashed through his mind.

By now Jose had run away to hide in a bedroom. I straightened up and said, 'You're right, I am fucking joking.' A wicked grin started to spread across my face. This took a while to sink in.

By now, I was laughing so hard I was almost crying, as Darren just sat there in shock. Finally, he mumbled weakly, 'You bastard!' and let out a ten-second sigh of relief. 'I think I just shit myself.'

'It's okay now, Jose, you can come out, it's not the cops,' I shouted into the bedrooms as I crossed towards the door. Jose reappeared, looking sheepish.

'Well, if it's not the cops, then who is it then?' Darren's brain was working again.

'It's two leggy birds in miniskirts with cropped tops,' I replied.

'Yeah, right,' retorted Darren, 'with Elvis Presley and Daffy Duck in tow.'

But it really was two leggy birds in miniskirts with cropped tops, accompanied by the boys with the sound system, Carlos, Antonio, cases of rum, beer, whisky and, of course, loads more coke, and about twenty more hangers-on. Wicked. The party had well and truly begun!

You may think that one party is much like the next, but not this one. I've been to thousands of parties, big and small, good and bad, but this one was mental. Day turned into night, night into day, and back to night again. We lost track of time, it was raining booze and snowing coke. I worked hard, I must have played my live set ten or more times, and how Darren manages to beat mix records so perfectly when the only reason that he's still standing up is because he keeps bouncing off the kitchen cabinets, I'll never know.

We were the foreign stars, flown in from Europe by Carlos to entertain his friends and he missed no opportunity to bask in the glory of it all, and for fuck's sake, this was only the pre-gig party, the fucking warm-up for God's sake. Unbelievable!

However, none of us worked as hard as the blonde girls in the miniskirts, because it turned out they were the free hookers who set up shop in one of the spare bedrooms, and anyone who wanted could just pull them in there, and well, you can imagine the rest.

Carlos was their favourite punter. He was in and out of there regularly. He had no shame. Even leaving the door open, so that when you were passing to go to the toilet, there he was, crazed on cocaine, riding one from behind while he slapped the other one on the arse to the techno beat. Shocking decadence! I couldn't help thinking Carlos would have fitted in just fine during Roman times. Emperor Carlos, the hooker-spanking party animal!

Over the next three or four days, hundreds of ravers were in and out of the party, and bit by bit, the place became more and more trashed. People were puking out of the windows if the toilets were busy, or just puking in the corner if they couldn't make it to the windows. Tables and mirrors were smashed, cupboard doors were hanging off. If you wanted to sniff a line, you just ran a credit card around the table beside the decks, and voila, a fat one appeared. How Carlos squared it with the hotel, who knows. Maybe he had the manager's grandmother tied to a chair in his garage or something.

Most surreal of all were the cleaning women. At some point every morning, well for the first few days anyway, the cleaning women would arrive to tidy up. They would go about their business as if nothing out of the ordinary was happening, hoovering up the piles of puke with an Aquavac, shovelling up the mountains of empties into sacks, and then dragging them over the unconscious revellers and into the elevator. Even a little dusting with a feather number on a stick, and once the place was shipshape – well, kind of – off they went.

Darren was a mess, a mobile disaster zone. How could he remain standing? Darren doesn't pace himself, he just consumes on and on, but the endless drugs and alcohol were starting to take their toll. Suddenly the music just stopped and I rushed in, to find Darren just standing there, staring at the turntables, eyes bulging, nose twitching, hands trembling, with spittle dribbling down his chin.

'Darren, Darren! The music's gone off!'

'Oh no! Oh no!' he repeated, over and over. Then the beat started again.

Now, I'm not saying I'm a 'just say no' drugs angel, far from it, but at least I try to pace myself. I like to be in a good enough state to at least keep the sound system running and deter the bad boys from making off with the equipment. I feel it's my mission in life, my divine calling you could say, but never in my wildest dreams had I imagined sniffing so much coke and with too much coke comes paranoia.

For the first few days, I was the life and soul of the party, chatting to all and sundry, (they mostly talked English, these upwardly mobile types, which was a good thing as I can't speak Spanish for shit), but as the days dragged on, I found myself hiding, sometimes for hours in my room, sniffing and drinking on my own, scared to go out, very anti-social.

I'm not sure what finally finished the party. A combination of many things maybe. The empty beer bottles being thrown out the windows didn't help. That finally brought some kind of complaint from the management, and a nervous-looking underling was dispatched to say the police had been round and could we please stop throwing stuff out of the windows. That's when I first realised that Carlos hadn't been seen around the place for a long time. A good twelve hours, in fact, and repeated failed attempts to raise him on his mobile didn't do wonders for my paranoia. Then the what ifs started to kick in.

Oh god, what if he doesn't come back? What if we get the blame for the damage? What if this? What if that? I thought, spiralling.

Without Carlos about, the free cocaine was running low, the booze also. The atmosphere was changing and a few arguments were breaking out. One of the hookers got into a slapping match with some girl who had caught her boyfriend sneaking into the spare bedroom. They left with faces like thunder. More fuel for my now rampant paranoia as I imagined gun-toting pimps arriving to shoot the place up, Rambo style. But more immediately worrying was the arrival of some very unsavoury types, eyeing up the sound system and other gear. Just great.

Darren wasn't going to be much help either. For Darren, the party had ended hours before. He was now completely unconscious, sprawled behind the turntables, and the latest DJ (who couldn't mix for toffee as you say in Glasgow) had to lean over him to play. My repeated attempts to wake him up had just provoked a violent reaction, so after receiving a few punches to the head, I just left him there in a pool of his own dribble.

The new DJ was bad, in fact, he was terrible. He couldn't mix, and insisted on playing the same four records again and again. He had to go.

'Ho you! You listen to me, pal,' I said. (My Glasgow accent flies back when I'm angry.) 'If you spin that shite one more time, I'm going to shove that record where the sun doesn't shine,' I told him in no uncertain terms as I poked him in the chest.

We went head to head in the kitchen, sending beer bottles smashing around us. If I remember rightly, he was a bit weedy and effeminate-looking and had definitely never been physically confronted by a cocaine-crazed large black Scottish man. He quickly folded and grabbing his pathetic little bag of tunes, he split.

That left no one to play. Perfect, it was time to wind this thing up anyway. I gently ushered out the bad boys, locked the door, stuck on a rap CD, and headed to my room for some well-deserved R&R. That's when I found Jose (the dirty little bastard) wide eyed and slavering and basically raping this semi-conscious cute little bird on my bed. Lovely, not. He and his squeeze were kicked out quick time.

Ahh. At last, alone, calm, and lying in my own bed, eyes closed and drifting, listening to the sounds of Dr Dre's Chronic 2000 album coming through the wall from the living room. I must have been in this beautiful state for all of... hmmm, twenty minutes, when all hell broke loose.

Crashing, banging, smashing and high-pitched screaming in Spanish could distinctly be heard coming from the other room and the music had stopped. This was not good, definitely not good! Already there was a frantic hammering at my door.

'Keef, Keef, come quick, help.' BANG, BANG! 'Help, my boyfriend, help, help.' BANG, BANG! 'Knife, knife. Naked!'

I recognised the voice immediately. It was Javier, the absolutely drop-dead gorgeous female friend of Carlos. Short black hair, in a boyish cut, athletic body, pert breasts, lycra top, ass to die for. You get the picture. Anyway, I woke from my trance, like a starving man in a baker's shop, and rushed towards the door, grabbing the only weapon I could find, a half-empty bottle of Red Label Johnnie Walker whisky (which I hate, so would have no problem crowning some arsehole with), and ripped open the door.

I've always been a sucker for the damsel in distress routine, it's got me in trouble before, and it will again. Anyway, there she was, gorgeous and distressed, so I had to act. Pushing her roughly out of the way, I strode purposefully into the living room.

The scene that met me was like a mini football stadium disaster. Everyone, well, everyone that could move, were trying, en masse, to force themselves through the narrow exit door. The TV was upturned, people were being trampled.

As the room cleared, I expected to see some coked-up knife-wielding maniac on top of poor Javier's boyfriend, cutting him up with a kitchen knife, but there was no one, no blood, nothing. Only the sound of Darren's snoring coming from the kitchen. Standing there feeling a little foolish, clutching my whisky bottle, I turned towards

Javier, half-accusingly, with a puzzled look on my face. But she was still frantic.

'No, no,' she replied. 'Window, window, he go that way, naked... knife.'

Sure enough, one of the living room windows was wide open. Strange enough in itself, as all the windows were fitted with safety catches that stopped them opening more than, say, the width of an empty beer bottle!

Rushing over, I reached the window with my heart pumping and sure enough, I could see where the ruined twisted catch had been forced open. Well, if he left this way, we'll have to scrape him up with a spoon I reckoned as I grabbed the ledge and leaned dangerously out, to peer down the one hundred or so feet to the car park.

Again nothing, no splattered corpse, no gathering crowd, no naked, no nothing. At this point, Jose arrived and tapped me on the shoulder, over-balancing me. Tottering on the edge, balls crushed against the sill, the blood rushed to my head as the cold hard concrete seemed to rush up to meet me. I thought my time had come, but luckily your body goes into survival mode at times like these and somehow, I swung my way back into the room. Safe but pissed right off with a face like thunder. Standing there breathing heavily, I turned to Jose, but what do you say to someone who has just nearly killed you?

'Jose, you fucking idiot, you could have killed me!' was a good start. My second thought was to throw him out. Jose must have read my mind and started backing away, palms outward and apologising.

'Sorry, I sorry, but it true. He naked, big knife, go window and gone, gone.'

'Look, calm down,' I insisted. 'Nobody's naked, nobody's gone. Come and look for yourself if you don't believe me,' I said, beckoning him forward with my hand

'Gone, gone,' Jose repeated, and started towards the window, then having second thoughts, he stopped dead. 'You push me, I know you want to push me,' he added, looking at me suspiciously.

Hmm, possibly, you could be right there, I thought. But I ignored him and turned my attention to Javier. She was on her knees, head in hands, sobbing uncontrollably. Looking down, it was hard not to follow the line of her black lacy G-string down, down... no, no, and thrusting these thoughts aside, I knelt down beside her, putting my arm gently around her shoulders, determined to get to the bottom of this.

'There, there,' I said comfortingly. 'Just calm down and tell me... WHAT THE FUCK IS GOING ON?'

So, between the sobbing and Jose's nodding and adding, 'Si, si,' bit by bit the story was pieced together. Javier's boyfriend, another Carlos, had somehow managed to take too much coke – haha, too much coke – and had become seriously paranoid. So paranoid, in fact, that he had decided Javier had been shagging her ex in the bathroom and was now hiding in the lift shaft. So, as you do, he had stripped naked, grabbed a huge kitchen knife, forced open the window and climbed up onto the roof to enter the lift shaft and stab his love rival. I tried to go with this, but no, it was just too fantastical. It just couldn't be true. We were on the thirteenth floor, for God's sake. Nobody could be crazy enough to climb out onto the roof, could they?

Crossing again to the window, I leaned back and out. Amazingly, it was actually possible to get onto the roof! Halfway up the window was a ledge running around the building. Above the window was another ledge, and running around the flat roof was a railing, for which one of the supports happened to be directly above. So, in theory, you could plant one foot on the ledge, reach up and grab the rail support and roll up onto the roof. Whether he stabbed his imaginary love rival or not remained unknown to me, but he made a damn good effort in the name of a coked-up love haze.

19

MADNESS IN DELHI

So, I came out my hotel in the Par Gange, Delhi, India, at about one a.m., stuck my plastic replica 9mm pistol down my pants (as you do if you're a little mental) and jumped on my beautiful new motorbike, the Yamaha Enticer. Cheesy name but a beautiful machine, all metallic purple and chrome, semi-chopper style, with big pads to rest your feet on. It was only a 125cc, max speed 70 mph, but who the fuck would want to go faster than that on a road in India? Not me, anyway. The day before, I had been cruising on what passes for a motorway in these parts when suddenly the road went right through a town, no warning or fuck all, and worse than that, I ran straight into a set of speed bumps! I mean for fuck's sake, speed bumps on the motorway? Luckily, I saw the sign, you know the one that looks like a pair of tits, and managed to slam on the anchors. But I still don't know how I managed not to go farming, and with no health insurance, it would have been a trip to the Indian National Health Service hospital, not good.

Anyway, where was I? Oh yeah, I jumped on the machine, sniffed a massive line of ket off the tank, and was gone. The only time to drive on the streets of Delhi is at night, in the day it's total gridlock, but at night (Delhi isn't really a twenty-four-hour city, like say London), it's wicked, wind in your hair, no helmet of course, empty streets, and you're off. But this time, I wasn't out for a cruise, or off to the five-star Indian international for a milkshake (one of the few places open all night), but instead I wanted some action; a bar, or club, maybe even a girl. Not easy in Delhi, so I'm driving and driving, out of my head, just about to give up and turn for home (at least there I could get a cold beer and sit in my hotel room), when I saw two lads thumbing a lift. They weren't dressed in the normal Indian clobber but more hip-hop style, which is unusual in Delhi, so I stopped and asked them if they knew of any open bars, and if they did, could we go there? I'd buy some beers and give them a lift up the road.

They were totally cool with this. They spoke good English and said they knew a bar, open for sure, and off we went, three up on the bike. So, we're driving and driving, and I'm starting to think these guys are full of shit, and also in the back of my mind, I'm wondering if maybe they're trying to get me lost, thinking I'm some easy tourist mark to rob. By now, we were in the suburbs, and the hood was defo getting rougher, so I decided to stop at an all-night chai stall for a cuppa and a chat. And test them out.

Telling them I needed a break, we pulled over and soon had three cups of steaming chai and were sitting on a wall, shooting the shit. They seemed ok but better safe than sorry. Standing up, I unzipped my hoodie so the butt of the automatic was just sticking out. It wasn't long before they had spotted it, and I could see them nudging each other and stealing glances at it while we talked.

Then one of them plucked up the courage and said, 'Is that a gun you've got there?'

'Gun?' I replied nonchalantly. 'Oh yeah, you can't be too careful these days in such a big city so late at night.' Hint, hint.

'No, no, of course not,' the older lad replied, trying to make it sound normal, but I could detect a slight quiver in his voice.

'Err, can I have a look?' he ventured.

With a quick sketch around to see if anyone was watching, I whipped the gun out, quickly passing it into my hand so in the dimly lit back street, there was no way they would see it was only fucking plastic.

'Sorry, no way anyone touches my pistol, mate,' I said and slipped it back down the front of my pants, zipping up my hoody. To say they were impressed would be an understatement.

'Okay, shall we go find this bar then?' I said, throwing my empty cup into the bushes and jumping back on the bike.

The younger one looked like he was about to bolt into the night, but the older one was up for it, I could tell, and they started talking quickly in Hindu or Urdu to each other. Now I can only speak a few words, but I'd bet a shit load of rupees that I knew exactly what they were saying.

Older one: *'Come on then, let's fucking go then, this is looking like a good night, this dude is fucking out there.'*

Younger one: *'No way, man, this dude is fucking nuts, he's got a gun, for fuck's sake.'*

Older one: *'Oh, come on, you pussy, let's live a little. Anyway, how the fuck are we going to get home from here, let him get the beers in then we'll split up the road.'*

And just maybe...

Younger one: *'Yeah, but you try to rob him and I'm fucking gone, man!'*

Anyway, we got back on the bike and continued our journey. Shortly after, they said to pull in, the bar was here. We pulled in but I couldn't see any fucking bar. It just didn't look like the kind of place, back street and all residential. I mentioned this and the older one replied that the bar was closed and pointed to a shuttered building to our left. I was doubtful, but it did have a beer sign outside. Now they said that round the corner was an illegal booze store, which I conveniently couldn't come to, and would I give them cash to pop round and get the booze. Haha, yeah, right, I'll just wait here then, did they think I buttoned up the back? I told them this, but they just shrugged and made to get back on the bike.

Wait a minute, I'd been sure this was where they lived and they were just trying to rip off a few rupees to jog off home with. But getting back on the bike? This was unexpected. I paused for a few seconds then decided. What the fuck, if I give them a couple of hundred rupees and they don't come back, fuck 'em. I could have got one to stay with me, but to tell you the truth I couldn't be arsed. It was almost 2.30 a.m., time to get back to the hotel, if I could find the way of course. Okay, I gave them some cash and off they went into the night.

Five minutes passed and I was pretty sure they had split on me, but looking at my watch, I thought to myself, I'll wait another ten minutes and if they're not back, I'm off. I was just considering having another little line of ket to pass the time when I thought I could faintly hear music. In fact, what were those bright fluorescent lights coming out of that building not one hundred metres up the road? Could that be a bar, or even better a nightclub?! I got straight off the bike to investigate.

As I approached, it was looking more and more promising. Wide steps leading up, lights, music, and even better, a fit bird sitting in a glass-fronted booth inside. She must be there to take the entrance fee, I thought. This is it. So in I went, climbing the stairs with a big smile, half-dancing my way up. 'Excuse me, is this a bar or a night club?' I asked, making a drinking motion with my hand. She just stared back at me nonplussed, if anything she looked a little scared! This wasn't getting anywhere and I was just wondering what to do next, when all hell broke loose.

Suddenly a curtain on the wall to my left was thrust back and a half-naked man leaped out swinging a large wooden baton at my head! Luckily, I hadn't had that other line of ket or I might not have managed to leap backwards down the stairs as the baton whooshed just past my nose.

FUCK ME! I thought, landing on my feet. I put my hands up palms outwards, ready to try to calm him down, but he wasn't having any of it, and face contorted with rage, he leaped down the stairs after me swinging wildly, screaming some shit at the top of his voice.

FUCK THIS! I thought, I'm off. And went to turn tail, just as fucking loads of reinforcements were piling out the door after him, and worse than that, they were all tooled-up even better than him! No joke, axes, chains, metal bars, knives, the fucking lot. OH, SHIT.

I was gone, running for my fucking life, with this crazy lynch mob hot on my heels, and they were gaining, looking back, one guy in particular was closing fast, swinging a mean-looking chain round his nut. These boys meant business. Running through my mind as I ran, was the fact I was going to die, alone, in the backstreets of a foreign land, in the middle of nowhere, hacked to death by these lunatics and I would never know why.

Then I remembered the plastic pistol, my only chance. Jumping sideways, I turned and pulled it out, cocking it as I did so. That stopped them in their tracks. This was do or die time, but I had the initiative, and meant to keep it.

Holding the pistol with both hands, I locked my arms to try and stop them shaking, and jabbing it at them, one at a time, again moving it quickly in case they saw it was plastic, I screamed, 'BACK OFF, YOU FUCKERS, OR I'LL BLOW YOU ALL AWAY, THERE'S NINE BULLETS IN HERE, EIGHT FOR YOU AND ONE FOR ME.' I put the gun to my head for a second to emphasise the point. Fuck knows if they understood, but I'm sure I must have come across as a pretty mental dude. Stalemate for a moment.

Initially, they had stopped dead, shocked by the sudden appearance of the gun, but by now they were collecting themselves, I could see they were thinking about rushing me, I hadn't shot anyone yet. Was it even loaded? I bet that's what they were thinking as they started to move to circle me. It was at that moment the lads came back with the carry out.

They jumped between me and the mob. I could have fucking kissed them. Things started to calm down, one talked to the mob while I covered them with my plastic pistol and the other talked to me.

It turned out that what I thought was a nightclub was in fact a fucking Sikh temple. And I had committed the ultimate sin of entering without removing my shoes or covering my head. Fuck me, it just shows how careful you have to be when in another country with a different culture. These fuckwits were going to kill me for that, the mind boggles.

Anyway, once the lads had explained I was just some foreign twat with a gun who just didn't have a clue, they lowered their weapons, and I made a big show of putting the safety on and sticking it back down my pants.

As they wandered off, I nearly collapsed as the stress lifted off me. Somehow, I had pulled it off, I was alive. I remember thinking no fucker back home will ever believe this. But you couldn't make this shit up. If I could, I'd be a bestselling author, not a rave promoter with a bit of a ketamine habit.

One of the lads passed me a beer and asked me if I was all right. I answered that I would be in a minute, once I'd downed this fucking beer and chain smoked some cigarettes.

Publisher's Note

It remains unknown what else happened on Keith's trip to India past this point as, although he shared the memories with his friends, the details were sparse. But it's safe to say that whatever else happened on his solo trip to Delhi, he slipped in and out of trouble with ease, emerging with a smile firmly planted on his face, like all those adventures before, as if it had all been part of the plan.

From this eventful night in Delhi to his last days in London, he always carried with him an air of spontaneity and unpredictable charm; his laughter was infectious and his need to help others – whether it be buying a troubled friend a beer on the promenade in Corfu or providing aid to orphans and soundtracking an indulgent night of techno beats for the war-weary people of Bosnia – encouraged all those he crossed paths with to be better, *do better*.

As you will see in the following epilogue and afterwords from those whose lives he affected, be it for one afternoon in London or countless nights behind the decks, Keith had his own gravitational pull, one that continues in his absence, or because of this absence, to draw people together in the larger-than-life space he has left behind. His legacy lives on in the memories and actions of others, his light never snuffed out.

EPILOGUE

BY RAY PHILP

The first and last time I met Keith Robinson was in the grassless courtyard of a business park in Walthamstow, London. He welcomed me by craning his neck out of the passenger side of a circling box truck, glaring at me like an enemy combatant. Not a promising start.

Keith and his Desert Storm sound system crew had just come back from a free party in France, and in a matter of hours would be off to another somewhere beyond the M25. For the afternoon that I had his attention, his phone was ringing, his crew was yelling, his mind was racing.

I was working on a profile of Keith for the now-defunct Red Bull Music Academy magazine. At the time I was living in Glasgow and had caught wind of a story, bit by bit, about this Scottish folk-hero raver who'd driven a sound system to Croatia and Bosnia during the war there in the mid-'90s.

Keith had other things on his mind. For a long stretch we talked about his time in the Territorial Army, which, until he'd mentioned it, was news to me. It went a long way to explaining the difference between the Keith in front of me – manic, verbose, theatrical – and the carefree one I'd come across in the documentary *Storming Sarajevo* and expected to meet.

In the film, a younger Keith led an adventure that seems unimaginable now. Living by their wits, he and his friends forged documents, installed gearboxes, packed aid, fixed doors, charmed locals and, of course, organised raves – all the while hurtling towards what for years had been an active warzone. They seemed thrilled.

If it's hard to think of a group of pals in their 20s doing anything like that now, it points not so much to a generational change as to Keith's sui-generis charisma and will-do attitude, a singular force that pulled everyone else along for the ride. What a guy to have in your corner, or, as the case may have been, a trench.

However much Keith had changed – 'I'll never go to many firework shows again,' he said, recognising an irreversible shift in his own bearing – what remained constant was his unflagging sense of right and wrong.

Whether he was ploughing through conflict zones handing out 'cultural aid', one earth-cracking kick drum at a time, or describing a nuanced insight about his mixed-race heritage, Keith represented a now all-too-rare figure in club culture – a walk-the-walk activist with an expansive moral imagination.

Not long before we parted ways, as the truck doors clanked shut and one of the crew leaning opposite me, a barely conscious French guy with bloodhound eyes, held onto a warm tinny for dear life, Keith asked me if I fancied coming to their next party.

'What, right now?'

'Yes, we're packing up, we're going!'

I said I had commitments the next day (which was true).

What if I'd said 'fuck it' and bundled myself into the truck? For a start, I would've written a better story. More importantly, I would've been privy to even more of Keith's. Among those that didn't make the original piece – my recorder was off – is a story about a regimental visit at which Keith's commanding officer made escalating attempts to stop him meeting Prince Philip.

To cut a long one short, he failed. Regular royalty met rave royalty. Better yet, Prince Philip got as far as asking what he did before the army.

'Rave promoter, sir!'

As Keith began to explain what techno was to the most senior male member of the British monarchy, he may well have enjoyed the peripheral sight of his CO having a nervous breakdown.

After the summer of 2015 I didn't hear from Keith again. By August of that year he was on remand in Pentonville Prison as a result of a dispute with Blue Door, the company through which Keith had enlisted as a property guardian of his unit in the business park. The charges were dropped a few months later, but his mission to 'rescue [his] life' thereafter ran aground far too soon.

One of the last things Keith told me foreshadowed what was to come. 'If someone comes in here and shoots me in the head right now, well, I can't complain,' he said. 'I've done it all.' But even in death, Keith had one mad adventure left in him: thanks to a 'space flight memorial fund' set up in his honour, his ashes are floating among the stars. Keith was the brightest of us; now he's where he belongs.

* * *

The conversation that follows is compiled from a two-hour face-to-face interview I conducted with Keith, which took place in May 2015, and an hour-long phone call about a week after. I've edited the transcript for clarity, but it remains largely untouched. As I turned on the recorder, I'd followed Keith into his office; he'd begun by gesticulating about the mess. (I'd seen worse.)

* * *

...Two days ago, [the office] was totally tittified, as my sergeant major would say – tittified! It was tidy, and now – look at it! I just can't do it all now. It's gotten to the stage now where I cannae do it. I can't get the staff. The free party thing is bad enough – that's hellish to get people to do stuff, because you have to use diplomacy and all these horrible tricks, and psychological tricks – like, 'Oh, that's a brilliant idea you had about putting out all those posters.' 'Oh, did I?' 'Yes, of course!', you know, that kind of stuff, to get people to do stuff! You have to write down, like, Agent A doesn't get up till eleven in the morning, and when he does get up he has a beer and a chillum. So he's bazoonga'd till lunchtime. So you've got to remember, you can't get him to do anything till lunchtime. It just goes on and on. Now I'm cracking the whip, because I joined the army and all that. I learned all about organisation.

When did you join the army?

When they attacked Glasgow Airport. You not remember, they attacked Glasgow Airport? D'you not remember, they attacked Glasgow Airport, they were doctors, [they] filled the car with... [John] Smeaton, leathered them. I saw him on the TV, I was in France at the time. 'Don't come to Glasgow, we'll set about yez.' And this phone started ringing, man, all over the place. I don't know about you and your friends, but we were all like, 'What, people have attacked Glasgow!?' There's people phoning from Australia and all that. 'What you gonna do?' I said, 'I know what I'm gonna do: I'm joining up. I want to fight the Taliban, take the fight to them.' You can't come to Glasgow – I used to steal cars in Glasgow – but there's no way people are coming to Glasgow and trying to kill people. They can forget it. They can just forget it.

How long did you serve for?

I was no spring chicken. I was thirty-six or something-something when it happened. I was too old for the regulars, obviously, and I didn't want to go regular, either, cause there's no way out. So I went TA – I joined the 52nd Lowlanders, it's like an ancient organisation, 6 SCOTS it's called – it goes right back to the Bonnie Prince Charles days. So it was one of the earliest line regiments in the army. Before the police, there was the TA. The TA is actually a very interesting organisation, because it goes right, right back, to the militia, you know where the local landowners, the elite, would raise men from the local area to try to keep the peace. So anyway, these guys, they feed 1 SCOTS, which is another amalgamation. What they did with the army was, there were too many regiments, the Blackwatch and all this. They merged the King's Own Scottish Borders and the Royal Scots – there's still tension within that group. But they had to do that because you end up with all these head sheds and loads of people at the top, and all these RSMs and all these ceremonial roles that they didn't need. It worked well.

So, 6 SCOTS feed 1 SCOTS. And 1 SCOTS are fighting the infantry line in the British army, so I went to Afghanistan with them. And, yeah, it was a bit tricky. I got what I wanted. I went to the recruitment office, they said, 'What do you want?' I said, 'I want to go fight the Taliban.' And the guy was like, 'What?' I said, 'Well, they attacked Glasgow Airport.' He said, 'Oh, you're the fourth one we've had in today.' He said, 'What do you do for a living?' I said, 'A rave promoter.' He says, 'Wait a minute.' So the captain comes in, and the sergeant's like, 'I don't know about this guy, man, he's a rave promoter, obviously some kind of druggie.' And the captain says, [mocks Etonian accent], 'Fight the Taliban? Damn good show! Basically, you're in, old chap, you're going to get your wish, sign on the line.' And I certainly did. Oh, my goodness.

The first three months, nothing happened. I was phoning home saying, 'Oh, we're doing a grand job here. Reconstruction, we're building schools. The locals love us! We'd go for tea with them... probably hashish! All that stuff you read about the terrible job we're doing is rubbish. But then I went to Glastonbury for R&R, told the same story again, and all my friends said, 'Are you okay, are you alive?' We'd only had a couple of minor skirmishes, y'know. What they used to do was, what was it they called it? 'Spray, pay and run away?' They were paying people $15 to come up *near* the base, but not that near, and fire over a wall. After a while we weren't even ducking. So this was the whole deal. But then, just before I went to Glastonbury, we arrested this Taliban commander. And I remember the meeting in a little base which was not much bigger than this place. PB Tofan, it was called. There was this meeting. 'Right, we're going to arrest this Taliban guy.' I'm a TA nosher. I'm an idiot, basically – I'm black, I support Celtic and I'm old! It was unbelievable – the banter's no true.

Most TA reservists get sent to guard the big base, if they're lucky. They're lucky if they fire a shot – they'll be cleaning pots. But somehow my life's never been like that. I get sent to PB Storm – PB Tofan means 'storm' in Pashtun. And I'm from Desert Storm Soundsystem! They weren't kidding about 'storm.' This thing was on the edge of the AO – AO's the area of operations, [near] the badlands. The sergeant was this crazy, psychopathic guy called Knoxy, and he wanted basically to take on everybody, the whole Taliban lot, he planned to do them all over. But this wasn't really a course of action I'd recommend, because, these people, it's all family. You can't destroy the Taliban because for everyone you kill, another two must join! By the Pashtun law. So say they're doing bricklaying or something. 'Oh, cousin Abdul's been shot in the head'. Tools down, straight off to join. There's no way, unless you kill them all.

So Knox has decided to take on the rest of the world. I remember the meeting. 'Is this definitely a good idea?' I did say a few things, but Knoxy's quite powerful, it's hard to fight against him, you know. This is a TA nosher. He told me, when I first found the base – this is brilliant. He goes, like, 'Corporal...' Ray, is it?

Yep.

[Adopts a gravelly, sleazy voice] 'Corporal Ray! Good guy.' Touch of the ass and that. He'd talk to me and he'd be like, *[adopts the voice again]*, 'Oh, no. Private Robinson. First, you're old. Second, you're black. Thirdly, you support Celtic, which is not the team I support! I'll choke ye!' It went on and on. But eventually, I won their respect – I had to! Because once I'd rescued the first guy from the... my big mistake was [joining] team medic cadre. I was a volunteer. I was a volunteer for everything – I had to get all the skills before I go there. They started saying. 'Apart from Robinson, who volunteers?' I thought I was like some battlefield doctor, like M.A.S.H. After my two-week course, that was me, I knew everything. But when it came to it – holy God. Cause you're all in ditches, hiding, while the fire's coming in. 'Team Medic! Move forward to the casualty!' 'What? I've got to move through the fire and get to the casualty, who's bleeding out there?' The enemy are using him as bait, you know? Aw, hideous. You get there and you can't remember your name, much less the first aid. I remember saying to the guy, 'Twoey, Twoey, are you all right, are you all right?' Which is not exactly what you're supposed to say. 'Do I look all right, I've just been shot in the legs, mate.' If the guy can recognise me as Robinson, and give me abuse, then he's not dead yet. Then you actually have done the first thing you have to – it's about response. That guy's no' dead. In fact, if there's a worse guy, you move on and leave him because at least he can start treating himself.

After we rescued a few casualties from the fire, I also found out that being shot at actually makes me really angry. The first time they tried to kill me, I didn't react quick enough. And I was kinda standing there, thinking, 'Oh, what's all that?' 'Robbo, get in the ditch!' I was like, 'What?' 'Robbo, you're going to die!'. 'Oh!' It's not your brain, it's when your body realises the danger, it moves like shit off a shovel. I've got

50 kilos on, it's 34 degrees or something. I moved like Superman into that ditch. Once your body realises there's real danger... I nearly died in the toilet. I got quite famous among 6 SCOTS for this I think. They started shooting at the base, and I was in the toilet, and I was like, 'No way am I dying in the kazi', cause it'll be remembered. 'Remember that guy, Robbo?' 'Ah, the one that died in the toilet.' I was like, no way. So I flung myself right through the straw door, with my trousers round my ankles – 'I'm not dying in the toilet!' It was a bit tricky. There was loads of fighting and casualties and nasty stuff.

How did the Balkans prepare you for that experience?

No, there's no dealing with that. It didn't help me at all. The training and all that, kinda. The army, kinda. But the reality of combat was mental. Like nothing else. The feeling of elation when you survive afterwards is immense. It's like being reborn. The feeling of being alive after a contact – even during a contact, the excitement is incredible. You're *shitting* yourself. Anyone who says they're not scared during a contact is either mentally retarded or lying. Because there's no way. I've seen grown men lying in ditches saying, 'I'm not moving, I've got kids.' That's regular soldiers. Once I realised I had a weapon that could fire back, I just went mental. I'd just jump up the top of the ditch and started shouting, 'Desert Storm Soundsystem!' And talking about their mothers and all that. I'd be shouting, 'I'm over here, I'm over here! C'mon!' And giving it to them plenty, man. I rattled them, you know. Cause that was my job. Not necessarily to hit them, because they're not standing up, and it's a 200 metre kind of range, is contact. I couldn't spot them at first at all. I couldn't see where the fire was coming from, and it was really scaring me because I didn't know where to shoot. And I don't like to just shoot anywhere – because you're not allowed to, for a start – you've got to ping the enemy, positively identify them. I just didn't want to end up shooting villagers or something. [Otherwise] it'd be me that starts World War III in Helmand by shooting some kid and I've got to rot in hell for it afterwards.

Anyway, this old soldier says, 'Aye Robbo – look for them in the shadows of the trees'. 'Shadows of the trees... I'll give this a shot, because I'll give anything a shot by this point. And sure enough, there they were. They're hiding in the shadows of the trees in the daylight, and you can't see because your eyes are looking at the brightness. See the trees, the shadows of them, that's where they were. Soon as I realised that, I was onto them. I was right on top of them. So I'm firing tracer, as well. So I'm using the sight just to get on the target and, *crack*, in wee bursts, watching the tracer, every fourth round's a tracer, just to bring it, walk it onto that target. So then I know their heads are down. And the reason for the head-down is so that the commander can get us together for what they call extraction; I called it running away. That was basically the plan. Get the hell out there. Cause what they're doing is they get you a casualty. And then they try to surround you and cut you off. They've got all the avenues covered – they know how long it takes a helicopter to come as soon as you call, 'Contact, contact' to control to send the helicopter. The other thing is the Quick Reaction Forces, you know, vehicles – but that takes a while, that takes 25 minutes. And I tell ye, 25 minutes, man, is a long, long time in a contact. The average contact is about 17 minutes.

Are you still with the army?

No, I left.

When did you leave?

Years ago. I went back to reserve and they promoted me to corporal really fast after my report from Afghan. And then they gave me a

PTLLS certificate, which is like a teaching thing. And they discovered that I was really good at teaching recruits. You ever seen that film, *Full Metal Jacket*?

Yes, many times.

I based myself off him, the Scottish, black version of that. I made it all really funny, but with a serious glint. But I was really good at it right away, like a duck to water. I've got the gab. I had a brilliant time. But the thing is, they offered me a full-time job. And the CO said [*mock Etonian voice*], 'Robinson, come on in, sit down. Got brilliant news for you, hea. Full-time job, 25 grand.' I was like, 'No, sir, I'm leaving'. 'What!?' .... I only joined to shoot... to get the people back from Glasgow Airport.

I was messed up in the head. I'm getting treatment for PTSD at the moment. The army never gave it to me, I had to get that myself, at Harley Street. It's working! I've kept a journal of it all. There's a girl that treats me saying that I could sue the army no bother for a couple hundred thousand, but wouldn't do it because I like the army. I gained things out of it. I've always had a moral compass, I've always helped people. As you see, you're having to live on the road and everything. You do get tarred with the same brush a bit. Other people's morals start to wear off on you in some ways.

When I came back from Europe after living in very difficult circumstances, living in Europe in trucks organising raves. My moral compass wasn't busted – it was better than most people's – but it was a wee bit skew-whiff. But coming out the army, it was perfected. Your loyalty, integrity, selfless commitment, respect for others, all this stuff. I'm not saying you've got to do that all the time, but you've got to aspire to it. I came back from that changed, definitely. I'll never go to many firework shows again. I don't like loud bangs, and I don't like people queueing behind me. I'm different now. Different!

You've been hardwired differently.
I see threats now. I look about myself completely differently now. When I look about, I am still looking for threats a bit. It kinda helps you. It's helped me with this – it might not look organised just now, but that's cause there's so much happening at the moment. It's happening. We're slowly getting together a new set-up.

You still put on events.
Yes.

And I saw a recording studio back there. Are you guys facilitating other people's music, as well?
It's just gotten to that stage, but we're getting kicked out! Some asshole – some slightly psychopathic... This woman, she's always had it in for us here, I don't know why. One of the tenants, the guardians. There's guardianships, y'see. She's managed to get us papped out. But then, little do they know... Ray, I'm now a resident of Walthamstow. Now, downstairs is Turning Point. It's like, for helping junkies get back to being members of society. Apparently, according to this cow, I'm a mad, smack, crackhead or something. And, I mean, I've been taking drugs now and again... Obviously, when I was in the army, I didn't. And I always did before. But I'm no crack, smackhead, I tell ye. But I'm gonna play this. If we do get kicked out of here, I'm gonna go to that balcony, cause I'm brilliant at living outside. But I've got other places – I've got the press, the local rag, and all that. You know, 'War hero forced onto balcony by horrible company.' 'Puts all his money from Afghanistan into opening an events business and gets squeezed out by these people and now lives on a balcony, eating baked beans',

or something. They'll love that. Thing is, I'll turn to Turning Point, and they'll set like four case workers on you. And they've got to get results. Or they don't get funding. Failure for them is horrible. So I'll let them help me, completely. Right into the house! That's my plan.

Now, I fought for this country and all that. I fought for free speech. I believe in free speech. But I tell ye: anarchists. See these middle-class, educated anarchists, they've not got a clue. If they got what they wanted – anarchy – they'd be the first to die. Because bad people, like me and worse, would just take over immediately. They'd be the first to die, because their education and stuff would not protect them. They don't understand what anarchy is. They've *no* idea. But I respect their being allowed to say it. Even a fascist – I hate Nazis, I fought against Nazis the other week here – I respect their being able to say their view. You have to respect a fascist in a way, because they're so focused and narrow-minded, and they're strong. I respect that in them. The same as the Taliban. I didn't like them, but I had to respect them. I like this country because there's such a mix of people can say what they want. The cops have not got guns. There's riots when... I know a couple of Met cops now through the army, and they said they were losing London – they were actually losing it – and they asked for the army, according to the people I spoke to, and they were told naw. Even that Theresa May, she's some kind of right-wing witch as far as you can make out, she said naw.

Since we've only got 15 minutes, cause I don't want to keep you for too long, let's move onto Croatia...

Let's quickly go through this, cause I can tell you this link-up bit...

The Criminal Justice Bill was counterproductive, because all these people met up at this demo that had absolutely no contact with soundsystems – they were not a force. They were completely separate entities doing their own thing. They'd never even heard of each other. There was no internet or anything. In Mixmag, once a month, that was your only contact with what was going on. So anyway, at that march, people exchanged telephone numbers, like busy-o. Cause there's mobiles now. A couple people had a mobile. I remember this guy coming up during the riot. I'm saying, 'Get away from the van', cause the cops are attacking it. There's blood on the streets, man. He says, 'Can you take my number, take my number?' I was like, 'You're mad!' He says, 'Naw, give me your number!' I write it down. *Scribble noise* I remember the guy, solidly. He had curly black hair and this crazy face, and he was Scottish – that's why I remembered him. So he gets back up the road after this madness, and I tell you, this madness never stopped at the demo. It went on and on. That's how we met Spiral Tribe and all this crap, and they were brilliant people. They were our mentors.

Anyway, so he's back up the road and we're sitting there, all of us, like, our brains bazoongad from this thing, man. The phone goes – 'Fuck's that, it'll be journalists'. 'Oh, my name's Paddy, remember, the crazy Scottish guy that nearly got done in by the cops trying to get your phone number?' I was like 'Oh, I do remember you! What d'you want?' And he goes, 'Do you want to take your soundsystem to Bosnia?' This is during the war! I was like, 'You what? Just a minute.' I look around the room and say, 'Guys! Who wants to go take the soundsystem to Bosnia? This is some crazy fucker from the march that we gave the number to. And a show of hands: all the hands are up like that. 'Mate, we're doing it'. And that was it. It was Worker's Aid from Bosnia. Some kind of Trotsky outfit.

You went at least three times, didn't you?

We got addicted [to going to Bosnia and Croatia].

How many times did you go?

I dunno, quite a few. We went with the aid convoys first. We were bringing cultural aid, as we saw it. Instead of tins of beans, which they didn't even like, it turns out. People were bringing tins of beans and sausages, to a Muslim country! Trying to feed them pig! I was like, no way man. If they'd found that out, there would've been riots! I think... we had a massive effect. It's been horrible. Everyone's dead – your granny, everything. But if these guys have come all this way in this crazy vehicle and they're doing a party, then it must be getting better. That's what people think. They're rushing out their houses, 'Whoa, I've made it, I'm alive'. From 70 to 3, there were people on the dance floor, and I'll tell you what, they loved it. They'd never heard any music like this in their lives.

What kind of music were you playing?

At that time, we were playing what was available from 23rd Precinct. We were playing, a kinda, a Carly Coxy techno, like techno with a 'ch', and orchestrally banging. I remember 'bang, bang to the beat of the drum' ['La Luna (To The Beat Of The Drum)' by The Ethics], all sorts of stuff. We were influenced by Colin Barr a lot from Fresh, I was influenced by him and his posse. But then I was influenced by DIY later, 'cause I met the house crew way up north. So I had a lot of influences. At that point we were playing, I dunno, pretty dodgy commercial techno, but it was all right. We've always played for the dance floor, Desert Storm, none of your pretension crap. We want people on the dance floor, that's our thing, dancing. And that's what it's all about, a party, isn't it?

How did locals receive the music?

They loved it. It didn't matter. Desert Storm have usually always played something [that], really, anyone can dance to it. We weren't playing gabber, we *never* played that.

One of the things that struck me about the documentary, Storming Sarajevo, was that it seemed hard to communicate with people. There must've been some tense situations, whenever you wanted to put on a party or if you needed help with something.
It was hit and miss. We had some dodgy moments, as you could imagine. Very dodgy moments. I remember when we were in Sarajevo once, and this guy, we'd been in this bar, and we said, 'We've nowhere to stay, we need somewhere to stay.' And he says, 'You can use my flat!' And I thought, 'That was nice.' We drive there and the place is really, well, fucked, and it says 'Welcome to Hell' on the building. 'What is this, man?' So we get in and he goes up the room and there's no-one else about. So he opens the place, and we're in there, and this guy, Sim, he's looking out and he asks, 'Is there a bullet hole there?' The Serb lines are up on the hill, and we know this and we, stupidly with the windows open, are staring up at it. And there's a hole in the window, and as I follow it from the Serb lines – we all did it – once we followed it down, and there's another hole in the chest of drawers, and opened it and inside was the sniper rifle, the front of it. We were like, Jesus Christ, man. We stayed there for a couple of nights but then we were away. That was hairy. There were a lot of hairy moments. There were almost too many hairy moments. After a few weeks of that life you lose the plot a bit.

What was the day-to-day experience of travelling across Europe in those trucks like?
We were with the aid convoys. It was interesting – there were so many different characters. There were people like the hippie move-

ment, the bearded lot – kept themselves to themselves a bit. Then you had the university students, there were Marxists. There was all this mixture of people. But anyway, we were quite friendly; we did parties wherever we went, so we used to get along with everybody. Then we got, finally, to Tuzla. It was the middle of winter. It got really, really heavy. You noticed, as soon as you came out of Germany, the tunnels – loads of tunnels – they started to get worse and worse. Until you got to Bosnia... I mean, the [roads] were terrible. They looked like nightmares. Leaking water and cracked pipes and huge potholes. The roads just became a nightmare. At that point the roads were really military controlled. So basically you went from one checkpoint to the next. Checkpoint after checkpoint. Some military stuff, too. Some shooting. Couple times you'd see people wounded and all that coming down. When they were fighting, it was only really buses they had. They were all loading onto buses. It didn't seem very hi-tech to me. And we saw some wounded on bonnets and a few things like that. The stories people tell that get you the most... You often get shot in your car driving it. By snipers. And then the family donate the car and give it to the neighbour. You often see these people, with their window taped up at the front, where they've been shot through. And you think, how did they survive that? And they're still driving about.

The [party] we did in Mostar... see, Mostar we did ourselves. The first couple [trips] we got to Tuzla and it was crazy – we drove about the streets and people just came out their houses. There's so many things that happened, it's difficult to pin down a couple of items. I can tell you one thing about Croatia. We went into this really bad town. There were Mercedes at the gates, in towns – that wasn't good at all. And you could see that these people weren't friendly. Bearded, large ones. We went to town, went to get a coffee. And the guy was not friendly – he was throwing the cups at me. I went out and said,

'I think we should just go.' As soon as I got out, this Mercedes came past the tables in blacked-out windows and one window went down and inside was this huge bearded guy with an AK pointed straight at us. We finished our coffees and left. Croatia was a bit more violent in some ways, in my opinion. Split, we went to this barn with a big shelf on the door. There's army calendars and the things they wrote on the toilets, like a little boy shagging a little girl from behind – just not friendly.

One story that really sticks in my mind. I remember when we did the party at the old police station, which was actually across Mostar Bridge, which of course was destroyed but they built another way across. And then I remember this guy came to me and said, 'I saw the lights in the police station and it took me right back – this is where we fought to the death.' He said, 'You'd be the last body, the guards there' – there were six of them, and probably had to have been like 20 that had died. He escaped through a tunnel he'd been shown by his Croatian girlfriend that went right underneath the river, a really weird tunnel. And they were trapped in there for days, they were freezing. It sounded terrible. Finally, he gets out at the river, and he swam across. He was the only one that survived, but he got tortured by his friends – they thought he was a spy! Wow. When he said, 'Thanks for putting on the party,' things like that make a difference, you know.

And I remember, oh my God, yes, of course, Sarajevo. When we were driving round – it wasn't the wisest idea, looking back, because the place was full of snipers. I remember standing by the side... I got a dictionary out, going through the words, bit by bit, and it said, 'Don't stand here – snipers'. And I suddenly realised, nobody else was standing [around] , and you're like, 'Right, good.' And I remember we drove past the market. There was no one who wanted to talk about it, but loads of civilians died in the market. It was one of the major turning points in the Kosovo conflict, because that's when a lot of peacekeepers died... like 40 people. We went to a high school that we were supposed to stay at. It said 'Welcome to Hell' at the front of it. We drove in! There were loads of holes, bullet holes in the window.

I remember the fucking asshole who nearly got me killed, I remember him. He was driving us in the truck. We were going through Sniper Alley [Ulica Zmaja od Bosne in Sarajevo, the city's main thoroughfare]. To get to Tuzla, you have to go through Sniper Alley. There's no way around it. There's Serbs up on the hill with anti-aircraft guns, not sniper rifles. This asshole kept flashing his lights – so that he could see where he was going – with the stick. Oh, man. We nearly died. It was the closest I came to destroying that convoy. Everyone's lights are off, because you can't have lights. They were going to shoot us dead, that's what we were told. No lights. Fine. This fucker can see where he's going, but he's shining them on a huge white truck. Fucking daft, man. I wanted to kill him. I've never felt so annoyed before, selfish fucker.

After you left, I know that you went to Italy...

Italy, Poland, Germany, Spain, Portugal – did we say that? – Goa, I've played the Caribbean, I've played Caracas, Venezuela... it goes on and on. You've got Montreal, New York, I dunno...

Eventually, we left [the UK] in 1996 and said, that's it, we're not coming back. We were persona non gratis here. Everytime they put my name up, the cops came up with 'subversive rave organising nut-job.' I got ran out of Glasgow an' aw. The head cop came round to my house, bang bang, Friday night. 'Robinson, get your black ass in the car, the boss wants to see you. You get out there.' And you're like, 'Oh, shit.' 'Robinson, there'll be no party this weekend. There'll be no party, or yous'll be getting the tin pail – you hear me, the tin pail!' So, that was the end of that. It was time to go. This was 1995. We had loads of problems. These were raves where we charge money. The trouble about money in Glasgow and clubs is, there's dodgy characters, it was a dodgy town. We used to get trouble. We're all from middle class backgrounds, from the West End. And these guys, they don't care! You've got guys on the door, there was this guy Webby. I remember he said, 'Keith, I imagine I have to let this man in now.' He came to the door and said, 'I'm on the guestlist'. I said, 'What's your name'? And he said his name, and I said he wasn't on the guestlist. He said, 'No, no, I *am* on the guestlist'. And he pulled out a huge machete. And I said, 'Well, mammoth machete, guestlist, you're in!' 'And here's my security tag, Keith, I'll no' be working for you again.'

After this, I thought, 'What am I gonna do?' I spoke to these wee dodgies from Partick – I won't say their names – and they said, 'Oh, we've got some guys who'll do the doors for you, they'll sort it all out – no more trouble'. We met this guy from Drumchapel, and [when I saw him] I thought, 'Well, this guy can do the door, he moves like a cat'. I've only met three other people who move this kind of way, on the tips of their toes and all of that – one of them was my kickboxing teacher, the other one was that Sergeant Knox, in fact, and this guy. He was obviously the real deal. So we got him on, and at first it was great. We lined up all these maddies from the town up from the Sub Club. 'You, MacCrimmon, naw, you're not getting in; you, give me your blade'. It was great! I didn't know who they were at this point. Obviously heavy dudes, saying to me, 'There's a guy climbing over the wall, what shall we do, Keith? Shall we stab him up?' 'Oh, no, no, no, please don't!' 'Just, eh, get his money off him and bring him in.' 'Oh, no problem.' So this relationship was going well. But then they started to take over. It all ended in tears anyway, to cut a long story short. We had to stop the parties for about a year, because they were taking over. It turned out he was the youngest son of a [gang] family in Glasgow.

One of the parties you did in Scotland was in a castle, right?

It was in Renfrew. What was it called again? It was a folly [Formakin House]. What this guy did, he bought some land somewhere out in Renfrew. He shipped this castle brick-by-brick from England, but he turned all the stones round the other way, so the weathered ones were inside and all the unweathered ones were outside, so it looked new. But he never finished it. So it's like gardens with... the Monkey House! That's what it was called. We persuaded this guy that we were doing a film shoot with 100 people. Me and this gyppo Bradley; Bradley's a brilliant guy. We arrived in Bradley's Porsche and rubbed the cream, as they say in French, and the guy believed it. I remember the day of the gig; must've been about 800, 900 of us. So he looks over the balcony into the courtyard: Andy Weatherall's coming in, we had everybody there. I said to the guy, 'Well, I think that's 100 in now.' There were 800 coming up the drive. And I thought he was going to punch me.

Do you still play at these events?

Aye... listen, Desert Storm makes me stratospheric. Stratospheric. The only thing you can't have is my money, my medal, and my girlfriend. Anything else is fair game. In my opinion, you can come visit me, interview me another year, and I think we've made it. I've got a few plans in progress at the moment, we're just gonna go stratospheric. We cannae fail. I mean – we can fail, but at least... it's always better to try hard and fail than... If it comes off, we're laughing. I'm about to do a Factory Records in this place. I've identified a fatal flaw in the business plan of the events industry, a fatal flaw which will allow me to – not take over, but exploit it massively.

Will you share that with me now?

Absolutely not. Confidential information.

This flaw's there. I'm a trained Brechin corporal now. I don't know why they did this to me. They took me to Brechin, and I can organise people now and manipulate people. I was always good at it before, but now I'm really good. As soon as I came back from the army into the events industry, I instantly identified a massive weakness. I could be wrong, but I'm not wrong a lot.

You said when war happens, music is always one of the first casualties. That really struck me.

It sounds like the kinda crap I'd come out with to sound good for the camera.

It did sound good!

I make it up as I go along.

Did that change your outlook on putting on parties, going to the Balkans, the significance of doing that for people who aren't just turning up, but almost needed that sense of release –

See, I like your thinking, and it's a really good idea, but, actually, naw. What it did to me was it said, 'If we can do parties there, we can do parties anywhere.' A party's a party to me. Bosnia, wherever it is, it's just a party. I like to come across in the media as profound and all that. I'm an intelligent person who thinks on my feet. But, at the end of the day, it's just a party. We just put parties on. That's what I do. Party, party, party, party. Apart from a small break to party with the Taliban instead, it's been party, party since I was 14.

You got into parties when you were 14?

When I put my first party on at 14 in my garage, 50 flyers, I thought 50 people. More like 50,000 people. The whole neighbourhood, it was swamped. Our parties have always been successful. Desert Storm's got the luck of the devil. Honestly, it's like cosmic shit, man. We always use the first warehouse we find. It was meant to be, Desert Storm, it was meant to be. It serves some purpose. This energy of the rave and stuff, it serves a purpose. And once you're on a roll, it just goes. The doors just open. It's not like normal life, where doors are hard to open – some open, some don't, some lead to things, some don't. Once you're on that wave, the rave thing, it just goes *whoooooaaaah*. And we're on it again, now. Doors are opening that fast, I've warned everyone to watch out for opportunities because opportunities will [also] take you away from it. There are so many opportunities now, at the moment, even the lights go green all the time now, everything's dropped into place. Something massive is happening. The rave is back, or music's back, there's definitely dancing to be done. People need to polish up their dancing shoes and start getting ready, because we're back. What was it they used to say? 'Lock up your daughters, lock up your wives / Lock up your back doors, run for your lives / Desert Storm's back in town.' Well, I tell you, we're back – and we're black!

This is a bit of an offcut now, but this bird I'm seeing at the moment, one of my favourite lines to white people – especially in the army – was, 'I'll be black'. 'I'll be black this', 'I'll be black that'. Just to break the ice. Taking the piss out of yourself is the best way to do it, and I think it's funny. I've been using this recently again, and the girl, she says, 'I'd like a word with you outside.' So she says, 'What's this thing about you saying you'll be black?' And I was like, 'Yeah?' 'You can't really say that.' 'How d'you mean?' She's as black as that sock, and

I say, 'What do you mean?' She says, 'You're not *really* black. You're really a demi-negro.' Now, she's black-black. A demi-negro is a really interesting phrase, because we speak French, both of us, and demi means like a half pint. So what she's saying, basically, is that I'm not black enough to say, 'I'll be black.' And this is a brilliant comment, because that was one of the best put-downs I'd ever had. I didn't know what to say about that. And now I say, 'I'll be half-black.' I can't say I'm black, cause she's right! I'm not.

How did you come up with the idea for Desert Storm?

Desert Storm itself was thought of in the toilet. I've thought of most of my main ideas in the toilet. Pissing, I don't know why pissing... Pissing, you're only using a certain part of your brain to piss, and it's a good place to think. I always have ideas on the toilet. We were doing this party in an old railway tunnel. It was our first ever Desert Storm [under Kelvinbridge]. We couldn't think of a name, we'd gone through all these stupid names. Saddam [Hussein] had been doing the first war by television, or the first war that I'd seen, the Iraq war. 'I know what we'll call it,' and I ran out pissing still, pissing everywhere, 'We'll call it Desert Storm, we'll call it Operation Desert Storm!' And that was it. Saddam's Bunker, it was called. Operation Desert Storm, Saddam's Bunker! It was Death or Glory and all that on the ticket, with Saddam's face on it and airplanes, warplanes.

Glasgow's a funny place. There's all these so-called hard people and all these so-called friends. When the cops came, they left me down the tunnel on my own, with all the cops, getting the tin pail. They all fucked off. The only one I forgive is my girlfriend at the time, Louise, who fucked off with the money, which I thought was a good move. I mean, that was fair enough. She was really apologetic afterwards.

I've had a crazy life. I wouldn't swap my life for anybody's. Kanye West, anybody – I don't give a damn. I've had the best life ever. If someone comes in here and shoots me in the head right now, well, I can't complain, I've done it all.

Ray Philp

AFTERWORD 1
DSTORM DAYS & SOUND SYSTEM LIFE
BY BSTORM

Scoraig: The First Time Our Paths Crossed

I first met Keith back in the early 90s, although we did not become close friends for some years later. I remember meeting him at the Scoraig free festival. I had travelled up from mid-Wales with some friends in an old Daimler; you know, the old curvy Jaguar-style one with twin tanks and leather seats? It was a classic car and luxury for its time, which would have been the '70s or '80s, I reckon. It was a long journey from Wales to Scotland. We were taking it in turns to drive so we were going nonstop all the way up to the Outer Hebrides, heading to Ullapool where we could catch the boat over to the festival site. An amazing, beautiful site out in the middle of nowhere, no one around for as far as the eye could see. Steep green mountains coming down to an open piece of land and then down to the sea – such a nice spot for a free festival.

When we arrived at Ullapool there were quite a few people in the car park waiting to get the boat over. DiY sound system was there with the Black Box rig. Quite a few of them had come up from Nottingham, some I would become good friends with over later years. We all got on the boat headed out to the site. It was probably a 30 to 45 minute journey up Loch Broom. We got off the boat and quite a few people were on site already – the tent and areas were all set up for the party while the boat headed back to pick up more of the waiting people and sound systems.

My mates and I were mulling around smoking spliffs and listening to music around the site and just generally taking in the amazing place we were in. I remember hanging outside one of the areas dancing to some music playing there, and then I heard, 'Ey, this is a banger, this one,' as Keef danced around next to me. I turned around to him and said, 'Yeah, fucking love this tune,' as I cut some shapes in the air. It was one of those classic early anthems of the era, Gat Decor's 'Passion', a total classic. We both raved for a bit and chatted like you do, questions like, 'Where you from?' and 'What brings you up here?', then we both went our separate ways. I saw him about over that weekend at the festival, but it would be some years later that we would meet again and become good friends.

Scoraig free festival was a special place and an outstanding, beautiful part of Scotland, a perfect place for a festival with sound people and good vibes. Who'd have thought that this chance meeting would lead to us becoming good friends later in our lives and end up with us doing all the things we did?

Nottingham: The Sound System Culture and Meeting the DStorm Crew

I was 20 or 21 years-old and I'd lived in Wales all my life. I was getting to the point of 'there has got to be more to life than hills, waterfalls and sheep'. I'd been doing parties and DJing plus producing music in and around Wales but was feeling a need for change and new experiences in life. I'd been going to Nottingham for the free party scene, out to quarries and outdoor raves that DiY and Smokescreen sound systems were doing. So, I decided to move there to do a music industry skills course at Clarendon College & Square Studios. Some friends of mine, Sam and his sister, Alice, had moved up there and as had my friend Ace who I'd known for some years.

We all got a flat together on Gregory Boulevard, Hyson Green, just round the corner from Radford Road – it was an area with quite a reputation but Nottingham has had a reputation for some years, just like a lot of cities. It can have its dark side but it also has its good side too – like the music scene. There was a big free party and club scene in Nottingham and the surrounding areas. Loads of different sound system crews and a diverse soundscape of underground dance music, and always loads of house after-parties or just gnarly people having house parties as there is a big student population. That is where I'd meet the Samovar crew and where I'd start DJing for all the parties and nights they were doing. I became friends with them all and a regular DJ at their events playing my sound at the time which was a selection of phat, heavy breakbeat, trip hop, big beat and jungle music.

Keith and the rest of the DStorm crew were living in the city doing parties and nights and someone said there was a house party going on somewhere in the city, so we rocked up. I had my bag of records with me and proceeded up to the decks to get a set – it's here that I meet Keith again and where I also meet the rest of the DS crew – Kerry, Amy, James and Liz. I got on the decks and played some of my banging jungle tunes.

The party was having it, people were dancing around the room the house was rammed; you know how it is – the kitchen crew people, those in the back garden round a fire pit, others in bedrooms chatting, the usual house party vibe. Keith came over to me and said: "Phat tunes, mate! What's your name? You should come and play at some of our other raves we do, come out to one of our free parties in the forest or down at the Sky Club! Come see us at our place over in Forest Fields, 71 Birrell Road."

I started going round, meeting all the DStorm crew and getting involved with raves and the protest movements going on in those days; Criminal Justice marches, Reclaim the Streets and DJing with them at free parties and club nights they were doing.

Amy and I hooked up, and I moved in with her at the DStorm HQ. We were going on missions to the teknivals out in Europe; Czech Teks in Hostomice and loads of others in Italy, France, Holland, Spain, Portugal, etc. Keith was a leader who always had a plan on what to do and where to go, but we all knew it was really the one we called the oracle in the DS crew who was behind the plans, aka Kezza. And when it came to setting up the rave and rig, etc, we were a nonstop rave machine. The DStorm truck was packed with everything we needed to get the party started and we pumped up the jam big time. The feet were stomping for sure!!!

Me, Ame and Ben decided to buy a truck together and travelled to Manchester where we met a guy in a yard who had a whole pile of Hovis bread trucks for sale. We ended up coming away with a Leyland DAF freighter – it was a huge eleven-tonne truck, but I only had a 7.5-tonne licence at the time, but the guy had told us we could lower it to 7.5 which was why we bought it. It had a massive box on the back of it, twenty-eight-feet long with dropdown doors on the side, a tail lift, etc. Lots of space in the back which we could convert into our living space; we put a partition wall just over halfway down the box for the living area and the back was for storing the sound system and everything else we would need for putting a rave on.

When we had finished the conversion, it looked great. A mezzanine bed at the front of the box and a U-shaped seating/sleeping area underneath with decks and record storage down the right-side wall, another seating area and burner down the left side wall, then the kitchen on the back of the partition wall. We were all ready to hit the road home on wheels, rave ready.

Reclaim the Streets, Teknivals, Warehouse Raves and Travelling

After quite a few RTS we did around the country we started to get a lot of heat from the Popo 5-0. We had lost the truck after the Bristol RTS. We got out of the demo okay but the next day, when James and Liz had gone to the truck to go get something, the police had been waiting, watching the truck where it was parked in an estate. As soon as someone showed up, they pounced and took it away. It took us months to get it back from that escapade.

We then spent a long time living out in Europe doing the teknival circuit, sometimes stopping in some of the countries putting on outdoor parties and warehouse raves. It was great interacting with all those different cultures in beautiful places with nice people – what a life, what an experience. I remember when it would come up to winter and we would all be thinking the same: let's head south to the sunshine! We all liked Barcelona as it's a very vibrant city and back in the mid-90s, there were tons of empty warehouses to do raves.

We also would go to Portugal and the south of Spain for the Dragon Festival, which was a regular. We did a lot of good parties in BCN and probably one of our pinnacle parties of the time in Badalona for New Year, 1999. We had this massive warehouse out by the three chimneys that was like a cathedral inside, the space was epic. We got to live there for over a month during the build-up to the rave (which was mostly unheard of at the time), being able to make sculptures and get all the art and backdrops up and around the building, plus a great-looking bar. We were travelling with other sound systems at the time: the likes of Lego, Subsound, Hekate and the Total Resistance crew who had just come back from their trip to India.

The party went off. It was a banger with music, DJs, live sets and visuals and the German crew were there with all the flame par cans on top of the sound blasting out massive bursts of flames, guys with flamethrower top hats with twenty-foot flames coming out of them, flaming aliens hanging off the bar. The place was full of sculptures, including a wicked totem pole and a clock whose hands spun around at midnight on new year made by the Totals. I made a few circuit board sculptures, a big one that went above where all the live sets were being played, and some around the bar which was looking great with cogs and wheels all over it, backdrops and graffiti all around the place, hexagon projection screens behind the rig and we had performers. Jonny from Mutoids was there with Spamzilla; a mutated car made into a dinosaur. There was so much going on! It was a pinnacle rave for us, showing what the underground scene was capable of, if given the right time and space to create an amazing place and atmosphere. Thousands came through the doors over the five days that the rave went on for – what an epic event!

After about ten years of non-stop raving, life moved forward. Life evolves and other projects come up, like it did for us at DStorm with the Bassline Circus project becoming our main focus and after ten years of underground free parties, warehouse raves and kicking in warehouse doors all over the EU, we were like, 'What's next?' We couldn't just stop and go get an office job. So, we bought a circus tent and formed a circus with friends from other sound systems and crews and the circus was born, but that's another story.

The Last Chapter: Life, Legacy and the Beat Goes On

I was living in west London near Bushy Park, a lovely place to live; nice and green, deer running round the park, big old trees and flowers, butterflies fluttering around, stag beetles wrestling each other and so on.

Keith had moved back after his last tour in Afghanistan. Things weren't the same, we had all moved on in life – I was living with Melissa and doing up a house, DS had been doing the Bassline Circus project and the whole DS crew had naturally moved on with their lives, family, kids and all that.

Keith was living in a squat in Limehouse just round the corner from a friend of mine, Mr Psik. We would sometimes stay round at Psik's place when we were in town hanging out or going out to gigs like Busta Rhymes at the Indigo Bar or Wu-Tang Clan at the Troxy.

We had done a few raves here and there around London in squats and the rig was going out to festivals as part of the Noise Control family, but we were not as active as we used to be.

I had been going round to see Keith as we were getting ready to go and do a rave out in Italy. We were painting the rig to make it look spick and span. Keith had a room at the back of the warehouse where the studio was, and I can remember him and Melissa having what I would call a healthy debate about the moon landing with Keith saying, 'Of course they landed on the moon,' and Melissa saying, 'No, it was all faked and filmed by the Americans in studios.' This banter was going back and forth, a debate that would inspire a tune, as little did we know, Keith had been working on a live set to take out to Italy and he had sampled himself and written a little 160bpm jungle tekno loop with a pounding kick and a rolling breakbeat where the synth line drops and in comes his vocal, 'Only a fool would believe we didn't land on the moon... [echo] moon, moon, moon,' along with the samples from 'Nasa, the Eagle has landed... Roger, we copy. Go, Go, Go.'

We had been at the warehouse all day sorting the rig, and me and Mel went to go crash that night at Tom's round the corner. The next day at the warehouse we were there all day finishing the rig and were was knackered. Keith had just had a shower and was chilling on the sofa. I remember saying to him that I was going to go and crash as we were packing the van and heading out to Italy the next day. I headed to Psik's around the corner to get some sleep, then at some point I got a call from someone saying Keith had jumped into the river.

I jumped up out of bed and headed to the river straight away, and as I headed down there, I was just thinking, 'What the fuck has just happened in the last few hours since I left him?' I got down to the river at the spot he had dived into; the tide was high and at that point it was obvious that the current was strong (you don't fuck with the Thames, it's a strong force). You have to respect it. I still to this day don't know what he was thinking diving in, although I know Keith was a strong swimmer. He had walked down to the river with someone from the squat and they had gone to a place where there are steps that go down to a beach area.

The person who he was with left him at this point and we don't know exactly what happened, but Keith walked around the corner and witnesses said that they saw him dive in over the barrier and swim around for a bit before disappearing. Maybe he was thinking he could swim back to the beach part which was nearby but he was out in a wide part of the river, known to be dangerous with strong undercurrents and maybe hypothermia was taking hold. By the time I had got the call and arrived at the river, he was nowhere to be seen. I was just staring at the water not knowing what to do, looking up and down to see if I could catch a glimpse of him anywhere but he was gone.

I was fucking devastated just thinking about what the fuck had happened in those hours after I had left him. The police came and talked to us about what he had been doing in the last few days and if there were any signs of him being suicidal (which there wasn't whatsoever). How could someone who had been so excited and invested in our Italy trip – writing music, printing clothing, painting the rig – be suicidal? He seemed fine, just the same normal Keith. Yes, he had his ups and downs over the years, but who hadn't?

I am sure that seeing the things that you see when you're in the army and out in Afghanistan in a war zone has some effect on you. Was PTSD a factor in all of this? Looking down the barrel of a gun and shooting at another human life is not something I could do being a pacifist, nor having to run for cover whilst being shot at – it must scare the shit out of you.

To this day, I still don't really know what happened in those last few hours after I left him on the sofa chilling at his. Had something gone on in those last few hours for him to do the things he did and end up in the river? For some time later it would cross my mind, if I just hadn't left him, would things have been different right now? But you cannot beat yourself up over thoughts like that. It was a very traumatic and devastating part of my life and I did not realise how much it affected me – it has taken years to get over it and I am not sure it is something that you easily get over, losing a friend in that way. I couldn't do raves for years after, I just couldn't after losing Keith, it just didn't feel right – he was the sound boy and I was the DJ artist. That's why I shifted the focus of DS to the record label, that became my focus – getting back into pressing vinyl again and starting the 4 Elements project for Keith: Earth, Water, Fire and Air. The first vinyl was a repress of Keef's last record that he made which some of you will know from the synth line which is off the old Electribe Morgan Tek. It's a colour vinyl, a yellow with green and brown splatter for earth and then we did an aqua green and blue splatter for water – we still have two vinyls to make to finish this project – fire and air.

There are more projects up and coming on the DStorm record labels, more tekno/techno (however you want you spell it), more electro breakbeats, jungle, jungletekno and experimental across-the-board electronic dance music. DStorm sound system will be doing more raves in the future, I think.

Going out to the US and watching Keef's ashes blast off into outer space on a rocket felt like a closure and it's now time to carry on with the music releases, more of Keef's and the rest of the DStorm crew's tracks on the DSR labels and get the rig out more, as that's what Keef would have wanted.

We are hoping to get the Moon Landing EP out, as this was the last thing that he worked on. It was going to be part of his live set for the Italy tour and was just some loops in Reason before I made his track for him. It's been remixed by the DStorm crew; D-Omen, Wendy Del Hardkore and Desert Frog and we plan to press 300 but it will be a mix of one hundred picture discs, one hundred colour vinyls and one hundred black vinyls, all in memory of Keef. Like this, we keep his legacy going. Even when we lose people, if we keep them in our thoughts, are they truly gone?

We are doing this with Keef's music by keeping his spirit alive in his tracks. He was a special kind of person and I'm not sure I will meet someone quite like him again or do the things I did with him. It was a once-in-a-lifetime experience; all those raves, protests, warehouse parties, festivals, the travelling and meeting all the people we met along the way. Something I will never forget. The sense of family and community you have when you're living that lifestyle is amazing and when I think back to it, it makes me laugh. How mad those days were and all the things we got up to.

There's lots more of this story to tell and the DStorm history to get out there but all in good time. This book is Keith's life story which he wrote before he left for the stars. I hope you all enjoyed the read and look out for more DS projects coming soon... And remember the only future is underground. DS forever ...

BTORM / DSTORM SOUND SYSTEM / DSTORM RECORDS, 2025.

AFTERWORD 2

BY BIZZY

Here are some memories as far as I can piece them together.

Jamie (Clanger) and I (Bizzy) were introduced to Keef through mutual friends. We had all grown up in the same area. Keef was a few years older than us, so we knew the older crowd and remember one of their early bomb experiments going off in a field nearby, attracting all sorts of emergency calls from worried residents. This stuff was attractive to younger guys – motorbikes, explosions and, of course, the parties.

Jamie and a few of us had a passion for music and had experimented with records and decks, then electronic keyboards and such. Jamie was always a ground breaker, the first on the acid house scene with the clothes, haircut, etc., the first with decks and then the first with a Roland TB-303 from the local pawn shop down the Barras market. £30 was the price paid.

The parties had stopped at the time due to an incident with the police, who had found some random charges on which to arrest Keef and a few others. The usual press nonsense was in full flow. They escaped any convictions, and when we met him, he saw our passion for music, so we agreed to give it another go.

I had an old Renault van and Keef mentioned the old canvas 2000AD Desert Storm murals were in the basement of a club in Perth that had burned down, and it may be worth us heading up to see if we could retrieve them. Keef had what both he and others recognized as charisma, along with a genuine sense of purpose—when he said he was going to do something, he meant it, and there was probably an adventure to be had along the way. Sure enough, we got there, Keef 'got into' the building, and the backdrops were indeed salvageable. They were immense and had a real presence, especially since they were painted in fluorescent ink. I later learned how important that was to Keef—the way strobe and club lights hit them made them glow brightly, adding a distinctive vibe and energy to the space.

Jamie and I were full in now. Everyone just seemed to have a role: from planning, taking donations to clearing up, ours was the music. Jamie and I started jamming at the gigs playing live with the Roland gear and a sampler: TR 909, 707, 606 some keyboards and the trusty TB-303.

It seemed to work for folks. A mix of Keef, Dan, Hamish, Eden and regular guests on the decks playing good house and techno with some live home brewed live acid house tunes thrown in. You will never get a better break down in a music set than the generator running out of petrol and everything slowing down to complete darkness. Usually the person in charge of fuel was having a great time. Then, the cheer once it's cranked back up, music back on! The parties were free from three a.m. until whenever and had a repetitive beat, perfect for a late clubber.

Jamie and I were the band, and this gave us the perfect cover - the parties were framed as video promos for our next musical release. We had a great videographer in Jim Rusk, who still has great footage of some of the parties including our trips to London to play at Spiral Tribe parties and the Criminal Justice Bill with the old Bedford Party van, our all night parties on St Andrews beach, Scoraig and a gig in the Ministry of Sound when Soma Recordings took us on a tour with them.

Jamie and I decided to record some of our bleeps and chords, and Jamie borrowed keyboards and better mixer to make a record. Jamie, like Keef, had great intention and when he set his mind to it then we normally got results. That day, in Jamie's bedroom, we wrote the appropriately named 'Desert Storm' track. Jamie then stated we need to visit Soma, a Glasgow quality electronic music label run by Slam. Their label was in its infancy and when we met them all they were like a family and took it on and agreed to release the track. They then asked us what track was on the other side? The problem was, we didn't have one! We got organised, borrowed the gear and made the B-side. Keef, Jamie and I were in Soma's office and they liked the B-side. In fact, they released it as a double A-side record. Soma's Dave Clark asked for the name of this track. Blank faced, Jamie and I hadn't named it. I'm usually awful at names but threw the name 'Scoraig' out. The three of us smiled and that was it.

Scoraig was a party Keef had agreed for the sound system to go to. So, off we went to Ullapool and boarded a fishing boat with the sound rig, record boxes and gear to play on a remote Scottish peninsula with no road access. Nottingham sound system DiY were also playing. Graeme John O, Bose, Smudge, Jamie, Keef and I all had a spiritual experience there. It was so unique and special, as we were in nature and so far away from civilisation. The cops would not be closing this down; the repetitive beat started and never stopped.

On some of these occasions the police would arrive and generally just watch and negotiate a finish time due to complaints, depending on the stage of the night. This was another of Keef's many strengths: taking on the role of a professional event organiser and video producer.

However, things started getting heavier handed after the Criminal Justice Bill became law in 1994. The police would shut down events on arrival, confident with their new legislation and organisers with the threat and reality of jail. This would eventually lead Keef to travel south, as Scotland is a relatively small place to keep going when the power had shifted.

Although we didn't keep in touch regularly after he left Glasgow, if he was up, we would connect. The reason the railway arch was hired was so that in one arch we could build a recording studio and party in the other. However, as Keef states, he was regularly involved with dodgy guys and we knew they wouldn't hesitate to take the studio equipment. So it was only used for Keef to sleep on occasion and parties on others.

When the trip to Bosnia came up, Jamie and I pulled out of that, and Keef went on another great adventure.

Brian Welsh approached me in 2018 when he was making the film *Beats*. He recorded lots of audio from myself, Hamish and a few others; Jim Rusk also provided original footage of the van and parties which they put in the film. I usually hate these things as I don't like the camera, etc. Even playing music, I'd rather hide out of the way. Desert Storm was perfect for that, hidden in the back of the van.

Brian had heard the stories of these Desert Storm parties and based the party in *Beats* around one. He was also fascinated with Keef's story and his life.

Keef left us in 2016 and, unfortunately, so did Jamie near enough to the day in 2019. It is nice to remember these times. There's loads I remember but as it's Keef's book I would only be adding my memories to it.

Bizzy, 2025

Keef, 1970s, Scotland.

Keef, suited and booted, 1980s, Pelekas.

Keef, the wedding, 1980s, Pelekas.

Dstorm crew press shot for the release of SO13 on Soma, March 1993, Glasgow.

Desert Storm & Spiral Tribe flyer, 1993.

Keef & James, Radio Tuzla first mission, December 1994, Bosnia.

Keef on the decks, Radio Tuzla first mission, December 1994, Bosnia.

Keef & James with Fish & Ben, two Bosnian refugees smuggled back in the DS truck.

DJ KRob and local youths in Bihac, Bosnia, 1996. Photo: Adrian Fisk.

DS truck, Mostar, bombed out building no man's land, summer 1996, Bosnia.

Keef, Mostar Bridge dive, summer 1996, Bosnia. Photo: Adrian Fisk.

Danny, Keef & James, Hotel Bosnia, 1996. Photo: Adrian Fisk.

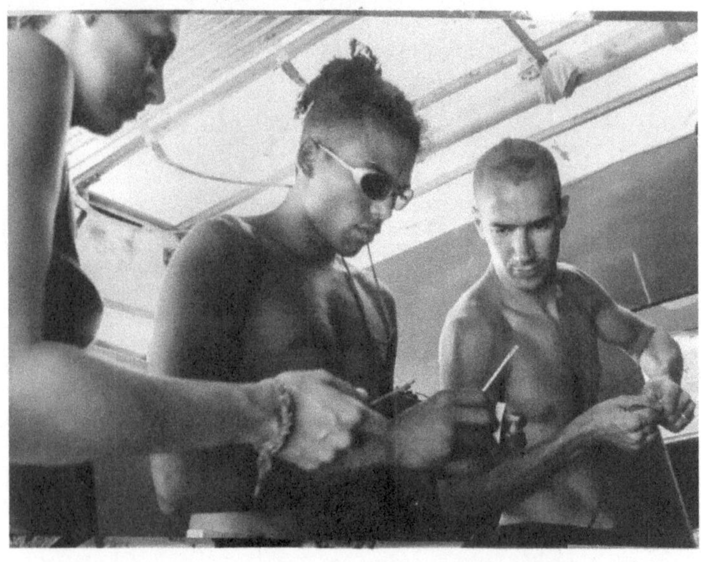

Liz, Keef & James, summer 1996, Tuzla with SP23, Bosnia. Photo: Adrian Fisk.

Keith at Reclaim The Streets, Nottingham, July 1997. Photo: Alan Lodge.

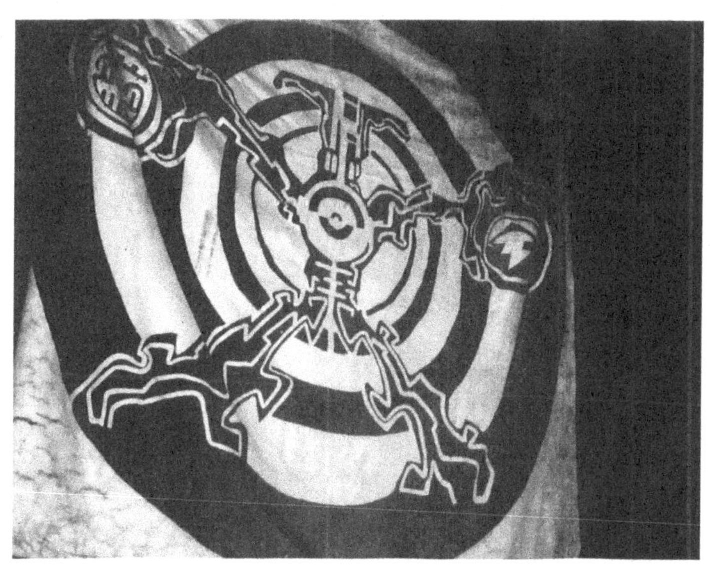

Dstorm backdrop, DS-SP23.

Dstorm rig, Roma, circa 1998.

Bstorm & Pekski setting up the rig somewhere in a field in Spain, circa 1998.

New Year's Rave, Barcelona, Sant Adrià de Besos 3 Towers rave, circa 1999.

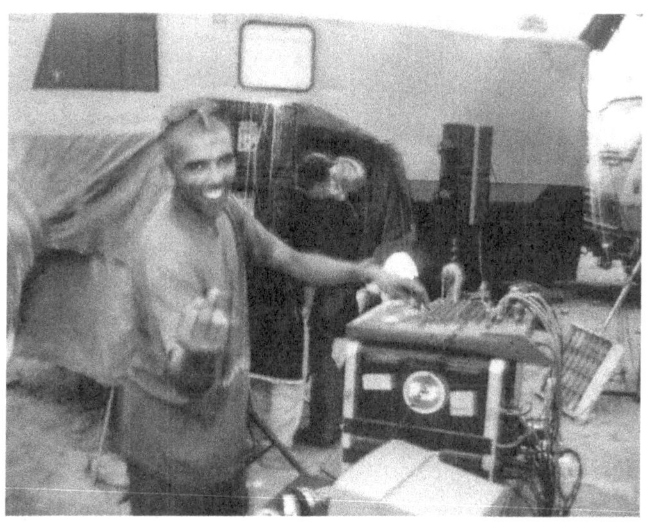

Keef live set, Barcelona, Sant Adrià de Besos, 2000s.

Barcelona, Sant Adrià de Besos 3 Towers Rave, 2000s.

Dstorm truck In a field somewhere, 2000s.

Keef - KDS23.

KDS23 live set, warehouse rave, London, 2005. Photo: Jaimie Taylor.

Keef, Birrel Road, Nottingham, circa 2001. Photo: My Julie.

DS flyer, Roma Festa 2002.

Keef the centurion, Exeter Road, Nottingham, circa 2003. Photo My Julie.

Keef & Alex LDN Underground, circa 2015.

Ostorm Sound System, Noise Control, 2015.

Keef, Nev, Bstorm & Alex, London, 2016.

Ray & Keef, TR-DS.

Keith in uniform.

Keef the raver, The Legend KDS23.

Keith in Scots Guard uniform.

Keef - DS23.

Keef, Rave in Paradise by Deams, Bristol, 2016

ACKNOWLEDGEMENTS

This book is dedicated to Keith's family & friends.

To Jenny & Sarah

To his Sudanese rebel dad.

To all the Dstorm crews past, present and future.

To all the ravers who ever came to a Dstorm rave, free party, underground warehouse rave, outdoor party, teknival, festival, tekno circus OR club night.

To all who have supported Dstorm in any way whatsoever over the years.

The old skool hardcore underground tekno jungle electro breakbeat rogue troopers cut rave shapes with you all.

To Glasgow, Manchester, Nottingham, Bristol, London, Paris, Roma, Barcelona, Amsterdam, Utrecht, Rouen, Lyon, Marseille, Aix en Provence, Toulouse, Perpignan, Narbonne, Turin, Milan, Bologna, Santarcangelo, Grosseto, Ostia, Anzio, Naples, L'Scala, L'Estartit, Mataro, Sabadell, Igularda, Villafranca del Penedes, Mipanas, Valencia, Orgiva, Cigarrones, Coin, Vienna, Bratislava, Prague, Warsaw, Krakow, Meilno, Bosnia, Hungary, Ukraine.

To all the sound system crews we ever linked up with on our travels around the UK and Europe.

To all the friends that did lights, visuals, lazers, fire, performance, sculptures, artwork, live sets, DJ, graffiti - your creativity is what made the rave.

To those that did the onsite cafes, the people that helped run the bar and the pizza.

To all the dogs that look after us.

To the underground free party people.

Kstorm & Dstorm...

Special thanks to everyone who pre-ordered the book

Francesco Annicchiarico, Ruth Baird, C Banks, Jeff Barrett, Helen Beaton, Nina Beinwachs, Pierre Blondet, Benjamin Bosch, Nicola Bradshaw, Mario Braun, Christy Brennan, Maxime Brouhot, David Burns, Michael Byrne, David Cameron, Marco Cangiano, Franca Casamassima, Lorenzo Cavallo, David Cecil, Mark Cheesbrough, Michael Cheesbrough, Nick Cohen, Will Conn, Darkmatter Soundsystem, Marc Davidson, Nicola Dirnberger, Steve Faraone, Elisa Fornero, Mason Garner, Damean Goodall, Hannah Grant, Brian Grieve, Matt Grimes, Gug Gug, Emma Hazelton, Christian Hirmann, Tim Hole, Wolski Hylander, Nick Jonas, Martin King, Alex Laurenson, David Lefranc, Rebecca Le Fey, Sharne Le Singe, Izzy Liney, Edwin Love, Joseph Loveridge, Carmine Maria Maggio, James Malone, Guillermo Martinez-Denegri, Dan Mayer, Ben Mitchell, Dave Morgan, Chris Mott, Graeme Muir, Norman Muirhead, Sonia Newman, William Oliver, Julian Percy, Adam Petts-Hannant, Lucie Potuzakova, Barbara Powell, Jonathan Richards, Mark Richardson, James Rollo, Ben Saxton, Andrea Scagliotti, David Slater, Craig Stock, Styfa, Karl Teifel, Mark van Harmelen, jan von treuton - treuton tribe: For All Free Tekno People, Sebastian Weber, Charles Weisfeld, Paul Wilson, Rhys Wilson, Thomas Wouters, Eric Zampoli

Massive thanks to all the people who funded the editing of this book back in 2020

Aurelien Fayolle, Sharon Taylor Kerr, Justin Kuncaitis, Matthew & Daniel Whiteside, Sally Young, Dan Ooops!, Karina Schwarz, Claire Beth Gibson, Jason Mccreadie, Adam Neville, Helen Savage, Stephanie Lees, S Palmer, Olivier Buquet, Tyron Slack, Ben Shouler, Zephyr Liddell, Andrew Pymm, Adrian Rennie, Victoria Leadbeater, Jane Nicholson, Luca Marongiu, Julia Longo, Flore Arnoux, Scott Wilkerson, Joe Fur, Vanessa Leigh, Rhydian Llewelyn, Flori Ss, Jam Soul, Mark Alchin, David Cameron, Justin Smith, Craig Stephenson, Bobby Kool Van Kleef, Derek Burke, April Mccabe, Rebecca Demarczcy, Sam Poole, Alan Lodge, Koen D, Natasja Owen-Jones, Richard Wenzel, Fabrizio Cantoni, Nick Webb Gary Hatfield, Nick Samovar, Neil Dilworth, Cassie Jackson, Barbara Powell, Claire Dickson, Norman Muirhead, David Slater, Matt Nichols, Charlie Watson, DJ Phasix, Nevine Malek, Hannah Ilett, Stevie Storm, Jo Gallagher, Mat Davies, Colin Mcgillveray, Alexander Simcock, James Corstorphine, Alan King, Jak Boydon, Sonia Burns, Jordan Patrick Conlon, Lindsay Bimson, James Laughton, Treu Ton, Marnie Devitt, Simon Noel, Kelda Platt, Craig Mcfarlane, Melissa Patissa, B Dorling, Manuel Iglesias Rendo, Mark Picton, Emma Bramley, Mark Downer, Lizzy Pritchett, Stephen Partington, Emma Goslan, Ciaran Gallagher, Dal3 Macdonald, Asia Catherine Newman, Helen Jordan, Jessica Hudsley, Agata Baranowska-Orr, Alice Appleyard, Alan Comerford, Manda Racz, Esther rose, April Mccabe, Alan Watson, Jo Finch, Ben Saxton, Victoria Leadbeater, Michael Griffith, Cassandra Jackson, Marc Bloomfield, Sharon Hitchen, Hannah Wright, Amy Tavner, Ruth Baird, Alan Stewart, Jon Swinstead, Nick Feldman, Michelle Harkness, Ally MacInnes, Vanessa Wright, Essie Richards, Steve Bedlam.